My Sequel

Wayne Reid

Lisa & Colin
Many thanks & much
Love Always
RiBSY xxx

DEDICATION

I would like to dedicate this book to my wife Laurel and our wonderful family across the world. To Linda, Karen and Trevor, Armando, Jesse and Edith, Daniel (Listo) Maria and Jewel, David, Maria, Julian, Pauline, William, Elizabeth, Sian, Christina, and Jordan.
To all our friends and those who inspired and helped along the way, especially Rich Mulligan, Steve Brophy, Helen and Nicky, Chuck Kershenblatt, Louis Elovitz, Phil Mews, Andrew (Ratfink) Wilson, Pauline Black, Jake Burns, Roddy (Radiation) Byers, Ian and everyone at Bat's Blood, Rob (Fazz) Farrell, Jeff Buckler, John (Rambo), Irene McDermott
and Eileen Daly.

Thank you all for the memories

Disclaimer

The contents of this book are for entertainment purposes only, do not attempt to replicate, relocate or even eat anything contained within.
Any resemblance of the names,characters and places within to any person, alive, dead or otherwise engaged, is purely coincidental. It's not about you, and never was.

x For Richard Dines x

CONTENTS

BUT THIS IS LIKE HELL

"And the air is cold she wrote me although the sun still burns my skin,
every blistered inch"- she cried, "will Winter soon begin?
Oh give me now a shelter here and take me once again,
down into the deep blue sea and drown me in your rain.
For this is like Hell for me, take me home again
Give me back your sweet caress and cover me again."

I read of how she needed me, I read of how she cried,
her voice still gently whispering as her tears fell from my eyes.

"Oh take me to your shelter dear-take me once again
down into the deep blue sea and drown me in your rain.
But this is like Hell for me, this is like Hell
This is like Hell for me."

1 (SHE SELLS) SANCTUARY

JFK airport, New York on a dark and rain sodden night. Not the worst place in the world to be nor is it the best. I clambered off my seat and headed down the airplane towards the exit and the warm humid atmosphere outside.

America hits your senses the moment you arrive, her smell is instant, warm and addictive. I queued politely through immigration, awaited my turn and eventually stepped forward to the Immigration officer sitting behind a small desk in what may have been a bullet proof booth.

"What is the purpose of your visit today, Sir?"

"Holiday" I replied.

"And where will you be staying?"

"Delaware, I'm going to visit a girlfriend I met in France"

"France, why were you in France?"

"I live there" I lied, knowing full well I had just left and was pretty much between countries at this precise moment in time.

"You live in France?" His eyes burned through the back of my skull, two searing heat rays scorched the roof of the building above and behind the back of my head, filling the room with acrid black smoke. Immigration officers have a knack of making me feel this way, worse than any school teacher, policeman or magistrate, these guys are cold and brutal, their hearts and humanity left firmly in the locker room at the start of each shift.

"I have a market stall, in the South, Montpellier"

"A market stall, what do you sell?" His voice unfaltering, flat, bland and full of suspicion. He was just doing his job, just trying to trick me into confessing that I was actually a Mule, my rectum currently stuffed with so many kilos of hard narcotic powder that I was in danger of farting up a snowstorm all the way to Nebraska.

"I sell jewellery, badges and T-Shirts, you know, fashion wear, whatever I think might sell to my customers, I buy wholesale in England and sell in France, not a bad living really." I looked at my passport in his hand.

"Thank you Sir, have a nice vacation." He stamped my passport and for a moment almost smiled as he handed it back to me. "Next!"

My rucksack eventually appeared on the carousel and once reunited I headed through the customs check area without so much as a second look. Maybe it was my leather trousers or the 'obviously too skint to afford a suitcase so I scrawled my address all over my virtually fluorescent green and purple rucksack' which just about contained all of my worldly possessions, but something seemed to get me through US customs unchallenged.

I'd left my records and important bits and pieces in England. My Mum was bound to have already sifted through everything and given away what she didn't like, sold, binned or burned the rest even before I'd left the ground at Heathrow. She was like that. She could look you in the face and say "Your Brother gave you this for your birthday" knowing full well she'd nicked whatever it was from another member of the family and thought we wouldn't notice.

Now that I was free to go I headed to the car rental telephones and called a number.

"I'd like to hire a car for a week, from JFK to Wilmington, Delaware."

"That's not a problem Sir, can I take your credit card number?"

"Credit card? No, I don't have a credit card, I deal in cash only"

"I'm sorry Sir, but if you do not have a credit card, you cannot hire a car."

A simple conversation which in today's world would be blindingly obvious, but in 1987 people still used cash, credit cards were a bad thing, spending money you didn't have was still an alien concept, something only con-men or students with wealthy parents would consider. Everybody used cash, real hard currency. Plastic was imitation money, the gateway to fraud and non-payment of debts owed, it was cash on delivery, cash and carry, cash with everything, everything it seemed apart from car hire.

"Bollocks!" I slammed the phone down and picked up my rucksack, this would need a rapid rethink, time to come up with Plan B.

Plan B turned out to be a bus from New York to Wilmington, simple, cheap and cheery travel, just like all the times I'd gone up and down the M1 in England on a National Express bus, tonight I could take a Greyhound and arrive safely without the headache of driving through the night.

I followed the signs to the taxi rank and before reaching the exit a well dressed man in a smart black suit caught my attention.

"You need a taxi Sir?" I was liking this being called 'Sir' thing, it made me feel even more like an Englishman abroad, in a good way, not a pissed up, fat bellied, lobster skinned football lout on the rampage kinda way.

"Yes mate, how much to the bus depot?" I enquired.

"$20 to the Port Authority, you want a ride-follow me?" He turned and led me out of the airport into the hot night air. We passed a row of Taxi's and he continued ahead of me until we came to a long black Limousine. "This is my car" he declared, smiling.

"That!" I'd never been inside a limo before, this couldn't be right,could it? "$20 you said, to the bus station, in this?"

"Yes Sir, normally I'd carry your bag too, but the yellow taxi cab's they don't like us private boys picking up customers from the terminal so we have to make like you're not with us until we get to our cars." He smiled and swung my rucksack into the cavernous trunk of his car. The trunk (boot, to use it's English name) was about the size of the van I had left at Heathrow for Plig to collect. When I called, it was Roz who'd answered the phone. I told her where the van was and that I was leaving for America and she wished me luck. Roz would then have had to pass the message on to her parents and suffer the shit storm that would undoubtedly have followed. Poor Roz, I liked her a lot.

I climbed into the back of the huge car, my driver having opened the door for me.

"Help yourself to a drink if you want one" he pointed to the drinks table in the middle of the floor. This thing was unbelievable, it was the size of our Grandad's living room, on wheels and plush leather seats all round. We pulled out of JFK as I hummed "If they could see me now..." I was living the dream, really, never had I ever imagined myself sitting in a chauffeur driven limo across New York, this was the stuff of dreams.

A short ride later we arrived at the bus depot, the Port Authority as my driver kept correcting me. He held open my door and I stepped out slowly and deliberately, one leather legged Dr Marten boot at a time, if I was being seen I wanted to be seen like a somebody. It was raining, it was dark, I had leather trousers and bleached blond hair, to top it all, I was wearing sunglasses and it was night time. Hipper than the hippest hipster in Hipsville, I had arrived to my audience, not that anyone was paying much attention, but if they had, they would have definitely noticed. I slipped my driver a twenty and a $5 tip as he handed me my rucksack, I would have gladly given him $50 for that journey, the boost I got, pretending I was somebody of note getting out of that car, was worth every penny.

Walking into the Port Authority building the atmosphere around me changed instantly, like somebody had just hit the volume button and turned it up to Motorhead. People flew by me in all directions, running, walking, shouting, talking, Tannoys reverberated from all around vomitting their inaudible messages in triplicate around the building. I was no longer the celebrity clambering out of the big car, I was just another invisible, overheated traveller on his fatigued way to somewhere else. I walked confidently and with purpose, this was the Big Apple, the city that never sleeps, and according to books I'd read as a kid, the hot murder capital of the world. I wouldn't be seen as a stranger, someone lost and vulnerable, easy pickings for the pickpockets and thieves that undoubtedly studied every passerby in this building. I walked past following the sign to the ticket office.

"I need to get to Wilmington, Delaware, next bus please, one way."

"If you buy a return ticket it's only $10 more and it's valid for a year"

"Ok, I'll have a return then" It made sense, but tasted bitter, I had only just arrived and was already planning my return.

"Take this ticket and go to Stand 121, your bus leaves in about an hour, have a nice trip Sir."

I followed the signs to departures, Stands 1-40, 40-80, 80-120 and then through a doorway to the street. This was not right. I was back outside the terminus in the rain, in front of me 2 homeless guys sat on a step smoking a joint and drinking from brown paper bags, just like in the movies but with added Smellyvision, there was a rank stench in the air and I wasn't too sure which one of them hadn't yet realised he was dead already. I turned and went back inside to check the signs. As I stood looking upwards a voice beside me asked if I was lost.

"No mate, I'm not lost, it's just that the stand I want isn't where it's meant to be" I said.

"Follow me and I will take you there, which stand do you want?"

"121, it should be just here-"

"Follow me, you've gone past it already"

I looked at the young black guy at my side, he seemed genuine enough but I wasn't entirely convinced he wasn't after something. As we walked past some more homeless people huddled in a corner, my guide informed me-

"You see these people, these are my people, my family. We live here, in the streets, the depot, we are family, we look out for each other man, when I get you to where you're going you'll look after me too, huh?"

I felt uneasy, and aware that this was not my home, these people had spotted me, they knew every nook and corner of this building, I barely knew my arse from my elbow and was carrying a rather large wad of cash in various places around my being, in pockets, my wallet, my travel wallet beneath my trousers and tied around my waist, my boots, rucksack and anywhere I could hide another wad of crisp green bills. I may have looked a million dollars in my leathers and bleached blond hair, but the sad reality was quite a bit less. I had a couple of thousand dollars about me, enough to last a few weeks, but more than enough to get killed for.

"I'll see you right my friend" I promised, but as the words left my lips another voice called across the divide, coming from behind us.

"Hey you! We've told you before-" Two policemen were heading straight towards us, "You and your friends, you're not allowed in here!"

I looked at the young lad and saw his demeanor change, he'd been friendly to me although I was wary, now he was like a frustrated animal, cornered. I turned away and continued walking, this was not my battle and I had no intention of being dragged into anything. I could already see the stand I wanted and although I was relieved that I was here and did not have to pay my guide, I also felt sorry that he had been denied a few dollars had our agreement been honourable.

I called Marybeth from a payphone, for the younger readers I should explain this is a mobile phone connected to the wall, it has no internet or text facilities but you can talk to people anywhere in the world just by dialling the right numbers and putting money into a slot, money being the heavy metal discs that older people collect in their pockets to exchange for goods and services. Dialling being the ancient art of putting your finger into a hole above the required number on the dial face, turning clockwise until it reaches the stop, on release it returns to it's previous position and you can select the next digit and repeat the process until all the required numbers have been dialled, at which point you are put through to your chosen friend. You see, your parents had to work so much harder for everything they've ever had.

"I'm in New York but there's been a slight change of plan, I can't get a car so I'm coming down by bus, I'll be in Wilmington in the morning, can you meet me?"

I boarded the bus and sat near the back so that I could smoke during the journey. I spent most of the time with my face up against the glass taking in all the lights and street signs I could see. I wanted to familiarise myself with the environment, to fit in, knowing my north from my south. We came out of New York city, across the state line and down through New Jersey. Huge swathes of industrial landscapes passed me by, factories the size of small towns, trucks the size of houses, and cars as big as Henry the 8th's codpieces. I was back in America, this time on the east coast, thousands of miles from my previous home in California. There was rain here, a different accent, a faster, punchier attitude and manner, but it was still a world apart from London or Coventry, it was a place for hopes and dreams, a place for living.

I was desperately tired, having worked the Marché Aux Puces in Montpellier, disposed of all my remaining stock and driven through the night to London, dropped off my personal belongings and driven to Heathrow to catch the first available flight to New York, fatigue was catching up on me and I dozed uncomfortably on the bus, my head occasionally bumping against the glass window as the scenery outside flashed by. I woke suddenly with every bump in the road until finally we came into Delaware and Wilmington itself.

Marybeth was waiting for me, along with her sister Jen, they'd borrowed their mothers' car and as I stepped off the bus I was squeezed to within an inch of my life. As exhausted as I was, I still had to endure the ritual of meeting her parents for the first time. If all went well I would be welcomed into their home, if not, I would have to go to a motel and take each day as it came.

We arrived at the house and I was duly presented for inspection, interrogation and summary execution. Her mother Pat, was kind and courteous, very friendly and I liked her a lot. I was pretty sure she liked me too. She was a nurse and naturally accepting of other people. Jen was very friendly too, she seemed more excited than anybody that I was there, I suppose she didn't feel the pressure both Marybeth and I did, about meeting her folks, winning the approval and support of their father. As it turned out he was every bit the hard nut to crack that I had feared. He worked for the DuPont company, held a mid-level supervisory role and therefore was neither accepted by those above or below him. We sat in their living room alone as he quizzed me about American football, my aims, aspirations and suitability for the job of sleeping with his daughter. As job interviews go, it was pretty lousy.

I was dog tired, almost hungover with fatigue, and in need of getting horizontal as soon as practicably possible. I really didn't do a good job of representing myself, or massaging his ego. It wasn't long therefore, before I found myself alone, horizontal and out for the count in a nearby motel.

I woke the next day in a state of half confusion, not fully sure of where I was, who I was, or what the hell was pushing the bed sheet up like a tent post. Long periods without proper sleep have the strangest effect on the male genital organ. When we really need it, the penis can be a pretty useless piece of anatomy, it's like the cat of the reproductive world, screeching incessantly for you to open the door, then when you do it sits on the stoop refusing to come in. When you don't need it, it's there, clawing at your lap, threatening to burst every blood vessel in your body with the power to lift a small bus off the ground.

Marybeth came to visit. Her father had decided I wasn't the right person for his daughter and so I was no longer welcome to visit. I was persona non grata, that was it. I couldn't hang around at their house, she couldn't spend too much time with me. She had a part time waitress job and I had no transport. Life was going to make sure that this relationship could not flourish.

We spent our afternoon by a river not too far away. There were huge rocks along the banks that I climbed over and down to the waters edge. I took photos of the river, of Marybeth, of the rocks. As I got right close to the water my foot slipped and I reached out to hold on.I managed to stop myself slipping into the fast flowing current but lost my camera in one of those slow motion moments when something happens and you can only watch it play out. The camera bounced from my hand and slipped agonisingly slowly down into the water. I saw it surface, once, twice and then it was gone, floating downstream towards the great Atlantic ocean, taking with it the memories I had captured of our first day together again.

I spent the next couple of weeks in the motel room. Marybeth took me out whenever she could. We visited Philadelphia, New York in the daytime and even drove down to Ocean City one day.

I called home from Times Square, New York, and told Mum I'd arrived safe and was having a great time. When I finished the call the operator rang back and said I needed to put another $8 into the phone, I said I'd think about it and hung up.

"Do you want to go up the World Trade Centre?" Marybeth asked as we craned our necks skyward.

"Up there?" I was getting dizzy at the thought alone.

"It's the tallest building in the world" She informed me.

"No it ain't, The Empire State Building is, everyone knows that!" She smiled back at me unsure if I was being serious or joking. I looked back at the sky wondering why I couldn't see King Kong anywhere. Don't they teach youngsters anything in school these days?

From time to time she would bring friends round to visit me, usually armed with pizza and beer. There was an all-you-can-eat buffet restaurant nearby. For $5 I ate like a hog, consuming tacos, ribs, pizza, Chinese food, Mexican chilli and anything else I could fit in my stomach. I bought Captain Crunch Berries to eat in the motel. These were a children's breakfast cereal that came in a variety of colours so alien to nature that you knew you were eating a chemical soup, but you did so because they tasted so bloody good.

"I have a friend who owns his own construction company, Mike, we're going to visit him at his house later" Marybeth informed me one day.

"Does he need anyone to work for him? I'm willing to give anything a go"

"I don't know, but hopefully he can give you some work."

We turned up Mike's house later that day. He was friendly, warm and welcoming and we got along pretty well. He told us about his house, it was haunted- or at least, had been.

"When I moved in things used to just move for no reason" he said.

"Things, like what?" He had my attention.

"Well, there'd be noises in the night, so I'd come down and the cupboards would be open, drawers used to slide open when nobody was around and chairs would not be where I left them. It was kinda funny at first but it got a little boring after a while."

"Was it scary?" I asked.

"No, never scary, I was never afraid of any of it, it just used to annoy me sometimes. So one day I came home, we'd had a really bad day on the job, everything seemed to go wrong and I was sure stressed and in need of a beer. I come on home and the son of a bitch has stacked all these chairs on top of the kitchen table. I walked in here and the cupboard doors were opening and closing by themselves and I just plain had enough, I went back to the front door, opened it and said 'This is my house now, I live here not you, now get out of my house!' and with that everything stopped. I was standing in that doorway and I felt something pass right through me and out of the door, I mean it passed right through me and never came back since, never. This house is as quiet as any other now, whatever it was, it's gone."

"Do you miss it?" I had to ask, just in case.

"No man, it's gone, I was never scared but it wasn't right you know, it didn't belong here."

It was an interesting tale, and Mike was an interesting guy but for all the promises of calling me tomorrow to go to work with him, I was still waiting, alone, a couple of weeks later, watching my money slowly waste away. I had to do something soon.

We went on a shopping trip to Philadelphia mostly just browsing, but I found a new shirt and a pair of trousers I liked, what I didn't like was the armed guard by the door of the shop. This was not the America I remembered from my time in California a few years earlier. I couldn't remember seeing automatic pistols on display in the hands of shop security guards, sitting next to the door in case of robbers or shop lifters. I never saw that in Los Angeles, Hollywood could be a rough place, but I never saw this level of security or paranoia. The streets of Philadelphia were a cold hard place to be in 1987.

I couldn't help but feel that the universe was conspiring against us. Chakra's were not aligning, the stars had it in for us, whatever it was, this battle had us on the losing side to begin with and it was obviously not going to work out any time soon.

Back at the Motel I called Mark Gazda and told him I planned on coming out to California. Mark was a friend I'd put up in London back in 1984, just before leaving for LA.

"Just call me when you are in town and I'll get you, you can stay at mine as long as you like." This was brilliant news, I suddenly felt hopeful of staying longer than I could if I had to continue in the Motel.

My next call was to Deanna, my ex in LA. It was through her I knew Mark.

"I'm coming over to California, maybe next week, I'll be staying with Mark but I thought it would be nice to meet up if we can."

"That would be great, but call me before you get here, we are moving soon, not sure when exactly, but call me, it would be great to see you. Mom sends her love."

There was no intention of rekindling our relationship, I had Marybeth, Deanna was with a boyfriend of her own, we were just meeting up as friends, that was all that we could be. I was in love with Marybeth and she with me, but it seemed we could do nothing right together. Everything was great when we were in France. I had work, money, somewhere to live-although that was starting to look as though it was coming to an end. The minute she left to go home things began to fall apart. The house, my trading ability, citizenship, everything. I had come to America in the hope of being able to put things right again, as if being apart was destructive. By being together we could rebuild something. But it wasn't to be. The universe, the gods, whatever had no plan for us. Not here, not now.

 I left Wilmington a few days later. Marybeth knew I had to go, we had no idea when I'd be back, but I promised I would. I had to go to California, I couldn't bear the thought of going to London, and anyway, it was only 3,000 miles away, just up the road really.

 There were two nationwide bus companies in America at this time, Trailways and Greyhound. I compared prices at the bus station. At $137 Wilmington to Los Angeles, and return, Trailways was by far the cheapest option. I couldn't afford to fly, the train was equally as expensive and anyway, travelling by bus was my thing. I got to meet people, see the country and most importantly, kill some time as cost effectively as possible.

 We said our goodbye's at the bus station, both of us clinging tightly, teary eyed. I waved through the tinted window of the bus as it bumped and lurched onto the road and out of town.

 Travelling south from Wilmington to Baltimore I noticed a sign, apparently we were on the John F Kennedy Memorial Highway , I- 95 . I sat in my seat at the rear of the bus, singing in my head the words to the Adam And The Ants' song 'Kennedy'. The video of JFK's assassination playing out in my mind's eye. "Kennedy's wife with his brains on her knee, poor Jackie...."

 By the time we reached Union Station in Washington *(No, not Tyne And Wear)* Washington DC. I was totally befuddled. Washington DC is Washington District (of) Columbia, that's what I was taught at school. But Columbia is in Canada, hundreds of miles to the north, unlike Colombia, which is thousands of miles to the South. So how come I now find out Washington is actually in Maryland, which is also a little corner of East London? It is often said that travel broadens the mind, well,it was confusing the fuck out of me.

 After a short coffee break and change of bus, we headed out along Constitution Avenue NW. On our left hand side appeared the Capitol Building, a large white building with a big dome, somewhat reminiscent of St Paul's Cathedral in London. It is the home of the US Senate and the House of Representatives, it looked pretty in the afternoon sun, green trees all around, blue sky up above and no washing hanging out of the windows to dry.

 We took the I-95 to Richmond, Virginia and then headed west on the I-64 to pick up the I-81 after Charlottesville. We were now in mountain country with the Appalachian range just on our right. Huge mountains covered in forests of green rose and dipped as far as the eye could see, or would see if it wasn't already the middle of the night. I'd seen the 'Blue Ridged Mountains' on TV, and imagined how they looked beyond the rain and the blanket of night time.

 I was getting tired and could barely stay awake any longer. I took a Gauloises (French Cigarette) from my pocket and had my last smoke of the day, then rested my head against the window. All around me, my fellow passengers had given up the fight and the sounds of heavy breathing filtered down the bus.

I slept through the rest of Virginia and was barely awake as we pulled out of Nashville.

Our next stop, Memphis was a longer break, we were able to leave the bus and freshen up in the toilets. I found a Taco Bell and treated myself to a couple of cheap burrito's washed down with a large cup of Dr Pepper, the fruity flavoured cola I very nearly got to advertise when I was in LA, 3 years earlier. It was getting hot outside and I was grateful for the air-conditioned environment of the bus, as much as I love summer, travelling west in August was always going to be a little uncomfortable at times.

We pulled out of Memphis, and crossed the Mississippi River, our driver waffling on about Elvis Presley, BB King and Johnny Cash having lived and recorded in this great city of Rock'n'Roll. Nothing was mentioned of the huge effort I'd had to put out attempting to poo before leaving town. Too much pizza, too little roughage and who knew how long it would be before we stopped next?

Little Rock was our next pit stop before joining the I-30 to Dallas. I scoured the landscape for Whitefork Ranch, hoping to catch a glimpse of JR Ewing, I wanted to slap him for all his wicked ways, but all I could see were the bright shimmering towers of the huge downtown office buildings, no cowboys, no Injun's, no horses racing alongside with masked bandito's threatening to hold up the stage, all the stereotypical images I'd held in my head, shattered. Dallas was just another big city in the middle of a big land.

It was another 9 hours to our next big stop, El Paso. I tried to get some more shut eye but kept waking up. It was dark outside and the motion of the bus was comforting but lack of exercise made it hard to really get any decent rest, especially when I couldn't lay down.

El Paso sits on the north side of the Rio Grande, to the south lies the Mexican town of Ciudad Juarez, a poor, overcrowded shanty town within plain sight of it's comparatively opulent American neighbour. Nowhere had I ever seen such obvious disparity between one river bank and another. Here it is plain to see why so many people give their all to cross the divide. Where Mexico pleads for alms, America say's "I'm alright Jack!" You can never blame the people for wishing to blur boundaries, for wanting better, to cross man-made lines in search of a better life. Governments and politicians the world over are protectionist, they ignore the pleas of their neighbours, humanity has no place in the halls of power and wealth and it always is the poorest that pay the highest toll. I had thought long and hard about this subject as a teen.

I had eventually distanced myself from Andy, my best friend from school, when he took to the right wing. I saw that by hating others, we were fighting amongst ourselves, denying each other access to things we should all have, peace, love, health, family, travel. Everything on this planet was for all of us, not just some, not just the privileged few, everyone. We were doing their dirty work, keeping the impoverished poor, creating a barrier and protecting the wealthy. This barrier, protectionist xenophobia, had already impacted on my life once, those same man-made barriers had forced Deanna and I apart, now they were forcing Marybeth and I to make choices we didn't want to make. Born on different sides of the divide like Running Bear and Little White Dove. The Rio Grande is for some the Barbed Wire Love that Jake Burns (Stiff Little Fingers) sang of. There is enough food, water, employment for everybody in this world, but instead of sharing we fight and wage war on each other, deny each other the essentials we all need. We create barriers, walls and rules stifling growth, starving the many as the few throw away their rotting excess. We are horrid, despicable beings that must change, for the sake of all humanity.

From El Paso we took the I-10 to Tuczon, Arizona. but before we managed to get too far into this leg of the journey, our driver made an announcement. "Ladies and Gen'lemen, we seem to have a problem with the air conditioning aboard this bus, I'm afraid it may get a li'l warm aboard but I'll just get in touch with control and see if we can get a replacement for the rest of the journey."

No air conditioning, in the Summer, in the desert, on a cross-country bus? Sometimes you just have to take the rough with the smooth.

"Ladies and Gen'lemen, I'm sorry but we have to just ride this out until we get to Phoenix, we hope to get it fixed there, in the meantime, open a window if you have one and let's hope we don't get too hot on board!"

Within minutes the inside of the bus had become a bake house. Sweat began to bead on my forehead, under my arms,down my back it trickled in a seemingly consistent manner. As time passed and we rolled ever deeper into the red sandy desert, the temperature inside the bus continued to rise. Older couples fanned their spouses, some passengers had bottles of water which they sprayed on their children first and themselves afterwards. I sat alone near the back of the bus, daydreaming of ice cold cola, a swimming pool, beer and parasols. I wished for a swimming pool to dive into, to feel the cool water remove the hot salty sweat from my skin. I wanted a sun lounger too, and a woman to rub sun screen into me as I lay naked in the heat of the desert. I was drifting off, half awake, half asleep but fully erect.

"Jeez!" I yelped, jumping myself awake. My fellow passengers unaware of my embarrassment as I changed position in my seat, attempting to cover up my involuntary growth.

More bad news was to come at Phoenix, AZ. The air conditioning unit could not be repaired and there was no replacement bus available. The sweat box had to roll it's way merrily along to Los Angeles.

The I-10 is one of my favourite roads in the world. It runs through hundreds of miles of desert, through the landscapes we grew up with as backdrops in spaghetti westerns. Barren dry lands with the occasional cactus, huge sandstone monoliths rising solitary from the ground. Deep blue sky and the threat of a rattlesnake under every rock. On our right lay the Joshua Tree National Park, named after the famous U2 album. We crossed the Colorado River near Blythe and headed ever closer towards our destination. On our left lay the remnants of the Salton Sea, a man-made lake that became the 'Ideal desert paradise' in the 1960's and 70's. Hotels, a marina, yacht clubs and bars had sprung up from the desert, thousands of people from Los Angeles and Palm Springs flocked to buy parcels of land along the shoreline. It was a haven for water sports enthusiasts, young, beautiful and well to do couples planned their retirements here. The Salton Sea was a modern day Sodom whose downfall came when the waters feeding the lake were cut off, the lake became saline, the fish died and paradise became a ghost town.

We stopped briefly at Palm Springs and then made the last 100 miles to East 7th Street, Downtown Los Angeles. As we approached the city from the low desert my adrenaline rose. I had sat on my arse for 3 days solid, with just the occasional 30 minute break here and there to stretch my legs, scratch my arse,eat, drink, piss and be merry. It was an exhausting journey, not helped by the loss of the air conditioning. I looked out the window as we passed San Bernardino and headed closer to my familiar old stomping ground. It was all so fresh in my head still. Hollywood, the Cathay De Grande, the apartment off Hyperion, Deanna and her mother, Joy. I was almost there. I just needed to call Mark and he'd come and get me, I can hang around for a while, see how things are, maybe meet Deanna and her boyfriend, maybe not.

Once I got off the bus I decided to ditch my rucksack in a locker at the bus station. I had already memorised both Mark and Deanna's phone numbers. I didn't need to be carrying the pack, looking like a tourist, a target in waiting.

I stretched my legs around the bus station and found a phone box, knowing I needed to call Mark I had saved a pocket full of quarters on the way over.

"Hello" It was not Mark's voice. Possibly his mother, or grandmother.

"Hi, could I speak to Mark please?"

"Who?"

"Mark" I repeated a little louder, just in case her hearing was off.

"There's no Mark here" She replied.

"Oh, I'm sorry, must have the wrong number,bye" I hung up.

That's odd I thought to myself as I mentally rechecked the number. I could see it in my mind's eye, just as it appeared on the page of my address book, which was in my rucksack in the locker.

I put in another quarter and dialled again.

"Hello?" It was her again.

"Hi is Mark there please?"

"There's nobody called Mark here!" She replied.

"Oh, I'm sorry, I seem to have dialled the wrong number again, sorry."

I hung up quickly, embarrassed at having called her twice now.

"Right, let's get it right this time....."

I put another quarter into the slot and very meticulously dialled Mark's number. There was a pause, and then a ring tone.

"Hello!" came back the old ladies' voice.

"Oh no, not again, sorry. I'm trying to get hold of my friend Mark, he's supposed to come and get me..."

"There's nobody here called Mark, now try a different number, he's not here." *Click!* She hung up the phone. Another quarter.

"I've told you, he's not here!" She was getting impatient with me.

"But this is his number, I've come all the way from England to see....." *Click.* Another quarter got me a similar response, and again. Finally I was down to my last quarter, I had started with 13.

"Listen Lady, I don't care if you're his Mum and you don't want me to stay, I get it! Just tell him I'm here, I'll stay somewhere else, I just wanted to see him."

"I don't care who you are, but you call me one more time and I'm calling the police, do you understand?" *Click.*

Mark wasn't home.

Plan B came instantly to my head, time to rally the troops, I knew Deanna's address, I could get her to call Mark and he could then come to Deanna's and get me, or, if his Mum really didn't want me to stay, I could hang out for a few days maybe sleep on someone's sofa, a friend, a buddy, a city park bench maybe. Now was not the time to worry about that, I could think about that later once I get to Deanna's.

I went back into the bus station and found a route map, there was a bus leaving in a couple of minutes from a nearby stand that passes the end of her street, I jumped into gear and found my way across the bus station, just in the nick of time. I jumped aboard and paid the driver a couple of dollars for the journey. I sat near the front so as to keep an eye on the street names, that way I shouldn't get lost or miss my stop. I hadn't been on a bendy bus like this one since I was last in LA. Deanna and I were going home one evening and were awkwardly surrounded by older evangelical women. They said nothing to us but the disdain was clear to see by the way they chewed on their dentures, sucking them to and fro in the back of their mouths, desperately wishing they were brave enough to pour out their hatred for us, for being 'Devil worshippers' or some such nonsense. One of the placards they were holding bore the words "Never trust a man with a shaven head." I'd just shaved the sides of mine that very morning, my Mohawk sprayed rigidly upright, my tattooed head in full defiant view of the placard, teased them to bring it on. I was in the mood for a good religious discussion, but it didn't happen.

I was starting to notice some changes in the city around me. When I had been here in 1984 everything was clean, tidy and welcoming. Now there was a different atmosphere. The streets were unkempt and a certain poverty seemed to hang in the air. It seemed as though the departing Olympic Circus, with all the world's media on board, had left the city in 1984 having stripped it bare of all it's beauty. The faces of the people around me were sadder than they had been just a couple of years before too, as if a relative had died and forgotten to tell anyone where they'd hidden their savings.

We finally reached the end of the street Deanna was living on. I got off the bus and walked up the road checking the house numbers. They had moved since I lived with them and so this was a strange neighbourhood to me, I had never been here before. After walking a few blocks I finally came upon the house. It was semi-detached, the stoop providing access to both properties' front doors. I made sure I had the right number and rang the bell. My heart was pounding from the adrenaline pumping around my system, I had not planned on being here, but now I was, I felt like squeezing Deanna and her Mother, I wanted to scream "I'm back!" and never have to leave again. I had missed them. My heart belonged on the East Coast with Marybeth, but something else belonged here, I didn't know what, suddenly I felt home, I felt as though I should be here, I hoped for some redemption, standing there on the stoop I could only imagine the surprise and happiness that would spread across her face when she saw me.

I rang the bell a second time and waited patiently.

I rang the bell a third time, less patiently.

"They've moved." Called a voice behind me, waking me from my thoughts.

"What-when?" I turned around to see the face of a 30 something year old black lady in the neighbour's doorway.

"Moved out yesterday" she said somewhat nonchalantly. I looked through the door window and saw for myself, the place was empty.

"Moved-yesterday? But, where-where did they move to?"

"North Hollywood somewhere, don't know where about's, just North Hollywood. You've got a funny accent, where are you from-Australia?"

"That's a joke-innit?, they haven't really moved?"

Not only had she awoken me from my somewhat intense and probably bad taste daydream, but now she was calling me an Aussie. My day was going from bad to worse to pretty fucking shitty on an immense scale. If this were Back To The Future I was definitely Biff crashing into a manure truck for the umpteenth time today. For the umpteenth time in recent times, I now had to come up with a Plan B.

I headed back to the bus stop totally dejected. Everything in this world was falling apart. I had nowhere to go. Nowhere to turn but the one place I least wanted to be, England.

Within the space of a few short weeks I had gone from owning my own business in France to being rejected in Delaware and now almost penniless and alone on the streets of Southern California. Hell, this was so bad I could write a book about it. I could write two, but nobody would believe me if I did, anyway. Plan B, was not forthcoming, there were no other doors open to me at this time, nothing else to do but bite the bullet and accept defeat. I took a bus to Hollywood and treated myself to a burger and fries, life always looks better after a decent feed.

It struck me now, sitting on a bench in the afternoon sun, that I had given it my best shot. I had come here to extend my stay, see my friends and kill some time, I already knew in my heart that I had to go back to London, again, but I had ignored the sign's for as long as I could. It was time to go.

Back at the bus station, I booked myself on the next available bus back to Wilmington, from there I would book my flight and get a ticket to New York. There was only a short wait in LA before my bus was due so I decided to phone Marybeth at the next stop and tell her of my plans. Curiosity made me open my rucksack and pull out my address book. I thumbed through the pages until I found Mark's name and number. It was the same number I had been dialling, the same number that had connected me 13 times to that poor old lady who- no doubt by now, had probably called the Police, the FBI, CIA and a compensation lawyer, to tell them of some crazy Englishman calling her multiple times to speak to Mark.Someone called Mark, who lived in Corona Del Mar, NOT Los Angeles, I'd been calling the right number from a different area code. DOH!

It was too late to go back, I was mentally beat and in my heart I knew it was time to go."Time to suck it up buttercup!" Time to get back to my roots and start again.

I called Marybeth from Phoenix, she sounded sad but agreed it was out of our hands now. I had to go back to England. I met some Swedish students who boarded the bus at Phoenix, they were headed for Dallas and I felt a pang of jealousy for them, they had another 2 years in America yet still. We all sat at the back of the bus waiting as the last of the seats were taken.

"Oh my god!" said one of them, "Look at that, she's beautiful." I looked to the front of the bus and saw a very attractive woman walking towards us. There were 2 seats left, one next to me and one next to the Students. She took the seat next to me and left the other seat to a younger boy who seemed to be travelling with her. As we settled into the journey and began to talk, it turned out that the younger lad was her little brother, they were travelling home to Dallas. As we talked I noticed an older man with his wife in the seats opposite ours, he was watching and listening to our chit-chat, he caught my eye and smiled, then gave me a 'thumb's up!' It seemed suddenly that I was the one everybody else envied.

Night was upon us and as the light's of the city disappeared behind, we settled into our seats, turned out the lights and relaxed. At first we sat upright, then slouched. Before long I changed position and she put her arm around me, a little while later she kissed me. The older man across the aisle smiled in the dark, again raised his thumb to me. I had no idea why she kissed me, she was beautiful and I was 4 days from my last shower, I had endured crossing the desert without air conditioning in the same clothes I was still wearing, I was unkempt, smelly and less attractive than my new Swedish friends. I also had a girlfriend of my own, but for some reason right now, I needed this contact. We were 2 strangers on a bus together, we held each other through the night, then kissed and parted in the morning without any exchange of contact details. I felt guilty for having done this, for betraying my girlfriend, but something about this encounter seemed almost destined. I needed this human contact and the beautiful, blond haired traveller who'd sat beside me, put her arms around me and lifted herself to kiss me in the night, she needed something too, it felt both wrong and right at the same time.

At Dallas I had bought myself some breakfast, used the toilet and had a quick wash before getting back on the bus. I felt a little more refreshed but was looking forward to having another sleep. Again, I sat near the back and decided to have a cigarette as we pulled out of the bus station. Seated next to me was another young lady, a brunette with plain features and a few freckles leftover from her adolescence. I offered her a Gauloise.

"Would you like a cigarette?" I asked her, offering her the packet.

"No thanks, not for me just now."

"Do you mind if I...?

"No, please help yourself, you're British aren't you" She was right, I am.

"Yes" I replied, lighting my cigarette. "But these are French"

"Wow, that's so cool." She settled herself into her seat and put her coat over herself like a blanket. I continued to smoke and eventually put my head against the window to rest. I'd just started to doze when once again I felt someone's arms pushing their way around my waist. I guessed this sort of thing happened a lot on buses here, but I had never experienced this in England before. I settled into my new position as a human comfort blanket, my head gently vibrating on the window with the motion of the vehicle. I dozed again and was shortly woken up as my new companion changed position and pulled her coat over her head which she now had placed on my lap, having already unzipped my fly. Again the thumbs up from across the aisle as I sat red faced, singing silently to myself "If they could see me now...."

We pulled in to Little Rock and I went to the toilet to quickly freshen up. I could not believe this was happening to me, well not exactly to me, I was quite happily allowing it, but what was going on? Is bus travel always like this in America? I had no idea.

As I came out the bathroom I was halted dead to the spot. The young lady who'd been so familiar with me on the bus but hardly spoken a word, stood in front of me. Behind her, her parents, a possible sibling brother, and maybe an aunt and uncle. A shotgun wedding? No, no, no, no, no. This could not be happening, I may not have resisted her actions on the bus, but I was not in the mood to be married off to her for it. I stood motionless, like a deer in the headlights as she stepped forwards.

"Here" she gave me a slip of paper and a photo of herself. "Write to me won't you?" Then she kissed me on the cheek and turned away. Her family smiled and waved to me before walking off, leaving me shocked and alone on the concourse.

"Could this trip get any fucking stranger? " I thought to myself.

Note to self: Don't tempt providence.

At Knoxville, TN, we were joined at the back of the bus by a small group of twenty-somethings, a white woman, a black woman and 3 young black guys. As soon as they sat down they switched on a ghetto blaster and subjected the back half of the bus to an impromptu Hip-hop broadcast. The music was not to my liking but it didn't bother me. They were a friendly bunch, and before long managed to get half of the passengers on board to join in singing along to the music. The bus took on a sort of party atmosphere, having been travelling for 6 days now, it was a refreshing change to listening to the dull drone of the engine, mile after mile.

The bus pulled in to a stop at the side of the road. According to someone who knew the area, we were close to a psychiatric prison. A couple climbed onto the bus and stowed their bags before taking seats near to the front. As they sat down somebody laughed at a joke and the woman, a rather obese lady in her late twenties or so, stood back up and frowned towards the group on the back seat. She obviously thought the joke was aimed at herself and took immediate offence. For the next couple of hours this same scenario repeated again, and again. Finally, the woman at the front of the bus came storming down the aisle.

"Who are you laughing at? Don't you laugh at me" She protested, nobody had.

"Nobody's laughing at you lady, we're just having a good time here." Said one of the guy's from the back row.

"Well don't, don't laugh at me." She turned and went back to her seat.

"What the fuck man? Who rattled her cage?"

"Stupid bitch, nobody's talking about her"

The music continued from the ghetto blaster but the bus seemed quieter all of a sudden. After another 10 minutes or so she was back, storming up the aisle with a face like thunder.

" You're doing it again-I told you not to laugh at me!"

"Nobody's laughing at you bitch, you need to calm the fuck down and get back to your seat, we ain't giving you no shit."

"The fuck you ain't giving me no shit! You're all shit and your music's shit and you can turn it the fuck down before I break it, bunch of bitches!"

Now, at this point I was all ready for handbags and false nails at 3 paces, but these ladies were holding nothing back, verbally. No punches thrown, no eye's gauged, face's clawed or ripped shirt's for the boys. This catfight was a verbal slanging match the likes of which I had never witnessed in my life. These girls had the bus in stitches, tears of laughter poured down my cheeks as the insults flew back and forth, both seemingly unfazed by the other's threats.

"You touch my black ass I'm gonna bop your li'l white pussy all the way to your momma's li'l hoe house, bitch, you got nuthin' on me bitch, ain't no li'l white boy gonna know which end to feed and which to fuck wid by the time I finish beatin' your bitch ass!"

"Bring it on bitch, I ain't scared of no fat freak motherfucker who can't sit still 'cos her ass so fat she got lard where her butt's 'sposed to be, yo' momma musta fed you straight from the doughnut fryer, you so fat and ugly yo'r daddy must'a been thought you was a manatee wid legs on the side when you's born, bitch!"

"Bring it on bitch- dang, you so ugly you must'a been been slapped both ends when you was born, you see this motherfucker-" The crazy lady from the front of the bus turned herself round in the aisle and shook her ass. "You ain't never gonna get what I got, You ain't got nuthin' on me bitch!"

I wasn't entirely convinced anyone wanted what she had, but she liked it and was more than welcome to keep it.

Hour after hour the insults flew. Up and down the bus came the crazy lady, each time sparking a new round of abuse and hilarity, I wish I could have recorded it, we had no mobile phones back then, no social media, or this would have been a global phenomenon. We laughed and cried all the way to Washington DC. As the bus came into town we were all invited to party at the nearest bar. "Hey guy's, let's all get some beers and hang out for a while, it'll be cool, you're all welcome except that crazy fat freak at the front!"

I would have joined them but I was on a mission now, I had to get back to England, I had to sort myself out.

"Ladies and Gen'lemen, welcome to Washington DC. I just wanna thank you guy's for being the best passenger's I could'a hoped for, and for making this a journey I will never forget, thank you for travelling with Trailways and I hope you all have a safe onward journey!"

I finally made it to Wilmington and to Marybeth. I never mentioned what had happened on the bus, just explained my decision to go home. She knew as well as I did that it had to be that way, but it broke both our hearts to have to part. Even though I had been unwittingly unfaithful, let's face it, I could have said no -but I didn't, I was hurting inside at having to leave again. I desperately wanted to stay but the barriers were up, we were to be separated again, not by the Rio Grande, but the vast expanse of the Atlantic Ocean.

I called home and was told I could move in with my brother Les. He and his wife Debby had a new place in Rainham and I could have their spare room. The plane touched down on Thursday morning, Friday I had to go to an interview with a company my Dad used to drive for in Barking. The Transport Manager was a family friend so the job was virtually guaranteed, all I had to do was turn up on Monday morning.

0800 Monday Morning I was met by my new supervisor and shown around the factory. I was issued a set of blue overalls and a pair of old wellington boots. The company refurbished old steel drums. 200 litre containers for carrying liquids, chemicals etc. At one end of the factory, used drums would come in and be rinsed clean with a mix of chemicals and high pressure steam. Then they would travel on a conveyor to a machine that reshaped the drum, using hugely pressurised air to blow out any dents in the drums. Next they were shot-blasted to remove any paint and residue, separated into various types of drum, open topped, lacquer-lined, Steel, side opening, etc. As each type of drum was required, they would sent on a conveyor to be lined, spray painted and then baked dry. They would then be stacked into vary colours, styles etc as per orders for the day, and then loaded onto trailers for dispatch. The factory was a noisy, toxic environment that could sometimes even be dangerous, and for £90 a week, it was to be my new home from home. My fall from grace was complete.

2 Room To Breathe

"Hello, I'm your nightmare and I've come to marry you, I wish I could say 'Sorry', but you'd know it wasn't true"

"That's a nice tan you got there, been on holiday? Anywhere nice?"
I got that response a lot from people when I met them. They didn't care where I'd been, what I'd been doing, they just wanted -for the most part, to brag about their forthcoming fortnight in the Gambia, Jamaica or Tunisia. "All inclusive" and usually on a guarded site, away from any of the locals. "They're not as clean as us, you gotta be careful when you're abroad."
I tried not to say too much, often letting them make up their own minds. No point trying to brag to a bigot, they only want adulation, empathy or understanding are beyond their conscious realms. It can even be hard to level with people who know already. Jealousy is an ugly trait, be pleased for those that do well, because when you're pleased and happy for them you smile and radiate a beauty that is more than skin deep, it glows in your aura and is detectable by all of those around you. When someone has something you like, be happy for them. When they achieve things you crave or aspire to, be happy for them. Be happy for them and happiness will be yours always, life is too short to be jealous of the achievements of others.
"I just got back from the States, had a couple of months out there, you know, took a bus from the East Coast to LA, had a burger and chips then back again. I lived in France for 2 years before that though, had my own business, in the South, beautiful it was."
"Sorry mate, I just gotta go see someone... (else)..."
Bragging rights do not gain you any friends, nor do they help you to reintegrate into a society you don't necessarily wish to be in. It was for these reasons I tried to keep my head down, keep quiet about the last few years, except for when I was with friends, people who knew. I was back in England, earning a living, stacking steel drums in noisy, dirty factory in the East End. Loading them into the back's of lorries, hundred's at a time, day after day. Once a week I would call Marybeth and chat briefly, one day however, we were on the phone for over an hour and when the bill arrived I lost everything I had been working so hard to save. I was getting nowhere, treading water and still struggling to stay afloat.
To help get through the weeks I would go to a club in Romford, The Rez. There would be live bands and plenty of good music, I met up again with friends I hadn't seen for a few years, saw a few bands and even destroyed one. After a long day of stacking, shifting and loading drums with the constant

noise of machinery, the banging and clanging of metal on metal, the hiss of compressed air and the occasional earsplitting explosion as a random drum gave up under intense pressure whilst being reshaped, the last thing I wanted to hear was a bunch of arty-farty types recreating the same environment in a nightclub and calling it Industrial Music. Industry has no music, it has noise, earsplitting, bone shaking, nerve shattering noise that dehumanises, humiliates and sometimes scares the living shit out of those unfortunate enough to have to work in it's environs. The dangers involved in working in a place like that were not artistic, it was not beautiful to see a man blown from one side of a building to another because a drum jam's in a machine and the whole lot explodes in front of him. It's not dedication to the art to have one's lungs burned with caustic soda, to have to handle unknown acid's, alkali's and whatever else passed through that stinking septic place. So when I dived into the middle of their performance, sending their nice clean and sterile 'Industrial' drums flying, threatening to kill every last one of the band, it was because (unlike the famous DJ John Peel , who was apparently their No.1 fan) I did not appreciate the 'Artistic Statement' they were making.

One old mate I reunited with was Ian Cruickshank, He was a couple of years older than me, didn't tend to attack bands in mid performance but he did know what was new, who, where and when. Ian had been around all the old haunts I had club-wise, so when I returned and had no idea what was on and where, Ian took me out and about. We would go to London at the weekend and be up dancing and drinking all night. Sometimes we'd just go for drinks locally and sit around chatting all night, having a laugh.

One night in Elm Park, we'd been out with friends, one of whom was a huge Toyah fan, so much so that in today's world he'd be accused of stalking, hanging around dressing room doors, waiting in alleys, eventually setting up her official Fan Club. We left the Elm Park Hotel and I wobbled drunkenly up the hill to the underground station. Ian and the others lived locally but I had to get the tube home, we'd arranged to meet up another time and I headed off alone up the steep incline. It was late and I walked straight through the barriers, no inspectors around, no ticket, no worries. As I walked down the long slope to the platform I saw a train coming in to the station. It was heading the opposite way, toward Upminster-I was going to Dagenham East so I didn't have to rush. I'd gone about a third of the way down when three skinheads appeared at the bottom of the ramp, heading towards me, they'd been up London for the night and were now homeward bound, drunk and loud. Knowing this could be awkward, I hugged one side of the walkway and kept my eyes low avoiding contact. This is usually enough to avoid any unwanted confrontation, but in this instance nothing was going to stop what was about to come. Of the three skinheads coming towards me it was the short skinny guy that made a bee line for me, and without warning dropped a headbutt full on to my nose. The pain was instantaneous, my vision blurred and I struggled to stay on my feet. I put my hands to my nose and felt blood running down my fingers. Not sure if it was broken or not, I pulled out a handkerchief to cover my nose and stem the blood flow. By the time I had got myself together, my attacker was walking ahead of his friends, laughing.

"Don't worry about it, he's had a bad night!" Called back the largest of the group, somehow thinking that made it alright then.

"He's had a bad night!" I retorted, "What about my fucking night, fucking arsehole...?" I wiped my nose again, then walked down to the platform.

"Last train westbound has already gone" said a voice approaching from the shadow of an underground sign.

"You what?" I said.

"Last train towards Barking has gone, no more trains now until the morning."

"Fucking marvellous, now I have to walk home too..."

The guard turned and walked away, only one more train from the city and then he could lock up for the night. Me, I had to run the gauntlet of getting out of here without being attacked again. My eyes were still watery, my nose throbbed and was still bleeding, little lines of dark red had already stained my face and neck. Fair play to the bastard, that was a quality headbutt, and I didn't fancy another one. I looked up the slope and saw them still hanging around at the entrance, they were in no hurry to leave. Just then something caught my attention on the tracks. Laying on one of the big wooden sleepers was a bolt, one of those used to bolt the clamps in place that in turn hold the rails. It was big, heavy and ideal for what I needed right now. The guard was gone now, so I jumped down onto the track and grabbed the bolt, pulled myself back onto the platform and walked assertively up towards the exit. By the time I got to the top, they had already gone. I watched them turn left, which was good, I was going right, down the hill and the long walk home. But as I came out of the station, I could see them in the taxi office next door.

Cue the Discharge song, Ain't no feeble bastard, no fucking scapegoat!

So I turned left and dived through the open doorway, past the two bigger lads and landed an almighty smack on the top of my assailants head. The bolt split his scalp and he flew sideways. I struck him a second time and third, the bolt flew out of my hand this time and suddenly I was aware I was being pulled backwards. My nose was bleeding again, his head was now pouring with blood and the two of us came nose to nose, blood ,snot and spit flying in all directions. I couldn't hit out as the big guy had hold of my arms from behind, in front of me, his mate was being restrained by his other friend.

"The Police are on their way, now pack it in!" Ordered a voice from behind the thick glass window.

"Come on outside" I heard behind me, the big guy not wanting anymore trouble in the taxi office, dragged me backwards onto the street. "Come on now, easy mate, it's okay, it's done now."

"Done? that fucker attacked me for no reason-"

"He's had a row with his girlfriend, don't worry about it, look it's finished, yes?" Just then the door opened and once more we were nose to nose.

"Look at my fucking head, look what you've done to me"...

"Your head? Look at my fucking nose!"

"Look at my fucking head!"

"What about my fucking nose, you fucking ....?"

"Enough now," called a policeman getting out of his car behind me, "Give it a rest or you're both going to the nick, now, what's been going on?" Another car and a police van pulled up, it was as if the taxi firm had his own police reserve in waiting. "You, get over here now."

We were kept apart and questioned for a few minutes. Eventually it was determined that if I didn't make a complaint for Assault against him, he wouldn't make a complaint of GBH (Grievous Bodily Harm) against me. Knowing this to be the best outcome, we both agreed and shook hands, him walking off with one mate, me sharing a taxi home with the other, the big guy. "He's alright really, just had a bad day, you two would probably get on any other day, we all used to be Punks, y'know, followed the Ants and everything, had some right laughs, d'you know Mad Max?" I knew Max, everyone knew Max, and Max knew everyone.

I hadn't been working at Steel Drums for long, maybe a week or so, when I made friends with one of the other lads there.

"You should come out for a drink one night with me and my mate Barry" he said, in his lovely thick welsh accent. "Barry looks just like David Bowie, but he's got a third eye in the middle of his forehead, it's a lump, he's always had it."

We arranged to meet up one night and have a few drinks together. When Barry showed up I nearly dropped my pint. Normally when someone say's "My mate looks like...." they invariably look nothing like whoever they're meant to, like me, I don't look like Francis Rossi from Status Quo, but you try telling that to all the people that keep asking me if I am He. Barry was David Bowie to a tee. He was an exact double of the man, maybe slightly older looking, but he was the spitting image, except for his mysterious third eye. He could have had it removed and earned a fortune as a Bowie impersonator, but Barry couldn't sing, just like I can't play guitar, Barry was Bowie's twin, I however, am definitely not Francis Rossi's twin.

Ian and I would go to a club by Marble Arch, they played some good music there but things had changed over the last couple of years. When Major and I hit the clubs in the past, we literally hit the clubs. Dancing now had become a non-contact sport, Saturday night was no longer alright for fighting. Punks had either developed into Goths or died in a heroin induced orgy of mediocrity. In my absence, the scene had moved on and I had some catching up to do. We went to see Balaam And The Angel, at the Lyceum. There was no Pogoing around, no fist fights in the crowd.

"Do you want to come with me to Holland? My mate Pieter, lives in Den Haag and we can stay at his place, there's a really great band playing, The Fields of the Nephilim, you know them, they're always being played in the clubs." Ian had a way of turning an invitation into a command of sorts. For some reason I was happy to be his run around, pick him up from North London after an all-nighter to take him home and sleep it off, I was his mate and sometimes, that meant going the extra mile. Going to Holland was different, that was a long way to go.

"We can get the train to Harwich, then overnight ferry to Den Haag, his Mum's doing us dinner, we go to the gig, stop at their house and get a lift to the ferry port Sunday, then back in time for work Monday morning. How's about it?" It sounded great, but I was skint. I wouldn't get paid until Friday and so would be running a bit close to the wind moneywise. I'd recently had to pay out £500 for the phone bill and was still trying, and failing, to save money in the hope of going back to America.

"Yes, I'm up for it, see you Friday."

I hadn't ever been to Holland-not that I knew of, maybe as a passenger in my Dad's truck when I was little, but I couldn't be certain. Nor had I planned this this weekend very well. I made it to the station, with my wages in hand, but the bank had closed. I couldn't exchange any money for Dutch Guilders.

"That's alright," Ian said, "I'll get the beers over there, you buy the beers on the boat."

The beers on the boat transformed into vodka's, then tequilla and before we knew it the sun was up and we were in Holland.

Pieter met us at the port and drove us home to meet his family. On the journey there, Ian kept pointing at the houses and calling out "Look, there's a Thingy-ma-jig!" or a "Oo-ja-me-flop!" Just about every house we passed had in it's front window a decorative object hung on a chain, an 'Oo-ja-me-flop!' Or another object, stuck to the glass near the centre bottom of the window, a 'Thingy-ma-jig!' These seemed to both fascinate and thrill Ian in equal amounts. They were decorative, but no more enthralling than an empty flowerpot. Something that did enthral me, however, was Pieter's Mum's dinner. She cooked us a chicken with a hot peanut butter sauce, and I would have married her there and then for that sauce, it was gorgeous, a national favourite in the Netherlands, and with me too.

I had never seen The Fields Of The Nephilim, but according to Ian and Pieter, they were the greatest band on Earth, they explained to me the concept of the band, their image, style and sound. I was really hyped by the time they came on stage, I was really looking forward to this show. By the time they came on however, the stage was a mass of fog, thick imitation fog, so thick that the band could hardly be seen. Behind me, their fans had built a human pyramid three or four tiers high, one person standing on the shoulders of another, standing on another. Nobody was dancing, arms twirled and hips swivelled on the spot but no dancing. I didn't understand what I was seeing, I failed to connect to the scene. To me, this was all alien, it was nothing like the raw energy of music I had grown up with. Not that it was the music that was wrong, the music was great, catchy and loud, but the growl of the vocal held back, seemed to dull the energy, I couldn't feel what I was hearing.The message, I didn't get 'It'. I have seen them many times since then, and I own some of their records, but I still don't get 'It'.

Ian's plan of being back in time for work Monday morning also came with a surprise clause, he had booked the day off, and morning meant any time before 12 noon. I made it to work just before lunchtime and was lucky not to lose my job. A simple mix of high employee turnover, and being family friends with the boss, meant that I had my wrists slapped, gently, and kept my position.

I was having a cup of tea one day in the work's canteen with Bob and Ray, the company's lorry drivers. Bob was waiting for me to load his truck, he was going to Liverpool and Ray was off to Caerphilly. It dawned on me that while I and the rest of the lads in the factory toiled away, these two were sitting here getting paid to drink tea and eat bacon butties.

"So how much do you normally get a week then?" I asked somewhat cheekily.

"With my night's out this week-"

"Night's out, you get paid to be away overnight?"

"Of course, they pay for our dig's and breakfast too, so all in I reckon I should be taking home about £180 this week" Said Bob, a rather portly, ginger bearded guy who obviously liked his bacon butties even more than I did.

"That's double what I get!" I thought about this, and then asked if I could drive their trucks.

"You'll need to get an HGV licence first, get that and you'll never be out of work" Bob winked at me. This sounded like a plan. My own father had always been a truck driver, he was paid to go all over Europe and was now earning really good money driving a petrol tanker. My Grandad too. If I got my licence I could get paid to drive all over Europe, and beyond. My mind skipped back to when I was on the beach at Marseillan Plage one day. I had been chatting with one of the drink's seller's who walked the beach all day with a cool box full of ice and cold soda's. He told me how he spent his year travelling the world. He began in Israel working on a Kibbutz or Moshav, he preferred the Moshav's as they paid more than the Kibbutz but were usually harder work. Then he would come to France to work the summer season on the beach before going on to Cuba to work the tobacco season there. Usually finishing his tour by relaxing in either Thailand or Bali, his exotic lifestyle sounded ideal to me. In a way, I could get a bit of this myself, just by driving a truck. I could get paid to travel the world, and driving was second nature to me. I wanted in. I wanted to get my licence, but first, Ian had invited me to a friend's party in Archway. Truck driving could wait until next week.

Contact with Marybeth had become less frequent, following my huge phone bill. She was at college and I was working, no matter what we wanted, it seemed that we were slowly drifting apart, life was getting in the way and would ultimately win.

I had managed to get hold of Fiona, she was back home with her Mum in Chalk Farm and we met up for dinner one night. It was great to see her, clean and healthy, happier than when I'd lived with her way back in Earls Court. We felt very close, like best friends. There was to be no sexual relationship between us. She had come out to France to visit when I was living there, at that time she had been training to be a croupier, now she was working and earning a lot of money. Her birthday was coming up and she invited me to go for another meal with her. I was pleased to accept and looked forward to it.

I arrived at her flat, fully suited and booted, looking the very essence of a boyfriend in waiting, flowers and champagne for the lady. I gave her a card and was introduced to her brother and his wife, as well as her Mother's new 'Friend'. We all hurried into a taxi and were whisked off to the West End. Somewhere between being invited and turning up on the night, I had forgotten what Fiona had said about the night. I thought we were going for a meal together, maybe back to the Texmex restaurant we'd been to in Hampstead a couple of weeks before. When we pulled up outside Langham's Brasserie I nearly had a fit. I became suddenly aware that the £16 I had left over in my pocket was not going to go very far in here.

We were seated between Russ Abbott and his party on one table, and some political bigwig and his buddies celebrating the fact it was Friday night, on another. I was so out of my depth. I'm talking goldfish poured into the Pacific kind of 'out of depth'. Throughout the meal I could think only of one thing, how many years of washing up was I to do to pay for this meal? When the bill arrived it was whisked away and despite my offer to pay, I was told not to worry, her Mother's friend was paying. The relief was almost orgasmic, especially when I noticed there were 4 numbers in the total to pay.

We arrived at a flat in Archway, armed with beer and cigarettes a plenty. A young woman Ian knew was having a birthday party in her mother's apartment. The flat felt like being back at Harold Hill, in Andy's mum's place, or Paul and Natalie's. The party was like a throwback to Wood End, people coming and going, nobody knowing who was who, concerned only with drinking more beer and hoping to have a good time. As the night wore on, the crowd thinned. There was a mix of local kids, the birthday girl and her friends, her mum and a couple of neighbours guarding the kitchen, a couple of Hell's Angel's, myself and Ian. I was in the living room talking with some of the local kid's when Ian came in to get me.

"Someone's crashed on her Mum's bed, we have to get them out 'cos he's desperate to sleep, come give us a hand will you?"

I walked into the bedroom to see a big hairy biker comatose across the bed.

"Come on fella, the lady want's her bed back now mate, time to make a move." No response. I tried again. "Come on matey, let's be having you." Nothing. He laid snoring on top of the bed, oblivious to our requests.

"Come on mate" I said, pulling at his boot. He shifted position and grumbled. "Hmmmnnnyoooofff, fff, fuck off!" He was not coming willingly.

"Oh well" I nodded to Ian who grabbed his feet and I pulled him off the bed by the shoulders of his jacket. He hit the floor with a thud.

"Woddyaaaaaphuuckinmmmmmm!" He was out for the count. We left him on the floor and let the woman of the house reclaim her bed, took another drink from the kitchen and settled back in to our conversations in the living room. It was about 20 minutes later that the door flew open, as if we were being raided by the police.

"Which one of you motherfucker's woke me up?" The biker stood in front of us holding a very sharp looking knife. The blade was about 8 inches long, thick, shiny and very dangerous in the wrong hands. I had no doubt this guys hands were not the right ones to meddle with, he was pissed off and very likely to do something stupid about it. Something in his demeanour said he had probably done worse than this before.

"Who the fuck was it?" He growled before turning and punching a hole through the wooden door. One of the younger girls in the room screamed and began to cry.

"Give it a rest mate, come on -you're scaring the ladies" Ian said.

"You lot, get out of here" he snarled at the youngster and her friends. They ran out of the room and straight out of the flat. There was only Ian, myself and 3 lads left in the room.

"Was it you?" He thrust the knife dangerously close to one lad's face, his eyes crossed as he looked down at the blade, I was pretty sure he farted quietly as the blood drained from his face.

"No, I..I..It wasn't me, I-"

"Stop snivelling you little shit. You're all fucking cowards, spineless fucking cowards pulling me off my bed like that-"

"Come on mate" I said, "you don't have to be like this, nobody's pulling anyone off of any thing here." The biker turned to face me.

"Was it you?" He pointed the knife at my face. Now was not a good time for honesty, diplomacy was needed, but it had to reflect the fact that he was armed, dangerous and had a massive ego to protect.

"Look mate, you don't have to do this, nobody here has done anything. The lady needed to have her bed back and that's all. Nobody has a problem with anyone and anyway, no one here is going to have a go at you mate, you don't have anything to prove to anyone, nobody's going to fight you, nobody here at any rate."

"If I find out it was you I will cut your fucking balls off with this" He wriggled the blade a few millimetres from my nose. It felt good to be complimented, he was acknowledging the fact that I did at least have some balls, though for how much longer I was not sure. One false move, one wrong word and he would definitely not give me another chance.

The flat quickly emptied, people headed off home leaving only Ian and myself alone with the crazy biker, to stop anything untoward happening to the lady of the house or her daughter. It was a long, quiet night.

I found out from my brother Les, that there was a Truck Driving School at a nearby airfield and arranged an afternoon's practice session. This was to see if I really did fancy having a go, and if I was actually capable of handling a truck and trailer. My first attempt at driving with air brakes was not hugely successful, I did as all newcomers do, hit the brakes as hard as I would in a car, almost sending myself head first through the windscreen. I could handle going forwards, reversing was like witchcraft, I didn't know how it was done but it had to involve sorcery of some kind, whatever I did with the steering wheel the trailer on the back would go the opposite way to where it was meant to be going. Suddenly I understood what it must have been like, to be a school teacher faced with me and Andy Nunn.

"You will do this."

"Nope."

"You will do as I say"

"Nope."

"Not like that, like this!"

"Er, nope."

"God give me strength...." But he never did.

I loved the idea of driving a big truck, travelling the world and getting paid for it, but there would be hurdles, not just learning how to do it, there would be the cost and the Medical too. Then I would have to get a job, and getting a job meant getting experience first, I needed some delivery driving experience.

I found an agency who supplied warehouse workers and van drivers to companies around the London area. After a short interview, I was placed on the books and told I could start as soon as I was ready, they'd give me some warehouse work and driving jobs to build up my skills and experience. I quit my job at Steel Drums, crossed my fingers, hoping I'd done the right thing.

My first job was a disaster. I was given a job to deliver some parcels around the West End in a Transit Van . I thought I knew the West End pretty well, this should be quite easy. But leaving the company's depot I took a wrong turn and was heading out of London on the A12. I tried to remedy this by making a U-turn at a roundabout, however a car on my right was going straight ahead in a hurry and we collided. Not knowing the procedure for this I gave the other driver my number and told him I'd pay for the damage. I carried on into London, with a bent front end and no headlight on the offside.

There is a huge difference between knowing your way around somewhere on foot, and having to drive there. Of the 12 or so deliveries I had on board, I returned at 6pm with 5 or 6 still on board, and a broken headlight, and dented front end. I blamed the traffic but really, I should have stopped and bought myself a map, planned my route according to my deliveries and all the other things I didn't do on the day, but it was my first day, and I had a lot to learn. The next morning I was called to the office to explain what happened and was told to fill out an accident report form. It seemed that any accident at work was covered by insurance and I would still be paid. That was a huge relief as I didn't have the money to pay for repairs myself, the downside of it was that I wouldn't be allowed to drive again, until I was trusted to do so.

My next job was in Whetstone, at a B&Q store. I was taken by minibus with the rest of the night crew and tasked with cleaning the place up and restocking the shelves. After a few nights of this I was asked if I wanted to work day's as there were some vacancies going, I accepted and when the night shift left, I stayed on and worked the day as well. Double shifting like this meant I would earn a lot more money a lot quicker, I was more than happy to do it. Until.

"Here, you can take this broom outside and sweep the car park clear."

So yes, Life. One minute you're somebody everyone looks up to. Your own business, money to do as you please, come and go at will. Jet setting around the globe, travelling in stretched Limo's, being eaten alive on long haul bus rides. The next thing you know, you're stacking drums in a dirty factory in the East End or some bastard hands you a broom and say's 'Go sweep the car park!' Beautiful isn't it. The array of opportunity, boundless.

I had been outside, making the car park look pretty, propping up my broom and smoking a cigarette when a car pulled in and parked right where I'd just swept. It was a convertible, MG I think, dark green and spotless. A lovely looking car. Whoever owned that didn't have to sweep car parks for a living. No he didn't, he just got had to get up on stage and sing.

I watched almost frozen to the spot as Dave Vanian and his wife got out of the car and headed toward's the store.

"Dave, Dave!" I called and leapt across the car park toward's the couple. "Hello Dave, fancy seeing you here, remember me? I interviewed you in Montpellier a few months ago, for my mates radio station."

"Yes, I remember, what are you doing here? I thought you lived in France"

"I did, but you know how it is, things happen, I went to America for a bit and just ended up back here, anyway good to see you, when are you playing next? Gotta come see you again, great show in Mont....." By this time they were already backing off at a gentle run. I could almost hear a voice whispering -

"Step away from the nutter with the broom, keep smiling, now run!"

One day you're backstage asking them about their careers, the next they're running away from you because you have a broom in your hand. Celebrity, it's a mugs game.

After a couple of weeks, I was offered a new placement, night shift with Fed Ex in Enfield. I was promised a long term placement, 3-6 months, with the added option of some driving experience if needed. I jumped at the chance and began straight away. It wasn't long before I had the job sussed and had made new friends with Geraldo (Gerry) and Russ, my co-workers from the agency. We hit it off immediately, and were constantly playing tricks on each other and anyone else unfortunate enough to come into contact with us. Gerry was Italian and lived in Dagenham, near Russ, a quieter but equally ruthless trickster with pale skin , red hair and glasses. Between the 3 of us, we could unload a trailer full of parcels in next to no time, everything loaded onto pallets according to their various postal code destinations. We loaded the trucks ready for the next morning's delivery's, often having to do the shunting (moving the trucks on and off the loading bays) ourselves. We were not allowed near any trailers, just the rigid's. I loved moving the big 17 and 18 ton trucks around the yard, I could imagine myself driving them around Europe one day, king of the road, a modern day nomad with diesel where my blood should be.

In a matter of weeks we had the place all wrapped up, and some of the managers too. We double and triple shifted, one week working a total of 120 hours each. We worked hard and played hard. When new workers came on site we sent them to the office for 'Sky Hooks', 'Tartan Paint', or 'Glass Nails for repairing pallets', my favourite being 'Long weights for parcels'. Always guaranteed to rid us of anyone we didn't connect with. We were bullies, of that I had no doubt, but when we shrink wrapped the Depot Manager and put him on a pallet labelled for the main hub at Nuneaton, he took it in good humour, even when we sent the photo's with a ransom note, addressed to the Area Manager, we got away with it. When Gerry crashed the forklift in the yard however, things got serious. Gerry and Russ were having a row, Gerry drove full speed at Russ who dived out of the way, Gerry then crashed into a pile of broken pallets and flipped the forklift onto it's side. This was a case of Gross Misconduct and they were in big trouble. Christmas was coming up and Russ needed to keep his job, he had a wife and kids at home, he couldn't afford to lose his job. Gerry didn't care, he already had plans for going to live in Italy, even though he'd lived all his life in London. Before he left, he had one last prank to perform.

We'd been told that we were to have a visit from the company's chief security officer. On the day of his visit we sat by the window of the canteen, with a full view of the car park outside. As if on cue, the Head of Security (UK) came from around a corner inspecting the outside of the building. He stopped almost motionless when he saw a cardboard box perched on a wall near the canteen window. The box had a label and was sealed with Fed Ex tape. He came straight over and reached up to pick up the carton, obviously thinking someone had been attempting to steal parcels from the warehouse. I saw him check the label, shake the box gently and then proceed to open it with his pocket knife. The silence in the canteen was evidence of some certain mis-propriety, but he was intent on getting to the bottom of this mystery package and paid us no attention. Wrong move. He put his hand into the box and felt between the styrofoam balls, his hand retreated and in his grasp he held a huge turd, one Russ had made earlier at Gerry's request. We howled with laughter as the Security Chief stormed off to the depot manager's office.

We were called into the Manager's office later that day.

"Lads, our National Head of Security had a nasty surprise this morning, and I am pretty sure we all know what that was. Now he's not a happy bunny, and is intent on reporting the incident to Head Office. So, please do me, and yourselves a favour, and calm it down a little. If you ask me I'd say he deserved it, but you didn't and I haven't, now get back to work and no more shitting in boxes, is that understood?"

"Yes Mike." We replied before being waved out into the warehouse.

The investigation into the forklift incident found Gerry to have accidentally put his foot on the accelerator, when tipping some damaged pallets onto the pile for burning, it was an accident and no further action required. The company took on a whole crew of Driver's and warehouse staff from the agency, contracts were sorted and the new team were due to start in the new year, we were not part of that team. Gerry went to Italy for Christmas on a one way ticket. Russell started a new job elsewhere and I was sent to Coventry.

I had only intended to visit for the holiday period, but once I got back to Cov I felt like I was home. I was back with my real family and had room to breathe, I Stayed with Helen and H, sleeping on their sofa. They were parents now, they had a little Daughter, Toni-Anne, and it was obvious they were both as proud as they could be.

"Why don't you come back to Cov?" Helen asked, "You could stay here until you get somewhere sorted."

The offer was too good to refuse. I felt stifled in London, like a square peg in a round hole. I had plenty of friends and lot's to do but I was not happy in my own skin there. Coventry felt more like home for me, and I was wasting no time in moving back. I wrote to Marybeth, telling her I was moving to Coventry, it was the last time I would contact her, the last time I would have to remind myself I'd let her down, that I couldn't be trusted. In a way, her father had been right, I wasn't good enough for his daughter, his rejection of me had become a self-fulfilling prophecy.

I had only been back in Coventry a couple of days when I got offered a job as a full time driver for a coal merchant and haulage company in Meriden, a small village just outside of the city. I bought myself a bike to get to work on, I hadn't ridden one for years but I needed to get to and fro at odd hours and couldn't afford a car yet. I reunited with Rich Mulligan, he just happened to have a spare room in his flat and so I now had somewhere to stay long term. I was grateful obviously, to Helen and H for putting me up, but I needed a place I could call home.

My new job was a mix of delivering exhibition goods, or contract work delivering heating equipment, boilers etc to construction sites all over the country. Other times I would be required to deliver sacks of coal to local premises around Coventry and Warwickshire. Delivering coal was back breaking work, seriously. I would have to load various grades of coal into sacks in our yard. The smokeless fuel was nice and rounded, more expensive to buy, but easier to manhandle. The largest grade of coal came in huge, odd shaped lumps, these jutted through the side of the 50kg (110 lb) sacks, digging into my back. They were awkward and painful to carry. Delivering coal is not for the fainthearted, it is hard, dirty work. There is a knack to carrying coal sacks, but they remain heavy, awkward beasts that could easily break a man's back, or cause irreparable lifelong damage. Coal dust is invasive, it gets into the skin, under your nails, in your hair, your ears, nose, mouth, in your eye's and under your clothes. You breathe it, eat it and sweat it all day long. I was lucky, I only had to bag it and deliver it to the end user's. I never had to dig the stuff, I never had to work below ground, trapped in a black cave hour after hour, day after day. Once a person is exposed to the reality of working with coal, he or she can only admire those that dedicate their lives to the industry, it is hard, back breaking work, and for the most part, thankless. The first time I tried lifting a sack my legs buckled and wobbled, I could barely walk in a straight line. After a few weeks I was carrying sometimes, two at a time. My back was strong, my arms muscular and powerful, I felt fitter than at any time in my life. Had I been a woman I might even have have fancied me, from a distance, in the fog after several tequila's when everyone else had gone home.

Rich was now DJ'ing at Busters, a club in the city centre above the market. The venue was done out like a cave and had a sunken dance floor. I loved it there and would spend all night thrashing around, throwing shapes and shaking my backside like Beyoncé before she was even born. This was the late eighties, a time of The Cult, Killing Joke and The Mission. New Model Army were big on the scene and yet we still threw each other around to all the old favourites, The Ramones, Dickies, Damned, even the Sex Pistols were still being played and enjoyed by folks who had grown up with their songs constantly playing in their bedrooms. Beer was swallowed in copious amounts and all the boys got together to compare notes on who had slept with who, or more frequently, who had been rejected and when. The more public and humiliating the put down, the more we revelled in each other's disappointments. Ronny, a short rockabilly lad who loved punk and The Stray Cat's equally, was a master at the art of 'pulling birds.' Nobody could pull a girl like Ronny, nobody, mainly because you just wouldn't.

There was a story of his, that one night, in the Irish club, he spent ages sitting with a girl buying her drinks, chatting her up.

"I thought I was in, I really did" he said. "Then this song came on, and I was a bit pissed and thought-yeah, let's dance. So I get's up, and say's to her 'Come on let's have a dance.' Are you taking the piss? she says. 'Come on, what's wrong with you? Let's dance!" It was at this point the girl in question gave him that deadly scowl, the one that say's something along the lines of 'How dare you sleep with my Mother when she's only been dead a week.' Ronny looked at her properly for the first time all evening and realised that she was sitting in a wheelchair. She was not going to dance. Ronny left the building, alone, early.

We had a little gang gathering together most weekends, Ronny the Rockabilly, Kent a postman with a knack for always being in the wrong place at the wrong time and upsetting everyone.

"Hey up, here comes Kent!"

"For fuck's sake no!"

This would be the normal welcoming conversation before he entered the bar with his usual high pitched, nasally voice.

"Y'all right lads? Not many 'ere tonight, what's everyone up to- hey do you wanna buy some socks?"

We were regular contributors to the till behind the bar at the Rose and Crown pub. Most people referred to it as the Rose and Queer, until a new landlord changed the name to The Courtyard and redecorated the place, as all new landlords do in an effort to get rid of the old customers. John Candy ran the bar and was an absolute scream, he could insult and bitch anyone better than any camp TV or Radio personality I've ever seen. With some good therapy, I may one day recover from his lightning fast quips.

Kent had been selling socks to people in the bar for weeks. One day the Landlord asked us to put a stop to it, so we devised a plan.

Kent turned up as usual on a Saturday afternoon, the Landlord was ready for him and the back room, where the pool table was, was empty.

"Kent, the landlord want's a word with you mate, better go see him"

"Cheers Ribs, what's he want?"

"I don't know mate, just asked if you'd go see him when you get here."

We watched as Kent went into the pub, and then followed him into the back room, silently.

"Now then Kent, it's about these socks..."

It was at that moment, myself, Rich, Decca and Ronny jumped on Kent. We pinned him to the floor and quickly grabbed a limb each, lifted and carried him outside where we had cleared a table ready. Kent was planted face down on the table, his hands lifted above his head, his legs pulled straight and within seconds he was bound with some thin rope to both ends of the table. For a moment, I thought that was it, we hadn't planned on doing anything else, but Decca stepped forward and heaved Kent's trousers and pants down to his shins. Somebody else pulled his top up and he lay there, prone, bound and semi naked.

"I have an idea," I said, rushing to the bar and returning with a jug of ice cubes. I poured them into a neat pile on the small of his back, wondering if this would make him loosen his bladder. Before I had the chance to find out somebody stepped forward with the icing on the cake, a red Rose. A solitary red Rose, with a stem, and thorns was inserted into his bum and Kent could do nothing about it. The howls of laughter attracted quite a crowd, and people were hurrying through bags, pockets and purses for their cameras. Kent must have been the most photographed individual on the planet that day, well, for the 10 or 15 minutes we left him there. Still tied to the table, de-bagged and with a rose up his arse, Kent did not give up, he lay there and tried chatting up the ladies as they came by to enter the pub. Anyone else would have died of embarrassment, not Kent, he wore it like a badge of honour.

I never really had a chat up line. I just seemed to wing it whenever I wanted to chat to somebody. I knew other lads who had certain phrases, lines or compliments they'd use to win a girl's favour, but me, I must have skipped school that day. When Animal and I hung out together, I'd approach a girl and ask if she wanted to see how many press up's I could do, throw myself on the ground and pump like a dodgy 70's porn star on crystal meth. Needless to say, this approach never produced results, but it made us laugh. Equally ineffective was our latest approach. Rich, Decca, Ronny and I all had our own pewter tankards which we kept behind the bar. We were loud and raucous, together, we would bash our tankards of beer and join in the call to arms.

"Gimme a "B!"
"B!" "Gimme another B!"
"B!"
"Gimme another B!"
"B!"
"Now put 'em together and what have you got?"
All together now for the chorus.....
"Birdin' Boozin' an' Brawlin' !" Yep, that was us.....

The Rose and Crown was a regular haunt for the Punks, Goth's, LGBT and others. It was also where John worked, on the door. John was the pub bouncer, or security guard. A short fellow about my height, with a dark moustache and equally dark sense of humour. We hit it off straight away, I was looking at getting my HGV licence, and so was John, as well as Ronny and Lisa -who I had known from The Butts college days. All of us were planning on becoming truck drivers.

John was ex-army, spoke very proper, almost like an officer but with added humour. I enjoyed his stories and how he told them. There were plenty of them too, and plenty of stories about John. He had a bit of a reputation around town and one night, returning from a pool match at another pub, some rather unappealing lads were waiting for him in the car park behind the pub. The rest of the pool team froze when confronted with an Iron bar and a couple of baseball bats, John took a step forward and calmly slipped his hand just inside his jacket. Knowing John's reputation, how it invoked the image of a gun toting psychopath, the bat wielding louts retreated from whence they came, taking their bats with them.

"What have you got in there John?" Asked one of the team.

John slowly withdrew his hand and showed him.

"Marlboro, soft pack."

I had not been living with Rich for long, a month or two I guess, when I asked him about someone he knew, someone I'd seen who'd caught my eye.

"Nikki, stay away from her, she's trouble, I mean it mate, she's bad news."

You know that 'Red rag to a Bull' thing, yes, as you already know, as a Taurus, I'm full of Bull, and if you wave a red flag at me I will chase it.

Other than the occasional fleeting liaison, I hadn't had a relationship with a woman since leaving America. I saw Helen and H settled and getting on with life. Other friends too were now married and having kids, My Sister Anne had a son, Michael, my brother had made me an uncle to Jack. Everyone was settling down and happy, except -I felt, me. I was beyond a crossroad in my life, I was way down the street, somewhere between the one way flow of the eternal Bachelor, and the car crash I was about to ride.

'That' girl was called Nikki. I kept seeing her out and about, she was pale skinned, had bleached blonde hair, and always had a smile for me, and I was a sucker for a smile. I was also a sucker for a sob story. Nikki turned out to be a walking sob story. Her father had died after a long illness when she was 14, and she spent the rest of her life blaming the whole world for her misfortune. I had heard Rich say not to get involved with her, but I couldn't resist, I thought I could fix her, make her happy. I had every intention of being the guy that gave her back her life, stood by her and made her happy.

Coventry had changed a bit since I had left. The Punks had changed a little too. There was a lot of 'Cock Rock' in the charts, lots of hair, lycra and spandex, bandannas had replaced many Mohawks, spiky tops had become greasy mops and everyone was into Guns'n'Roses. Boys looked more like the Girls than the girls did, especially from behind. There were new bands around town as well as the old. Annex UK, Blitzkrieg Zone and The Primitives, a band that had a song in the charts called 'Crash'. I saw the singer in The Rose one night, she was just the same as she looked on Top of the Pop's, same clothes, same hair, same height, she was only little and we only had a little telly. There were still some old die-hards, like Rich, myself, Decca, Sharif and Mince, as well as the new kids on the block, Little Rich, Kent, Ronnie (the Rockabilly) Big Nosed Dave and Raoul. People came, people went, that's life.

Something else new, was Comic Relief. People raising money by dressing up and doing strange things for charity. 1988 was my first experience of this phenomena. Blitzkrieg Zone were playing in the back room of The Rose and all I had for fancy dress was a wet-suit. So there I was, at a gig, in the overcrowded, hot, sweaty back room of the pub in a wet-suit and Dr Martens, I still to this day can't understand why that look never took off, so practical in the British Climate and you don't even have to stop chatting up the girls to go to the toilet. *(Don't try that at home kids, your mother won't like it!)* A lot of beer was drunk that night, and a lot of money raised for charity. I got the feeling it might just catch on.

Much to Rich's displeasure, Nikki and I got together. Because she was barred from his flat, I spent more and more time in her bedsit, as did some of our friends, to the point where some days I got back from work to find other people sitting on the bed when all I wanted to do was bathe and sleep. Little Jacqui was a regular visitor, she had a lot of problems too. I was at work one day when Nikki had left her alone for 5 minutes. Jacqui found the medicine cupboard and by the time Nikki got back, the cupboard was bare. By the time I got home, a very unhealthy looking and apologetic Jacqui was still alive on the bed. I gave her a lecture about the dangers of doing what she had, but she assured me she had simply wanted to get stoned, I wasn't convinced. Jacqui was a troubled soul, she had a big heart but even bigger demons.

H had started working with Helen's Dad, Stuart. He had a shed and fencing company near Hearsall Common and some Saturdays I would help out. We made fence panels from scratch, laying out the framing and nailing the boards together on large wooden benches, carrying them outside and dipping them in a water based treatment tank. Once they'd been stood to dry we would load the van and deliver them to houses around the city. The shed's were also made from scratch to a basic design. Firstly, we made the floor and roof sections. Then we'd make the sides, back and front. The workshop rang out with the sound of electric saws, air guns and BBC Radio 2. The air and floor were thick with sawdust. The small toilet was stained dark brown and would freeze in winter. The kettle, weighed down with a century's worth of limescale, was constantly in use.

"Stick the kettle on Bones" Stuart would say, and I would. We didn't have milk. We didn't have tea. We drank black coffee, instant, no sugar, a nice thick layer of sawdust was all the sweetener we would need.

Saturday mornings we would receive a delivery of timber and boards. Our first job would be to have a coffee. Next, we'd unload the delivery truck, by hand. Each time I took 6 boards, H took 8, so I'd take 9 and he'd have to carry 10. We competed incessantly throughout the day. When taking panels outside to dip I'd take 1, H would take 2 and I'd return for 3. It wasn't possible to carry more than 4 panels, not on your own, we tried and failed continually laughing at ourselves for even attempting. When it came to moving shed panels, we did the same, competing to carry the biggest or heaviest panels, it was fun and we loved our work. We were covered in woodstain, fed on coffee and sawdust, chocolate and crisps. It was hard work but we loved it and the extra money came in very useful.

My first visit to Nikki's childhood home ended rather abruptly. I had been told how her Father had died in their front room, that sometimes Nikki hated being in the house, but I was not ready for my experience. We'd popped round in my new car, recently acquired with the tip's and extra money I'd earned at Euroshed's, and by saving some of my wages from work. As soon as I entered the house I felt strange. It was an overwhelming sense of something or someone being all around me, almost suffocatingly present in the air. Nikki went upstairs to get something and left me in the hallway. I felt it, I could almost hear it saying I was not welcome, and I was convinced I wasn't. Something, someone, did not want me in that house. I quickly left and waited in the car outside. When Nikki came out, she asked me what was wrong and I told her what had happened. She didn't seem too surprised, as she had already told me that she too had often felt uncomfortable in the house. On subsequent visits the atmosphere lightened, but I never felt truly comfortable in that house, I always felt as though somebody was watching me.

There seemed to be a lot going on in Coventry at this time. The UK Subs came and played a brilliant gig in Longford one night. Other bands were playing in and around the city centre. Busters was always busy, and there was the Sir Colin Campbell and the Hand & Heart that were also putting band's on. Our neighbour upstairs, was a well respected DJ and old school punk called AL Jones. Al was nocturnal for the most part, up all night working, playing records, mooching around. Trying to sleep in a bedsit, keeping a regular job with some very early start times and a night life, was a huge task. It was obvious we would have to move, and soon.

I got stuck in London one night and had to stay overnight, so I decided to visit Fiona. I called Nikki, she flew into a jealous rage and before I could do anything, she arrived drunk and spitting profanities at Euston Station. I was embarrassed by her actions, nothing was happening between me and Fiona, we were friends but Nikki didn't trust me, not now, not ever.

We started saving for a place of our own, not to buy, to rent. I was working, Nikki got a job with an agency and we somehow managed to get a council flat, on the 16th floor of a tower block, overlooking the canal basin and city centre. We decided to get married on the 17th May. We chose this date as it was 3 days after her birthday on the 14th, 3 days after mine on the 11th, it seemed to make sense at the time, and it was a Saturday. I invited members of my family, friends from Coventry, and others. Fiona came up from London, Capsule from France- with a gift of the Bérurier Noir LP, On á Faim. There was a great turn out and we had the back room of The Rose & Crown, for the reception, followed by a late finish at Busters. I had a bright red Mohawk and

Nikki had died the tips of her hair red too, to match her wedding dress. H gave a speech, something along the lines of "Cheers everyone!" Between us we must have drunk enough to drain the Coventry Canal. It's purely coincidental that coastal sea levels around the UK rose that night, though we were doing a grand job of pissing for England.

I woke up hungover, married and unsure I had done the right thing but determined to make a go of it. I'd had some room to breathe, some time to sort my head out from the years of instability, insecurity and hedonism I had immersed myself in during the past. Now it was time to settle, make a home and move onward.

3 Sounds Of The Suburbs

"One thing I can't give you is the one thing you adore, and the one thing that I cherish, I shall love forevermore...."

We were at Helen and H's one night, it was getting late and we'd been drinking cheap lager since we finished working earlier in the evening. "I loved Adam And The Ants, you know, their earlier stuff mostly." Slurred H before waving his half empty can around in a full circle in-front of himself. His eyes seemed fixed on a spot of the skirting board, way off in his middle vision, somewhere between intelligent conversation and 'I fuckin' luv you!' H was pissed, drunk, and still holding his own in the conversation.

"I saw them once, at Lewisham, brilliant gig. Adam fell off the stage at one point and all the seats collapsed." I said, recounting the events of the night.

"Was that when they'd brought out Kings of the Wild Frontier?" H asked.

"Yes, there was a support band on with them, pretty good but not brilliant, what were they called?"

"Hel, didn't Dave Pep play with the Ants?"

Helen looked up from the baby she was trying to breast feed, Toni-Anne was half asleep and three quarters full of milk.

"Yes, but I don't remember when."

"God's Toys!" I exclaimed, having recalled the support band's name. "God's Toys, that was it. They did a song 'We are God's Toys, God's Toys, God's Toys!" I sang, stretching out the last words as the band had done that night.

"That's it, yes, Dave Pep played for them."

"Dave from Blitzkrieg Zone?" I asked, I knew Dave but not that well, I'd spoken to him a few times in the pub and seen him play a few times.

"That's him, yes, he used to play for God's Toys"

"I remember watching the keyboard player mostly, she was well fit."

H stopped waving his can as a puzzled look came over his face.

"The keyboard player?"

"Yes, I thought she was lovely."

"The keyboard player?"

"Yes."

"Dave Pep was their keyboard player....."

Saturday nights were usually spent like this, laying around drinking beer and talking about music, politics, life. I didn't always find out that my teenage desires had actually been men in skintight leggings, this was a one-off, never to be repeated incident.

No sooner than we'd settled into our new home on the 16th floor, Nikki fell pregnant and suddenly we were parents in waiting. She was on the pill and this was not planned. It was welcome, but not planned. I reckoned it was because of all the speed she'd had when we moved in. We bought a whole load of amphetamine sulphate, enough to keep going for a fortnight without stopping. While I was at work, Nikki helped herself and over the course of a couple of days had consumed the lot. She was running around like a whirling dervish, decorating the flat in next to no time. She also had to go to work in the mornings, her pupils the size and colour of a lump of Anthracite, she cooked and served for police officers and prisoners, at Little Park Street Police Station's canteen. I didn't mind the unexpected pregnancy, I was excited at the prospect of becoming a father, knowing there would be a little bundle of love that I would see grow and become a full human being in time.

Becoming a Father meant changes, it meant having to be mature and saving money, buying for the child first, a loving home environment, safety, security. My carefree travelling days were over and I could not have been happier. I wanted this new phase of life so very much. My biological clock was not ticking, it was screeching in my head. I was ready, I was 23 but felt nearer to 33 and a third, with my life having been played on 78. I had had all the heartaches, girlfriends, one night stands and true loves I could have wished for. Now was the time to knuckle down and be an adult.

As Nikki got used to the idea of having someone growing inside her, I changed jobs and booked myself onto a HGV driving course. Once I had that licence, my wages would almost double and we would be more able to provide for our new family member.

We had a spare room in the flat, which we had planned to let out to a gay couple that were interested in moving in to. Fortunately they decided they'd prefer a place of their own, so when we found out about the pregnancy we were glad they had not moved in. We were to need the spare room for our baby, and all it's paraphernalia. Something else we needed, was the all-clear from my GP. I wanted to know if I had anything wrong with me before bringing another life into the world. I was not keen on the idea of finding out I had some communicable disease that I could be passing on to our unborn child. I was tested for HIV, Hep A & B and a host of other ailments. Everything was negative, the Hep from my younger days was gone. It was explained to me that I had probably had a type of Alcoholic Hepatitis, Jaundice of the eyes and skin brought on by an excess of alcohol. I was beyond exhilarated, I was being given a brand new start, a whole new lease of life, a new beginning with a family of my own. My upbringing had been good, in comparison to others, I had had it easy. I hadn't been abused or mistreated, but I had been cut off by my father. We hadn't spoken for years, nor would we. According to my Mum, I was better off out of it, I was better off living my own life, away from the arguments, the fights, the lies. I was better off, but I was also losing out, as were my family. We were all being pushed apart and played against each other. Whatever was going to happen, I was determined to be the best father I could for my kid. I didn't want an environment where the parents fought, where the kid suffered because the adults couldn't get their own acts together. My children would be loved, and raised with love.

We were in town one night, possibly at The Lanch. The girl's were up and dancing when a bit of a commotion broke out. Somehow during their dance, Nikki had stepped backwards and onto Bev, her high stiletto heel passing through the top of Bev's foot. Bev was in agony and hardly able to walk on her injured foot. Nikki apologised but that wouldn't fix Bev's foot, she needed to get to hospital. Seeing as she was so small, Bev was about 5 foot tall in her heels and weighed in at somewhere around the average for a 6 year old. I decided to take her there myself. I picked her up and walked with her in my arms to the A&E unit at Coventry & Warwickshire Hospital, about a mile away. I have always liked Bev, she was well travelled, had a sense of humour and was one of 'Us', whoever we were. She clung onto me, scared I might drop her, her arms gripped tightly around my shoulders. Nikki was getting annoyed with me, her insecurities making her jealous of me carrying Bev. If she had been the one with the damaged foot, I would have done the same, but in her eyes I was in the wrong.

Jealousy and insecurity were to become a continual distraction in our marriage. Nikki believed I was having affairs with every woman that I met. No one person was safe, none. I wish I had been so lucky back then, I'd probably have worn myself out by now though. Expired with a smile on my face and "Who's that on my lap?"

Morning sickness came and went, sometimes not appearing until evening, sometimes immediately morning came. I did what I could to help, but as all parents know, the expectant father is not much use to a woman with morning sickness. The 'Look what you've done to me' snarl, and "Don't you ever think you're putting that thing in me again" sneer, kind of fills a man with dread. We do what we can to help, but invariably all our efforts are in vain. We become the target, the enemy, the person that did this to them, and for at least 6 months of the pregnancy we are doomed. Nothing we do or say is relevant, advisable or even possible. Everything in the house becomes a lethal projectile -except for the soft stuff, that becomes tear stained and covered in make-up, snot and the dregs of whatever meal was last thrown at you. Nikki was highly volatile and constantly depressed. She drank and smoked, unable to fully stop but reducing as best she could throughout her pregnancy.

I began my HGV driving course. Each morning for 2 weeks, I cycled to Nuneaton where my training began. I shared the course with 2 other trainees. 3 Students and 1 instructor squeezed into an old Bedford tractor unit. Behind us a 20 foot long, single axle flatbed trailer. From Nuneaton, we drove down to Coventry, Kenilworth and Stratford finally coming to a halt at Long Marston Airfield. Here we were taught to reverse and made to back our vehicle into a coned off area. We repeated this most important of tasks over and over again. Occasionally taking one or more cones out, our skills improved with the practice. To break up the repetition, we would often practice our emergency stops or 3 point turns. We also sat around and drank a lot of tea. Dave (-not that one) would tell us stories of his colourful career as we sipped our brew.

"So what was the most valuable load you ever carried?" I asked him one day.

"Oh I don't know, a few hundred thousand pounds maybe, but a lad I used to know, he was an owner-driver, had a flatbed trailer and the dirtiest sheets you've ever seen in your life. Anyway, he got a job one day and rolled up into a very secure yard first thing in the morning. The guy on the weighbridge told him to leave the truck there with the keys in, go to the canteen and have breakfast, everything was free and they'd come and get him when his truck was loaded." We listened with keen interest as he continued his tale. "So about an hour later they come and get him. His trailer fully loaded, sheeted and roped absolutely perfectly, better than he could have done it himself. He was given his delivery address and told to go straight there, no stopping, no breaks, no diverting from the route he was given. He'd already been told to fill up with diesel before he arrived in the morning and so started to think it was all a bit odd. Anyway, he gets to where he's going and is told to leave the truck on the weighbridge. Same deal as before, lunch was free and waiting in the canteen for him. An hour later they came back. The truck was clear, sheets rolled perfectly and his ropes coiled neatly. Before leaving, he asked the guy on the weighbridge what it was he'd been carrying, he wasn't supposed to tell him, but he did, it was 24 pallets of used bank notes for burning."

I was constantly surprised at the length of the trailer behind the truck, I had never driven anything this big before and it seemed huge. I loved driving, and I loved the challenge of driving something this big. I relished in my fantasies of driving an artic across the desert, a real globetrotter, pushing the boundaries beyond Europe, driving to the ends of the Earth. In the real world, I was now working for an agency. I got the occasional van driving job, but for the most part I worked as a warehouseman for a handful of companies around Coventry.

On the day of my actual test, I felt quite confident. We'd practised driving the route the previous day and I thought I had it sussed.

"You'll be fine" assured my instructor. "Keep the nerves at bay and just drive as you have been doing, you should pass no problem."

I did as I was told and was doing fine, very fine. I stayed away from clipping curbs, except maybe once or twice. My lane discipline, use of the road and observation were going really well until the examiner uttered those unforgettable words:

"Continue along this road, unless the road signs instruct you otherwise." I knew this was coming, we'd practised this one too. This was that road that turns right just at the top of the hill with a side road joining straight ahead, I had to turn with the road and not continue straight ahead, we'd done this junction yesterday, it was fresh in my mind, it was a doddle, it was... Not the same road. As we reached the brow of the hill there was a turning to the right and the road carried on ahead, but it was not the same junction we had practised on our route, this was different. Everything suddenly looked wrong. I hit the brakes and indicated to turn right at the same moment as my mind screamed to continue ahead. My eyes told me to continue, my mind's eye had already seen the road going off to the right, everything competing in a split second for my immediate attention.

"Bollocks!" I yelped. This was a monumental fuck up and I knew it. It wasn't enough that I had nearly turned into a housing estate, but to throw the examiner forward so that he almost headbutted the dashboard was a complete no-no. The look of hatred on his face told me I didn't need to bother too much about the drive back to the test centre.

I was back at the test centre a month later. We stopped for a tea on route and Dave (-not that one) gave me a couple of small brown tablets.

"These will take the edge off your nerves" he said.

"What are they?"

"Pro plus, caffeine pills. They just give you a slight edge, help you concentrate a bit better."

I concentrated much better and gave an absolutely perfect drive, probably the best run I could have ever done. No clipping the kerbs, no crazy panic, everything was perfect.

When we got back to the test centre I was beaming. I looked across the cab to my examiner as he wrote out my paper. He handed it to me and was gone from the truck before I could say a word. Dave (-not that one) jumped into his seat and asked how it went. I passed him the paper.

"Failed? what happened out there? I thought you'd passed, the way you were smiling ."

"I did too-I gave him the best drive I've ever done, I don't get it"

He jumped out of the cab and returned a few minutes later, climbing in on the driver's side.

"Off the record, he said you gave a really good drive, but he remembered you from your last test and didn't feel certain you could be trusted alone out there yet, you need some more practice."

Another month passed by and I was back for a third time. Following on from my previous experience, I topped myself up with Pro Plus before leaving home. When I was handed more at the breakfast bar I took those too.

"I'll have a word and see if I can come out with you on this test, sometimes they let us tag along, just to see all is going ok."

I took my test feeling like I'd just snorted a whole jar of Nescafé. Behind and beside me, Dave and the Examiner chatted about all things Campanology. Yes, my examiner was a fucking bell ringing, rope tugger. His lack of fingerprints no doubt paralleled his lack of friends and equal lack of humour. They drew pictures of bells, talked about tones, and casting, sequences and notes. I drove like I just didn't care, and I didn't. I was destined to fail again. No god fearing rope tugger was ever going to let me loose on the road with a truck. I had tattoos, an inverted cross on my arm and a flaming skull on the side of my head, not to mention 'BEEJAY' on my neck. I was a sinner, a sex mad infidel who would burn forever in the depths of Hell, while he played the very bells that would summon the good folk to witness my destruction. I was doomed.

We pulled into the test centre and they both climbed out of the cab. I slid across to the passenger seat, as was normal practice after an exam, just in time to be handed my Pass Certificate. I'd given my worst drive, half cooked on Pro Plus, and yet he passed me. He may have been a rope tugging bell ringer, but for a split second he was my bestest friend in the whole world.

I had a new job now. The company I'd worked for in Meriden had no articulated trucks, only 'rigids', in plain speak they had trucks, but not trucks that pull trailers. I wanted to drive the big trucks, the Artics, I wanted to be a 'King Of The Road', none of that Tonka Toy nonsense for me, I wanted to go big, and now I had my ticket, nothing was stopping me.

I'd started with a company called Double D, AKA 'Dodgy Deliveries.' It was bargain basement haulage, the bottom of the pile. As soon as I started I knew it was not to be viewed as a long term position, a job at Double D was only ever going to be a stepping stone to something else. As is still the case nowadays, you couldn't get a job if you had no experience, and you can't get experience if you have no-one willing to give you your first job. Double D would always take on anyone, no matter how green they were, because the turnover of drivers was a constant problem. People came and went on an almost daily basis. For me this was no problem, I was planning on doing a couple of months, 3 -6 at most- depending on how things went.

John passed his test before me and was doing agency work to get some practice. As soon as I started with Double D, I got John a job there too. He started on one of the Artics while I was still on 7.5 ton rigids. Now I'd passed my test, I wanted to get out on the road in one of the old Leyland Marathon's we operated. I went to see our boss, an old bearded Irishman, also called John.

"I finally got my ticket John, I passed" I announced happily.

"Good lad, I'll get you out in one of the units as soon as I can, for now I need you to go out with John tomorrow, double manned, come in for 5am, your loading for Southampton."

The following morning John and I met in the yard. The yard was a dirty, greasy area on a small industrial estate just around the corner from where I used to live with Fritz and Greg. There was a tatty Portacabin that masqueraded as an office on one side of the yard. Alongside it, a row of of old Bedford trucks in various states of disrepair, rot and destruction. The red cabs had seen better days, most of the engines had been to the moon and back several times, but on differing mornings would refuse to start without a blast of easy start sprayed into their air intakes. At least once a week, even this would not be enough to wake up the dormant, aged beasts. Behind the office was the garage/workshop. We called it the workshop, but it was more like a battlefield hospital for dead and dying pieces of British Road Transport history. Our mechanics, the hospital butchers, were trained neither as mechanics or butchers, they were ex-drivers that happened to possess a set of overall's and the occasional spanner. Because the yard was a rugged mass of hardcore with a thick coating of oily mud, it would be quite slippery, there were permanent puddles in some areas that were ankle deep in drought conditions, in bad weather I imagined how easy it would be to wipe out the entire fleet should I lose traction whilst manouvering in the mud. Despite this, John arrived in the yard spotless.

"Are we ready?" he smiled a wicked grin.

"I've got the keys but I haven't done any checks yet." I had only just arrived myself, unlike John who looked clean and smart in his Dealer boots, blue jeans and leather jacket. I was sporting work boots, and oil stained, dirty overalls and a beanie hat.

"You dip the oil-I'll fire up the boilers" John took the keys and was up in the cab before I could open the bonnet.

Leyland Marathon's were a real truck. A throwback to 1960's Middle East trucking. They were designed and built for the long road, easy fixes and 'comfort', I use that word very loosely.

I wasn't allowed to drive until my full licence came back, so riding shotgun with John was the closest I would get- for a few days, to being a real trucker.

We headed off and made our delivery in good time, but as we headed back up the A34 we noticed something wasn't right. As it started getting darker our lights began to dim. It seemed that our alternator wasn't working and our batteries slowly running low. John drove on, we switched off the heater, fan, radio and all other electrical units we could do without. We were still 2 hours from the yard and it was getting dark. The further we drove, the less our lights illuminated the road ahead. It wasn't long before they were so dim we couldn't see the road ahead, nothing was reflecting the dim yellow light of our headlights. As we neared home there was a bump, the cab dipped and I was thrown off my seat. John bounced back into his seat before we hit another bump and again we took to the air.

"What the fuck was that?" I shouted.

"Fuck know's, I didn't see anything, did you?"

"Nothing mate, I didn't see a thing."

"We'll check the truck when we get back, if there's any blood on the bumper I'll say you were driving , Hahaa!" John laughed.

"I'll wash the blood off but you're crawling underneath to scrape the brains from the sump."

By the time we reached the yard we were crawling along in the dark. Candles would have been preferable to the pathetic amount of light now coming from the truck's headlights. A quick check of the front of the vehicle revealed nothing, no blood, no dead animals or persons unknown, nothing. It was about a week later that John informed me what it was that had thrown us from our seats. A friend of his was settling down for the night in a lay-by. He was just about to get back into his truck, having just completed his last duty of the day, watering his wheels, when a truck raced through the lay-by like a bat out of hell.

"It seemed to have almost no lights, and bounced back onto the road with a thud heavy enough to break the back of a warship."

The lay-by was on a bend in the road, unable to see the road, let alone the lay-by, we had raced through without realising we'd left the road. It seemed the god's were on our side and thankfully, no-one was injured.

I went to see the boss, it had been a week or more since I got my licence and I was getting irritated with having not gone out on the road alone, in an artic.

"I'll send you out next week" he promised.

"If you don't, I'll be out of here. I got my licence to drive artics and that's what I want to do."

"Look, I'll pay you class 1 rates, this week and I promise to have you in one next week, on your own, how's that sound?"

It was more than fair, I was being something of a diva but I had a point to make, and I really didn't want to lose the hang of driving with a trailer on. Sure enough, the next week I was sent out on my own for the first time, in an artic.

I loaded with packaging materials and headed to Tottenham. The load was higher than anything I'd ever carried before, it was almost 16 feet from the ground and the trailer was 40 feet long, the longest thing I had ever driven in my life. I was excited and scared in varying degrees. Excited that I was finally doing it, and scared that I was finally doing it too.

My first day out on my own came as a bit of a learning curve. It's one thing to think you can get out on the road with a large trailer and a load, but a totally different feeling when you are out there. It is you and your skill that will get you home safe at night, or get you dead, very quickly. You soon learn to secure your load properly. We used flatbed trailers so we could load any shape or sized goods, pallets of packaging, car parts in steel stillages, timber, reels of paper, anything we could. Every item had to be tied down with rope tied so tight that nothing would become loose, even after hundreds of miles of on the road vibration and motion. The truck driver's knot of necessity is the 'Dolly' knot. To create one, just take a length of rope, at one end you have to secure it to the trailer by making a small loop with the rope, twist it over a rope hook and then twist it again to form another loop, put that on the rope hook above the original loop and pull. It should now be secure. Coil the remaining rope and then throw it over the load on the trailer, taking care not to catch any power lines, phone cables or low flying aircraft. Cross to the other side of the trailer and pull on the rope until all the slack is gone and the rope is positioned over the load in such a way as to secure it in position. Then make a dolly knot. Make a small loop, pass it over the main piece of rope and then pull another loop around it creating a nice tight top end, hold this with one hand whilst feeding another piece of rope through the large loop you have already created and pass that piece around the chosen rope hook and back through the bottom loop whist pulling tight on the free end to take up all the slack from the knot. If this is still not tight enough, add a second, third or fourth dolly to the rope and without crushing your load make sure you have created a chord tight enough for Dire Straits to get all boned up about. If this is not working, find yourself a trucker whose hands are gnarled, dirty and friction burned to the point of being one large callous with no determinable palm prints, slip him enough money to make him smile and let him show you how it's done.

Once the load is roped and not going to fall off anytime, you then need to protect it from the weather. Bearing in mind, you are already outside most of the time, you are probably already soaked through to the skin having had to secure half a dozen full coils of rope, about 20 times on both sides of the trailer. You have already walked the length of a half marathon going from one side of the trailer to the other, tying dolly's, burning your hands with the rope and not slipping in any puddles. Now you have to pick up your sheets. Two green canvas sheets usually 25' long and 20' wide each. If you don't know how big that is, think of a piece of heavy material, twice as thick as a pair of denim jeans, and about the size of your average council house back garden. Take both of these- one at a time, and put them on top of the load. That's right, climb up on top of the load and place one rolled up canvas sheet near the front, and the other near the back. If you are fortunate enough to have a helpful loader, he may use his forklift truck to put your sheets up in position for you, if not, place the sheet over your shoulder and climb to the top of the load, 100 lbs of dirty, sopping wet canvas over your shoulder as you climb up a load 10, 12 or 14 feet above the ground. Now you have to roll out the canvasses starting with the rear one first, making sure that they are not upside down. Once the rear sheet is fully unrolled, climb back down to the ground, and now, using the sheet's rope ties, secure the sheet to the trailer. You must start at the back and ensure the sheet is tight, covers the load and that all corners are neatly tucked so that the flow of air as you are driving, does not make the sheet billow out and obscure your view or become a hazard to other road users. Once the rear sheet is done, climb back up with your top-sheet, (a waterproof tarpaulin usually about 50' x 15' which goes over both canvas sheets to waterproof the load) and place it near the back of the load. Roll out the front sheet and climb back down to secure the sheet, ensuring the front end comes down over the top of the trailer's headboard, and the back overlaps the front of the rear sheet. Now you are ready to climb back up to lay out the top-sheet. Once this is secured and you are back safely on the ground, you may well be ready to roll. This all sounds very simple, but try doing it on your own, in windy conditions, rain, sleet, snow, ice, or even hot summer sunshine while suffering from hay fever. This was the lot of the Trucker, King Of The Road and seasonal snot monster. If you managed not to fall off a load, slip down a taut sheet, or get parachuted to Narnia while clinging to your tarpaulin, you were doing well.

Once unloaded, I rolled my sheets back up and tied them down on my trailer before heading home. Day 1 of my career behind the wheel of a very large automobile, was-in my opinion, a success.

Day 2 was a different matter. I loaded at 3 different customer's premises in Coventry for different locations in the North East and Scotland. I was going on a long haul journey, well, long enough anyway. I was expected to be having 2 nights out away from home, sleeping in the truck for 2 nights, it seemed like an adventure. I was a real trucker at last. I headed off from my last collection point in Exhall, and joined the M6 north. Climbing up onto the motorway and towards the services at Corley I managed to reach the grand speed of 35 mph. The Marathon was not happy about this heavy load behind the cab, but she plugged along anyway. I pressed my foot hard on the throttle and still she groaned. Changing gears was an adventure in musicianship more than it was anything to do with mechanics and driver abilities. The gear stick swam around like a ladle in a porridge pot, sometimes there would be a gear at about the 11 o'clock position, sometimes it was more like 9 o'clock, usually it would be around 3 pm before I actually found one that worked. The engine groaned, the gears crunched and I played every tune in the Billboard Chart to get the gear stick into position. I took the A38 towards Derby crashing and shearing metal teeth as I went, all the while listening to The Buzzcocks, The Members, Stiff Little Fingers and Penetration on a compilation cassette that sounded like a far away muffle on the truck's radio/cassette player. The tinny sound complimenting my over the top vocal as I cheerfully sang along to the songs.

"Every lousy Monday morning, old man's out" *Cruuuuunchh!* "-washing the car. Mum's in the kitchen-" Cruuuunnnnccchh, crun-crun-cr-crunch, crunch, cruuuuuu-

"This is the Sound, this is the sound-" *Cruuuuun* "of the suburbs!"

I found my way to the A1 north and stopped for fuel and a break just before Scotch Corner. When I tried to restart I found I had no gears at all. The truck's clutch was gone. I called the boss from the petrol station and was told to wait for a recovery truck. I was to be towed to Darlington and given a rental truck to use while mine was in the workshop being repaired. It was already getting late, so I decided to leave early in the morning, that is, once I had the new truck. Sure enough, it was early morning by the time I had been towed in and given the replacement truck. Having picked up my trailer, I headed out of the repair garage and into a thick morning fog. I managed to find my first delivery in Sunderland, then my next and my third delivery. By lunchtime I was ready to go to Edinburgh.

I came out of Newcastle and the fog was still thick, I headed north and kept going, the road seemed to go forever, zig-zagging through the countryside. Signs were few and far between, so few in fact, that I couldn't remember seeing one for a couple of hours, still, the Bedford hire truck was so much more comfortable than the Marathon I had left in Darlington. I was a long way from Darlington now, in fact, it felt like I was a long way from anywhere, and I still hadn't seen any signs. I began to look deeper into the fog and eventually my efforts paid off, there was a road sign, Carlisle 16 miles. I had somehow taken a wrong turn in the fog and was now on the wrong side of the country. Instead of going north, I had turned east somewhere, somehow and was now a long way from where I wanted to be. I consulted my bible, the A-Z Trucker's Atlas of Great Britain. According to the gospels on page 27, I could take the A74 to Glasgow and then catch the M8 to Edinburgh. This was a plan and I was back in charge. I continued into the valley of death bravely slaying every cloud that dimmed my vision. The road turned and twisted, rose and fell with great regularity, there seemed to be no such thing as flat land this far north.

I drove and drove until eventually coming to a stop at a service station on the M8, it was late, and I would do my deliveries in the morning.

Thursday morning I headed into Edinburgh and drove through the quiet wide streets, I was early and the city still slept. Large, square granite houses seemed to smile warmly as I drove past. They appeared indestructible, solid buildings where generations of family would cohabit and take turns to become the elderly grandparents. I immediately fell in love with the place and began to hark back to my roots. My mother had told us for years that we were part Scottish, the name Reid being a typically Scottish name for people with ruddy complexions. Later on, she would claim we were of Irish descent, travellers, possibly coming from East European Roma people. She would claim a lot of things, usually dependant on her audience, but whatever she claimed, it invariably left you doubting you'd ever heard a word of truth from her in your life, especially when it came to family matters.

Once I had finished my deliveries, my sheets neatly rolled and tied down on my trailer, I headed back towards the A1. Again the fog descended and I decided to look for somewhere to park up for the night. Visibility outside was pretty awful, I could only see about 30 feet in front of my truck, which was better than it would have been in the Marathon, because the heaters in the Bedford were working, unlike the pitiful dull glow of air that was meant to help demist the Marathon's windscreen. I had been heading for Berwick on Tweed, but somehow had been led astray once more and found myself in a lay-by near Jedburgh. I consulted my bible once more and found I could continue and get back on route at Newcastle, all was not lost, but I had missed my chance to drive along the rugged North Sea Coast road.

Friday morning I left for Darlington, and made it to the garage in one piece, despite having gone back to the same roundabout 6 times because I'd forgotten where the garage was. My truck was being off, so I dropped my trailer outside the yard and sat around for the rest of the day drinking coffee and reading old copies of Commercial Motor, Trucking International and Truck & Driver. I read them all and found myself particularly drawn to the stories of driver's heading off oversea's. Such glamour, sunshine, scenery and adventures enough to thrill just about everyone. In the parts department I asked if they could make me a number plate with my name on, which they did, 'RIBSY' was duly handed over to me for the princely sum of £5. I would attach this plate to all workhorses from now on, I was a real trucker, I'd been to Scotland and everything.

Returning home I was not met with a fanfare. There was no welcome home for the weary traveller, just a simple "You took your fucking time, you were meant to be home Thursday night, not Saturday!"

Nikki was unhappy at me being away, she was unhappy when I was home too and the fact that I was still breathing was a source of constant irritation to her. She had given up her agency work soon after becoming pregnant, moping around the flat all day didn't help her, and socialising meant having to go to the pub and drinking soft drinks all day on her own. Nikki was becoming more isolated than she was happy with, it was difficult enough living on the 16th floor of a block of flats, nobody wanted to visit you. But living on the 16th floor, and being pregnant while your husband is away at work sometimes for days on end was really tough, especially when being pregnant brought you out in big boil like spots and you felt like your skin was toxic, and less and less people liked you because you were constantly moaning. Nikki was becoming a pain the proverbial, but this was just the start.

Everyday at Double D was an experience, mostly due to old worn out vehicles breaking down, not starting or dying a long overdue death before being taken apart and left as naked spares to seize up in the yard. Both John and I stayed on purely to gain some practice out on the road, before leaving to take on better positions elsewhere.

For me the end came one day after a coach tried to wipe me out on the M1.

I was heading south with a load of bricks, sand and cement. The trailer was heavy and I felt concerned that the truck wasn't going to make it to Kent. Anyway, somewhere by Northampton I saw a coach in the hard shoulder, driving along with his hazard lights on. I looked in my mirror and saw another truck just about to overtake me and knew I couldn't change lanes. Then I caught sight of a vehicle parked in the hard shoulder and before I knew what was happening the coach pulled out in front of me. I locked on the brakes and a huge cloud of smoke billowed from the trailers wheels, as I burned away 6 months worth of tread. The trailer wobbled a little and then swung out just missing the back of the overtaking truck, I stepped off the brake and then pumped the pedal as hard as i could, all the while watching the back of the bus getting closer and closer to my windscreen. I was waiting for the inevitable crunch but the bus pulled back into the hard shoulder in front of the broken down car and AA patrol guy that was working on it. He too had a narrow escape as my trailer swung back around and almost took out the car and his yellow van. By the time I stopped I was almost jack-knifed and the load was hanging precariously over the side of my trailer, everything had shifted. I crawled along the road and into a service area about 2 miles further up the road to secure everything. There, in a parking space I saw the coach that had caused me to nearly crash.

"What the fuck were you doing back there?" I berated the bus driver.

"Getting my bus here to the services, the clutch has gone, it's cheaper to get a repair here than a tow off the motorway."

"You nearly killed me, and other people, to save a few quid?" I was infuriated and called the police. By the time they came, I beside myself with rage, how dare this guy think it's perfectly OK to cause my death for the sake of a few pounds, how dare he deprive me of a life, of ever seeing my child born and grow, just because he wanted to cut corners.

I called my boss and told him about what had happened and that I would be delayed.

"Is the truck okay- what about the load?" He asked. The Load- what about the load? Nobody cares about the load, it was the driver who should have been your first priority. If I was raging before, I was positively apoplectic now, was my life really worth so little, worth less even than a few hundred bricks, some sand and cement? Really? It was probably a build up of frustration, anger and shock, but when I finally got to Edenbridge and was told I'd have to wait until the morning to unload, I dropped my trailer and drove home. It was my last journey for Double D, my last ride in a Marathon.

I went back to working with H for Helen's Dad Stuart. I would get some agency work from time to time and was able to pretty much just about make ends meet. It was okay, but I needed a full time job. I needed the security and the extra money.

A few weeks later I answered an advert for a job, and after a successful interview, I began working for a firm based near Carlisle, no- not that one with the green motors. Dayson's had 2 trucks based in Coventry, near the airport at Baginton. By day, they ran south with timber from Scotland, or coke or fertiliser from Cumbria . The coke would go to Sheerness steel works in Kent, the fertiliser to Moretonhampstead, Devon, and the timber could go anywhere, Woolwich, Cardiff, Swansea, Kettering. Once unloaded, we would call in and be given our collection details, normally reels of Paper from the docks, or timber. Sometimes steel from Sheerness, sometimes tractors from Basildon. Everyday meant driving to the delivery, un-sheeting and unloading, which would take about an hour, driving to the collection point, loading and sheeting, then driving back to Coventry. 15 hour days were a regular occurrence, it was hard work, my hands were calloused and hard lumps of skin developed around the side of my hands and under my fingers. Rope burns were reshaping my hands, and from time to time, arthritic like pains would wreak havoc with my joints. I was tired, under-slept on a daily basis, and felt permanently fatigued. I was in total sympathy with my child-bearing wife. She however, had no sympathy for me. I was still being hounded, where had I been, why was I late, what did I mean-traffic? Everything was questioned to the point that I began to wonder about her own motive, was this a cover, a ruse to get me to admit to something I hadn't done whilst she was doing as she pleased when I was at work? Her insecurities were not just irritating they were getting in the way of us having anything like a normal, trusting relationship, I had no desire to be chasing other women now, we were married and I for one was committed to our marriage, but she was either too young, too immature or too hung up on her own past -or possibly present even, to let things be, she was suspicious and jealous for no reason I could fathom. It was spoiling our relationship and would often lead to arguments.

As the arrival date for our baby loomed , I had the opportunity to change jobs, to do the night trunk to Carlisle everyday instead of working daytimes. My new position was simple, 4 1/2 hours to the yard at Southwaite, swap trailers, 4 1/2 hours return with an hour break in Southwaite to refuel and swap trailers. In other words, regular hours so I could be home for the baby, when it came. And came she did.

Sian arrived on Friday 5th May, with a slap on the arse and a snip of her cord, she was handed over in a little white blanket. Sian was beautiful, she was almost hairless when she was born and stayed that way for a long time. I loved her immediately and wanted to hold her for all time. Nothing in this world was ever wanted as much as our little girl. She would be loved and cared for all her life, she would never want for things we could give, she would always have a loving home, and parents who would be there for her, to care, nurture, teach and grow. I made every promise I could to my little girl, and I would do everything I could for her.

Soon after she was born, Sian was introduced to her Grandmother Patricia, her Uncle and Aunt, and her Great Grandfather. Nikki's family were all over her, it was lovely to see so much enthusiasm from them after month's of mixed sentiment. I don't think they were truly impressed when she first fell pregnant, but once they saw Sian, they all fell in love with her. It sounds very Mills and Boone -but it's the truth, she was both adorable and adored. The greatest thing to happen in a man's life is the birth of his 1st child. Relief, fear, joy, expectation and adoration flood through the veins like the greatest rush a man could ever experience, this is my legacy, this here is the future, a fresh start and new beginning. A life created of love. When I am gone she will live on and carry in her all my memories. These are some of the myriad of thoughts, dreams and prayers that we have, an honest desire to do for our own better than was done for us, to improve, to love and to nurture. Any person not feeling these emotions on the birth of their children is either devoid of feeling, or a danger to those around them. It is natural to want to love, teach and grow with a child, it's programmed into us just as much as the desire to put everything we come across into our mouths when we are little, food, flowers, boot polish, even dog poo. These things are hardwired into us so that we continue to reproduce, grow and prosper. Being a parent is the pinnacle of evolution, the moment we have achieved our purpose in life is that moment when a child reaches out and touches us, knowing we are there for them. We will protect, care and serve them all our days.

Mother and baby were both fine, healthy and home in no time at all. Nikki's friend Toni came round to the flat to help me blow up some balloons to welcome them home. It may sound strange, I can front a guy with a knife or gun, charge at 100 kid's running at me to beat the crap out of me for the honour of their school, I can face anything, anything but balloons.

I took a week off to help Nikki and Sian get settled. I soon got used to the crying at night, the demanding and endless needs put upon me, and when I'd sorted Nikki out, I'd take care of Sian. I learned to put myself last, no matter how tired I was, I had to be there and I had to be strong and dependable for both of them. Nikki was not a natural mother, she struggled and would often break down in tears, as time went by these episodes became more frequent. She was constantly jealous of anybody that came near me or took my time, often accusing me of the most ridiculous charges. Her insecurity blossomed after the trauma of childbirth, as bad as she was before she was pregnant, she was much worse now.

Back at work, I returned to day shifts as the money was better. The long days were a grind and I started to think about changing jobs again. I was constantly tired and the regular battles with traffic around Dartford tunnel were getting ridiculous.

One morning at Dartford, as I was heading to Sheerness, a plumber's van cut me up terribly and the red mist descended. I jumped out of my truck and banged my fist on the driver's window.

"What the fuck are you playing at you stupid bastard?" That's a lesser known Coventry saying for 'Good morning to you, kind sir, I think your driving is rather is somewhat erratic, please desist!'

With one look at my ugly mug against his window, the driver decided to welcome me to Essex by opening the door and threatening to bash my brains in. Judging by the size of him, he probably could have too. I trapped his leg in the door and held him in limbo for a few seconds, once ready, I let go of the door and punched him in his face. He recoiled slightly and then surged towards me. We were both standing on the motorway now, the traffic moving around us as we exchanged blows. At some point I grabbed his hair, turned him and smashed his face into the roof of his little silver van. He seemed to want to stop then, so I let him go, but instead of leaving it be now, he grabbed an object from next to his seat and smashed it down on my head. If he'd hit my stomach I may have gone down, but my head is a thick as the tyres on my truck. He swung his weapon again, it was a length of rubber hose with a metal core, he missed me as I turned and ran to my truck. I wasn't running away, I was evening the odd's. Next to my seat was heavy steel wheel brace, I grabbed it and ran at my challenger. Just as he was about to get in his van I swung the metal bar and connected with his head. He fell into a heap next his vehicle and I walked back to my truck, victorious. We parted company there and then, he drove off at speed with a sore head and I jumped back into my seat and turned up the volume on the stereo just as the Blitz song, 'Never Surrender' began to play. Sometimes life is just like that. To this day, I've never received a Christmas card from that driver, strange really, I thought we were getting along really well.

Once Sian arrived we were unable to go out as much as we had been used to, our spare time was no longer our own. Nikki swore she'd never be like other Mum's, she wanted to still go out and have fun, dance, go to gig's have friend's round for parties and have more fun. But that ideal was never going to work, the first thing about having fun with your friends is that you have to have some friends to have fun with in the first place. She'd made a career out of pissing people off for as long as some people had known her. She was an attention seeker, a well to do middle class kid from Suburbia who wanted to play with the city kids, worse than that, she was from an expensive village in the sticks, part of the London/Birmingham commuter belt. She didn't really fit in with the punk crowd, I don't think she'd ever gone without much in her life, except love and affection. When I breezed into town it was like a wave of fresh air had come to rescue her, to start afresh. I was her access to the in-crowd, I was her ticket to something she aspired to be but never could. In reality, I was nothing more than a fart in a very slow elevator, I knew shit stank, but she thought it was all a game, a nice place to visit. When we were out she'd get herself worked up if her ex was around, playing up to get his attention and getting into fight's with his girlfriend. At Buster's she'd wiggle her bum around to Wayne County & The Electric Chair's song, 'If you don't wanna fuck me, baby, fuck off.' and then collapse in a drunken heap, crying because nobody wanted to, nobody that she wanted to anyway.

I turned up for work one Friday morning and set off for London with a load of timber on board. I checked the load and all seemed well even though I couldn't see under the canvas sheets, everything seemed okay. I pulled out of the yard and joined the A45 south, but my journey was abandoned even before I'd got into top gear. I noticed a bulge in the sheets as soon I went round the first bend near the Peugeot factory at Ryton. The load had shifted and I had to get it off the road and back to the yard as soon as possible. I called the boss and told him of my problem.

"Can you not reload it?" He asked.

"There's a timber yard nearby, I did some agency work for them before, maybe I could borrow a sideloader and get it sorted, but there's nobody in for a couple of hours yet. "

"Good lad, let me know how you get on." He hung up, I knew he thought it was my fault the load had shifted, but I hadn't done anything, I hadn't swung the truck around enough to lose a load that's for sure.

I hung around in the yard and tentatively loosened some of the ropes on the load, as I did so, some of the timber shifted and a few planks fell off the side of the trailer.

"Bit of a mess you've got there" came a voice behind me. I didn't know the voice nor the little guy with the long shorts and dark sunglasses who had crept up without me noticing.

"The load shifted, I'm just trying to sort it out, I reckon it'll be alright if I can get a sideloader on it and get the sheets off."

"You'll be here all day re-stacking that lot."

"Well, I reckon so, but I can't go anywhere until I've sorted it." I said.

"You should come and work for me" he smiled.

"Work for you? Where? Who are you?"

"That's my Daf behind you-" He nodded towards a plain white Daf 3300 that was parked in the yard, behind it, a plain white Tilt trailer with red chassis, the type of trailer the continental guy's used for trips beyond the English Channel.

"Your's, you own it?"

"Yes it's mine."

"Where d'you go in that, then?" I asked, expectantly.

"I'm loading tomorrow, for Spain." Now he had my full attention. "Got to pick up a full load of axles from Wrexham, take them to a new warehouse in Barcelona, probably reload with onions in Valencia and back home."

"That sounds like a good job-what's the money like?"

"The money's good, I make a living out of it, I mean, what are you earning? I could give you £300 a trip and you could do it in a week, that's more than you're getting now, right?"

"Yeah, I get about £200-250 if I do 6 days a week."

"Well, if you fancy it, I'll give you £50 to load this tomorrow, if you want to go to Spain, you can ship out Sunday-have you ever been before?"

"No mate, I used to live near Montpellier in France, but I've never been to Spain, I've never driven a truck over the water either, I wouldn't know what to do really."

"It's a piece of piss, if you can drive that here-" he pointed at my truck, "You can drive that over there, and you'll get a suntan."

I think he had me at Spain. I had to go home and talk with Nikki, but this meant a significant pay rise (and a suntan), and a great opportunity to advance in my industry, and get a suntan.

I reloaded the timber, got everything safe and ready to be delivered on Monday before having a chat with Nikki. She was keen and thought it might be worth a try, especially as she could come with me on other trips, it would be like having a permanent holiday, and a suntan, and getting paid too, bonus!

I called my boss and gave him the good news, he was a little taken aback but said if it didn't work out, I would be welcome back.

I loaded the next morning in Wrexham, and met my new boss Bryan, in a pub the following lunchtime. I was keen and ready to go. Bryan, not so, but after two more pints of beer, he was ready and I drove us to Dover. Once we'd been through the custom's facility and got our paperwork stamped and checked, Bryan took me over to the export lounge. Here we met up with some other drivers, some who were also from Coventry, knew Bryan.

"Where are you going?" Bryan asked a group of drivers.

"Switzerland" said one.

"Milan" said another.

"Beauvais, then into Paris."

"You should come and work for me" he said to a blonde haired woman called Sandy. I had only just started with him and here he was trying to give my job away to somebody else. "-I'll buy a new truck for Sandy, you know I'd look after you."

"No thanks, Bryan, I don't think Malc would be too pleased if I left him to work for you, anyway, I like what I do and Malc looks after me as it is." Malc was the 'Big Boss ' at Express Freight Services in Coventry, his driver's were considered the best in town, well paid and well travelled, I was in with the in-crowd and liking it, especially the beer and suntan bit. By the time we left

Calais we had polished off a jug of red wine each and I was on the bunk, Bryan drove through the night.

I woke up near Le Mans and took over from the boss. It felt good to be back in France after such a long time away, but it felt different too, driving a truck abroad was a new experience for me, I was quick to learn and soon had my road positioning down to a tee. Bryan was pleased, and tired as well as a little hungover, so I told him to sleep and I continued to follow the route he'd told me,down to Saumur then the autoroute towards Bordeaux.

I woke Bryan from his slumber as we approached Saumur, just as he'd asked me to.

"Nearly at Saumur now Bryan." I said, prompting him out of his slumber.

"Humpfrlhmmmmmnnifwrith!" came his half sober reply, then there was movement, he farted, and slid off the bunk into the passenger seat, his face as red as a good Burgundy wine. He swapped seats with me before getting to the Autoroute, I leaned back in the passenger seat, fatigued and with the smell of his fart lingering in the air, I watched the world pass by. We pulled off the motorway at St André De Sangonis, where we picked up the N10 and stopped for the night at a truckstop called Claude's. Here we ate supper and drank more red wine and beer with other British drivers on their way to Spain. By nightfall, the place was heaving but when we woke up next morning, only a handful of trucks remained.

Bryan took 1st shift and noticed there was a fault with the engine, the alternator was playing up.

"There's a Daf garage up the road, we'd better take it in there." he said, heading back towards the Autoroute.

It was mid afternoon before the truck was repaired, a wire had become disconnected somewhere, it took longer to find the source of the problem than it did to fix it, but at last we were back on the road, sober and full of strong, French coffee.

Bryan drove us to Bordeaux, around the ring road, over the big bridge spanning the river Garronne and then south towards Toulouse, Perpignan and eventually Barcelona. Before we entered Spain, we had to transit the border at La Jonquera. Cigarettes changed hands, permits swapped and stamped as required, so as to be usable again on the next trip. Everything on the border seemed to work smoothly, if you knew how to smooth things over that is. Money and Marlboro were not just currency, but the language of international trade itself.

We reached the TIR (Transports des Marchandises Internationaux par Routier, or 'customs' if you prefer) area at Zona Franca, in time for supper.

"Dos tortillas con jamon y queso por favor, y dos cervesas." Bryan said confidently as we reached the bar.

"That was a bit of a mouthful mate, how long have you been coming here then?" I asked.

"About 10 years or so, on and off, I used to do Iraq, Saudi and the gulf but the work dried up, so it's best to stick local now, the rates are shit out there now and it's getting dangerous, too many idiots with guns, I wouldn't go past Turkey nowadays, it's just not worth it. Cheers!" We clinked our beer bottles together and awaited our omelettes, Spain was looking good so far.

Next morning we queued to get into our agent's office, there were about 20 other loads in front of us. We put our papers in and were greeted with the same reply as all the other drivers, "Manana" (Tomorrow).

"What do we do now?" I asked Bryan.

"Nothing else to do, we go on holiday, come back tomorrow morning, but we won't be cleared until lunchtime anyway, it's always the same here."

We dropped our trailer in the TIR park where it stood, the trailer couldn't leave because it had the load on it, which was now under customs control. Until our papers were stamped and returned, that trailer was not leaving the compound, today, tomorrow or ever. The tractor unit was free to come and go as we pleased. According to Bryan, on days like this the drivers would all head to the beach or Las Ramblas, which was where he took me. We parked by the port entrance, at the bottom end of Las Ramblas.

"Pull your curtains closed and lock your doors, it'll be safe here, the guard's in the port will keep an eye on it, they're as good as gold like that here."

We wandered up and down Las Ramblas, window shopping, watching the scantily clad women walk by.

"Prostitutes," said Bryan "- watch out for the dirty ones, her there, see, do you see them marks behind her knees? She's a junkie, you stay clear of them ones, if you want a clean one you have to go into the bars, come on, I'll show you a good place up the road here."

We entered a bar, just an ordinary looking, dimly lit bar you could find anywhere in the world. Bryan ordered two beers, picked up a newspaper from the bar and began to slowly read it through his thick 'Reactolite' sunglasses. I looked around the room and noticed two young, scantily clad women approaching. Bryan ignored them, his head firmly wedged in the newspaper.

"Hola!"

"Alright" I replied courteously, it was as close to Spanish as I could manage.

"Eengleesh?" came the reply. "You wan buy me dreenk? Mebbee we go hopstair be reelly good fwend? You look good lover, come hopstair?"

"No thank you, it's very nice of you but no, I'm just having a beer with my mate here, we're alright thanks."

I looked at Bryan, no response. He seemed totally oblivious to what was happening, all consumed with his newspaper and fizzy Spanish beer.

"You two...?" Asked the other woman, pointing an accusing finger at Bryan and myself.

"Yes, he's my......" I started to say, but they had turned and were giggling to themselves as they walked away. ".....Boss...."

I turned back to my beer and Bryan slowly raised his head.

"If you want a go, I'll give you the money and take it out of your wages next week" he offered.

"Thanks, but no, I'll wait 'til I get home." Bryan sniffed loudly and returned to his newspaper, I sipped my beer in silence as it dawned on me what I had implied to the prostitutes, now busily giggling and staring from the other end of the bar.

We eventually returned to our truck to find a quarter-light window smashed. The cab had been ransacked, but our passports and other papers were left in clear view on the dashboard. All they'd wanted was cash. Our clothes had been sifted through, our cigarettes and duty free booze gone.

"Bastard's!" Snarled Bryan, "The fucking bastards, they've had my emergency money, bollocks. I thought we were safe here, my fault I guess."

"Why your fault?" I asked, how was it his fault someone broke into the truck?

"I should have bunged the security guards over there some money, they must have seen them do it, probably did it themselves, the bastards."

We tidied up the mess and returned to the bar in the TIR Park. We continued drinking into the small hours and when we left to go to bed, we were followed by another Englishman who was having trouble locating his truck. We wandered around for a while trying to find it for him, but with no joy. Eventually it was decided it had been stolen and the Guardia Civil were called. The driver was distraught, all his papers, passport, clothes, everything, gone. His boss was not going to be too happy with him either. The truck and trailer gone from the TIR Park while he sat in the bar all night. As it turned out, however, the truck was still where he'd left it, on the other side of the park.

We joined the queue at the agent's office, just in time to catch a Dutchman losing his temper. His load could not be cleared until Monday morning but he didn't have enough diesel in his refrigerated trailer to last through the weekend. As he had a wagon and drag combination, in other words a rigid truck with a trailer on the back as opposed to a tractor trailer, the prime mover was also carrying a load and so could not leave the Customs park until the load was cleared. Following much voice raising and swearing, the Dutchman stormed out of the office frustrated at having not filled up his tanks before coming in to the Custom's Park. The agent cursed under his breath, lifted a huge pile of papers, then put the Dutchman's file at the bottom of the stack, he was in for an even longer wait now.

We were finally cleared on by Friday lunchtime. I was relieved to get out of Zona Franca not just because we'd been there too long and I was losing money, but because I'd fed every bloody mosquito in the TIR Park. I had been bitten from top to toe and was covered in little red itchy dots. Bryan drove us to a brand new warehouse which had just been built, our load being the first to be delivered on site. The manager of the place came to meet us and apologised that we wouldn't be unloaded until Saturday morning. As compensation for the delay, we were taken for a meal and free drinks. This European Truck Driving malarky seemed to always involve plenty of drink.

Bryan thought we would reload onions from Valencia, so once we were free to go, we headed south and eventually stopped at a Truckstop outside of town. He called our agent but as it was the weekend, got no response.

By Monday morning we had had just about all the sunshine, Bacardi and beer we could stomach. Bryan finally got through to England and had a face like thunder by the time he got off the phone. We had driven over 350 km (200 miles) South from Barcelona, expecting to load in Valencia, but we had no load here, we were to load the following morning at a farm South of Toulouse in France, another 650 kms back up the road.

By the time we got back home to Coventry, it was Friday night and having been away for almost two weeks, I returned home with around £100 wages. Bryan had lost a lot of money on that trip.

I had a chat with Nikki and we decided to see how things went on the next couple of trips, if we could make a living out of it I would continue, if not, I would come home and work in the UK again. Being away from home had been hard on her, our little girl Sian, and myself, but if I could do a few trips within a week each time, then the money would be worth doing it for. Yes, there would be delays some weeks, but other times things would work out fine and it would all balance out. I just needed to get some time at home too.

4 Safe European Home

"Though the deepest bluest ocean never touched you as I swam, and the brightest hottest sunlight never warmed your paling skin, you were there beside me as I swam so far alone, alone I swam, so slow I swam, with you on my mind....."

Tuesday morning I loaded a couple of JCB diggers and headed for Portsmouth. I was booked on the night ferry to Le Havre. I hadn't slept on a ferry since I was a kid, and now I was driving a big ass truck on my own, feeling like the master of the universe, king of the road with all the imagery of freedom and adventure that came with it. Truth be told, I was a slave to the job, a prisoner in a mobile box, but it was to be a long time before I realised this. For now, I was living the dream, heading for the sunshine, window open, the wind in my hair and Slaughter And The Dogs on the cassette player, 'Where have all the bootboy's gone?' I'll tell you where, they all went south, following the sun.

In Le Havre I was checked by French controls, a paperwork exercise to determine the goods and paperwork corresponded, the truck was legal and I had no contraband on board. Once cleared to transit, about an hour after arrival, I headed off towards Bordeaux. I spent the night at Claude's and then ran to the Spanish border at Irun. Entering Spain meant transiting from the border to my delivery point Alcala De Henares, just east of Madrid. Clearing at the border meant finding an agent and taxi rides to and fro, an experience I was later to endure on other trips. I presented my permits and handed over the obligatory packet of Marlboro, the pack was whisked away and thrown into a drawer bursting with cigarettes from all manner of countries. Stamp, stamp, stamp and the sweaty, moustachioed official handed me back my papers.

"Adios" and I was free to go.

I followed the road south through San Sebastian, I was in Basque territory, there had been much unrest in the area over the years. Basque separatists had killed and kidnapped many people here. There had been car bombings and shootings in the streets. The whole area was covered in graffiti, words written in a language I couldn't attempt to translate, I barely knew any Spanish, let alone the Basque tongue. I kept going, on to Vitoria-Gasteiz and down to Burgos where I pulled in to park at Victor's, a Truckstop frequented by all the other drivers. I treated myself to my favourite Spanish drink, Café Con Leche. A weak milky coffee made with sterilised milk that has a creamy smooth texture. I rang home and spoke to Nikki. No matter where I was, I would always endeavour to call home in the evening, I always kept a pocket of coins and made sure to report both my safety and whereabouts. I would always ask how Nikki and Sian were.

The following morning I set off nice and early. I had never been to Madrid and so I had to trust the directions and tips I had been given by other drivers I spoke to on the way down. I managed to find my way around the city well enough, heading toward the airport and then picking up the road out to Alcala De Henares. I got close to the town but somehow missed my turn off, turned around and came back again missing the exit to where I needed to be. I was getting hot and befuddled and by the time I reached the site I was too late to clear customs that day. I was now to weekend in this factory. There were 2 other British trucks on site, the whereabouts of the drivers was unknown.

A Security Guard told me there was a water tap in the warehouse I could use to fill my water container, or rather, he would have if he spoke any English or I spoke Spanish. In reality, he'd pointed toward an open roller door and I wandered over with my recently purchased 50 litre container, in search of a tap. I found one, the pipe feeding it led directly up to the roof and I thought that maybe that was to keep the pressure up and the temperature down, even though it was actually nearer the sun than I was on the ground, and it was pretty hot down here. With no company, nothing to do, I retired to bed with a bottle of beer and a book, and another beer with a beer chaser, for the road.

Next morning I was up and away. I wandered into the town and spent the day people watching from outside a variety of cafes and bars around the central square. I walked back to the factory around tea time and set about cooking myself a 'Camion Stew', a truck driver's term for a meal similar to a Balti in that one large pan is used and anything goes in it. Corned beef, potatoes, beans, an egg and a generous chunk of cheese. Topped with ketchup and washed down with a bottle of red, it was the perfect end to a relaxing day in the sunshine. Looking at my map, I noticed a lake up in the hills nearby, by nearby, I mean closer than the coast, several hundred clicks away. Having had enough of people watching in the dust bowl that was Alcala, I invited my newly returned fellow English neighbours, to join me in the morning on a trip to the lake, about 100 km's up the road.

There were 4 of us in all, a husband and wife from Essex, and an owner-driver from Staffordshire. The couple sat together on my bunk, the other passenger on the spare seat. I drove east, past Guadalajara and up into the hills, to the Embalsé de Entrepenas, eventually pulling up by a 'Playa' (beach) at the lakeside. Towels were laid out, sunscreen applied, ice cream and beer consumed with gusto. The lakeside was a popular destination, after we arrived, the Playa filled with cars and campers of all descriptions, people swam, bathed and played in the sun and water to their hearts content.

"So where did you fill your water carrier?" Asked the owner-driver.
"The guy at the factory told me to use the tap in the warehouse" I replied.
"Not the one by the door by any chance?"
"Yes that's it, it was a little warm but-" I stopped myself mid sentence as his his mouth turned upwards and he burst out laughing.
"Hahaha, you do know where it comes from, that water?"
"The roof?" I hazarded a guess.
"That's right, it's an open tank, collects the rain water, but the bird's like to bathe and shit in it too, you haven't drunk any of it have you?"
"A little bit, yes"
"Well don't drink anymore, it's full of maggots and all sorts, that stuff will kill you if you're not careful."

When he wasn't looking I took a peak inside my nearly new, once filled water bottle. Sure enough there were tiny little maggots, worms, or whatever the hell they were floating around in the water. Thankfully I hadn't drunk too much, but I couldn't help feeling a little sick when I noticed just how green the water was looking. A thick line of algae was forming around the bottle at the waterline and I shuddered to think what would happen had I continued to drink it.

As evening fell we clambered back aboard my truck, families and other groups around us were packing up too. Our exit was limited and at one point, weaving between camper vans and picnic boxes I turned to head back to the road but the truck stopped dead, the earth beneath us had given way and we were stuck, up to the axle stuck and nothing was getting us out of there. We tried everything we could but nothing worked. I needed to be pulled out by a recovery vehicle. I was in deep shit, Bryan was not going to like this.

The other's managed to hitch rides back to Alcala De Henares with some locals heading home. I spent the night alone, looking at the stars, bogged down by the lake contemplating the long walk home, and how much of my own gear I could carry.

"I've got a problem-" I started to tell Bryan.
"What? You did what? You're where?" I struggled to get a word in edgeways. "Ring me back in an hour and tell me your fucking tipped or god hell me I'll.." He slammed the phone down." How the fuck am I going to get tipped when I'm stuck in the mountains 60 miles from the fucking trailer you prick!" I shouted into the muted mouthpiece. Just then a JCB came around a corner and drove slowly along the road. If ever there was a an example of divine intervention, this was it. I chased the driver, waving a 1,000 Peseta note.

An hour later I was backing under my trailer and feeling pretty happy with myself, despite having got stuck in the first place.

"I'm empty" I informed my boss shortly afterwards.
"Good, now wait there, Ian is coming to meet you, he's driving Don's truck, and tipping there today, when he's empty, head to Cadiz, I've got you a load down there."

Ian eventually turned up the following lunchtime and we did as we'd been told, we headed to Cadiz. We were given the address of a farm in the middle of nowhere. We had to follow a local passerby we'd flagged down, for about 15 miles we trekked cross-country until we came to a cross road. I handed over some more Marlboro and the old man smiled, pointed right, mumbled something inaudible in Spanish and drove off in a cloud of dust. We were at the entrance to a farm, miles from anywhere it seemed, but the name matched the details we had. Unfortunately for us, there was a Belgian truck on site already, and when we arrived we were told it would take the rest of the day to load him, our loads would be done tomorrow (Thursday).

Ian and I pulled on our overalls and mucked in, it's what you did, helping each other out. We were all family, truck drivers were a united people, we knew how hard the job was alone, so we always helped out when we could.

Between us we stripped the Belgian trailer down to the floor, the tarpaulin, roof bars, frame and timbers, everything laid in piles nearby as we loaded farm equipment onto the trailer. The load was roped and strapped and then the trailer rebuilt around the load. We did an excellent job and the Belgian driver was grateful for our help. He was delivering to the same place as us, Spalding, Lincolnshire, but he was going home for the weekend first.

Ian and I were shown where there was a shower and washroom, I asked one of the farm hands if there was a shop nearby where I could buy a bottle of wine for our supper.

"I take you, you come in car, me car, me take you." I got his drift and told Ian to put some dinner on, I was getting the wine. Five of us clambered into a pick up truck, the driver plus one in the front, the rest of bounced around in the back for a hair raising, bum breaking 10 minute drive to the nearest bar. "We drink" I was informed and followed the guys into the bar. In typical Spanish style, the bar was surrounded by a million discarded tissues, the patrons greedily swiping another tissue and wiping their mouths between every sip of their drinks, before throwing the paper onto the floor, and taking another. I was given a glass of Bacardi and coke, two thirds white rum and a tiny splash of cola, in England that would have been a quadruple shot with a double on top and squirt of coke for colouring, in Spain, it was a normal serving. Before I could finish another appeared, then a third and fourth. The farm hands were finally getting ready to go home now, I somehow managed to thank them for their generosity and drunkenly ordered a bottle of wine for our supper. The driver, and I guess lead farm hand, mentioned something about a local festival and said Ian and I could come along, he told me to be ready for about 8pm as he would pick us up, he was as tipsy as I was when he drove off, unlike Ian, sober as a judge with a saucepan full of stew and no wine.

Now I'm not going to tell you the rest of the night's story unless you promise not to tell anyone, I do have an image and reputation to uphold, so please, this is purely between you and me, nobody else need know about it.

After our camion stew and cheap, rather sharp, bottle of wine, Ian and I were bundled into a car and taken to a house in a nearby town. The house was full of people, and tables full of food and drinks. We were introduced to everyone in the house, Mum, Dad, brother, sister, uncle with a dodgy moustache and the an aunt with a cleavage big enough to hide a tank in. Food was handed to us, glasses of more Bacardi, the people were so very generous to us but seemed to be rushing us to finish. When we did, we were driven to another house and the same scene played out, the whole family welcomed us with open arms and heavy bosoms. Food and drink was lavished upon us and then we were whisked away again to another house, and another. Finally, when we could eat and drink no more, we were taken to the Fiesta in the town square. There were hundreds of people, food piled high on tables, beer and wine flowed like the rain Lancashire, and there was music, and dancing. A stage had been set up for people to dance on. The night was warm and glorious, the generosity of the townsfolk was incredible, and I was pissed. I was very pissed. So pissed that I started dancing to Rick Astley, the only English record that was played that night.

At 6 am we were taken back to the first house we'd stopped at. Ian and I promptly puked our guts up in a flowerbed at the front of the house. At 7 am we were woken from our slumber on the living room sofa and taken back to the farm. The Sun was up and it was already warm, our heads were thumping as we started to strip our own trailers down. It was 6pm before we were ready to leave. We were like the living dead, and we had to get out of Spain before 10 pm Saturday night, when the border closed to heavy trucks. We had 28 hours to complete a 20 hour drive, hungover, desperately tired and overheated. We made it to Irun and onto French soil at 9.50 pm Saturday night, then through the night we kept going, as tired as we were, we kept going, stopping for fuel, coffee and the occasional half hour cat-nap until we reached Calais. It was a miracle we hadn't been caught for running on a Sunday (which is illegal in France, except for perishable loads). Monday night I was home and slept soundly into Wednesday.

Nikki wasn't coping too well alone at home. So I took her with me on my next trip, both her and Sian. Now only a few month's old, Sian was still being breast fed when we shipped out of Portsmouth with a load of frozen chicken for a coldstore in Madrid. Our reload was from Murcia and we managed a couple of days off at the Meson Del Moro, a hotel near the Mas Blanca customs facility about 30 km's from Murcia. The hotel staff loved Sian and gave us a room to stay in for free. We were paying for food and drinks, as well as the swimming pool, but giving us a room was a wonderfully generous and kind offer.

I did a few more trips for Bryan, but being paid trip money was not working out. I was earning less than when I was home every night. Nikki was going stir crazy too, being left behind was not her idea of domestic bliss. I was obviously having too much fun without her, and that had to stop. I gave in to her tears and quit my job. It was an experience driving to Spain, but trip money was a con and I needed more regular income.

I returned to working with H again, Helen would sometimes come in on a Saturday if her mum, Diane or Sister Nicky, babysat Toni-Anne. It was a proper family business, everyone helped out when they could.

I was bringing in some slats one day when a cry went out from one of the benches.

"Fuuuuuuuuuccckkk!" It was Ian, another lad who worked full time now with H and Stuart.

"Fucking bollocks, shit, fuck, fuck, fuck it!" He held his hand against his chest and ran past me to the office. Inside the workshop everything had stopped.

There was blood all over the electric saw Ian had been using to trim the boards to length, and somewhere in amongst the sawdust, I found the top of his thumb. Stuart took him to the hospital, and a few weeks later he was back at work.

It wasn't long before Nikki fell pregnant again. There had been much talk between us about having another child so that Sian would not be an only child. I wasn't quite prepared for it to be so soon, we were still living in the flat, way up above the city skyline and getting one baby, ourselves and our shopping up into the flat was hard enough, having a second child would be almost impossible. I got my old job back at Dayson's, the money was good and we were able to get a mortgage for a house on Blythe Road, Hillfields. Being the posh git I am, I preferred the area's other title, Lower Stoke, we were still in Hillfields, but Lower Stoke sounded more upmarket, we were turning into Yuppies, before they were fashionable.

Stiff Little Fingers were playing in Leicester, at the De Montford University. We headed over with Helen and H and were having a great night, the band were playing a fantastic set and everyone was jumping around. I kept an eye on Nikki as she was being shoved around in the crowd, when all of a sudden someone turned and punched her straight on the nose and she went flying. I dived into the crowd as Helen helped Nikki to her feet. Full of rage I lunged at the guy who'd punched her and grabbed him by the throat, my fingers locked behind his windpipe as I pulled him off his feet and dragged him through the crowd. He seemed to go limp and heavy, but pure anger gave me the strength I needed to pull him through the compacted audience. Once at the side of the throng, I slammed his body into a wall and he slumped to the floor. My fists were clenched tight, my right arm pulled back as taught as steel spring ready to deliver a paralysing blow to my target. The guy was out cold and I was pulled back by H.

"Leave it mate, he's done!"

Helen took Nikki to the toilets and I went to the Gents kicking the wall with frustration, the anger I had prepared to release on the guy who'd punched my wife, was now released on an inanimate object, pent up energy freeing itself from the constraints of my bodily muscles. The security guards tended to the unconscious guy in the auditorium before showing him the exit. Nikki reappeared with a swollen nose and her makeup spread around her face, not a look that would catch on with the locals, not yet anyway.

Arriving at a building site one morning in Swansea, I followed the track to where a crane sat awaiting the concrete pilings on my trailer, before I could get to it though, I had to negotiate a tight corner where steel rods protruded from the ground on one side, and two tipper trucks were parked opposite. I found the drivers in a Portacabin, drinking tea. They were more than happy to move their trucks a few feet for me to get round, and as I jumped up into my cab they returned to their own. One truck was facing one way, the other faced the opposite direction, I looked up and immediately as I did so, the world slowed, everything slowed down. I looked over in mute horror as one truck reversed at the exact same moment as the other driver opened his door. The sound of metal on metal crumpled through the air, followed by a muffled scream.

"NOOOOOO!" I tried to shout out but the words caught in my throat as I leapt down from my cab. The door of the second truck was ripped forward by the rear corner of the first. Between the two, the burly, bearded driver knelt in the mud, his eyes clenched tightly shut and his right hand clutched to his chest as the left covered his injured hand. I grabbed him under his arm as his mate did the same on the other side. Between us we marched him to the Portacabin and then I ran to the site office to call for an ambulance. Returning to the trucks, a small group of workmen had gathered to see what was happening. The drivers door was crumpled outwards, it was almost unnatural, the interior spattered with blood. I looked down to the floor and found what I had suspected to be there.

"What are doing, what's that?" Asked one of the labourers as I delved in the mud.

"It's his fingers" I said, picking them up from the mud. The labourer wretched as I turned and took my find to the Portacabin, hoping the hospital could reattach them. Some years later, I met a driver from the same company travelling on the Eurotunnel. I asked if he knew the guy involved in the accident.

"Yes, he's still with us, doesn't do much driving now though, he's getting on a bit, but no,they couldn't get his fingers back on, they were too badly damaged."

When Nikki got closer to her term, I returned to night trunking up to Southwaite. I slept all day and spent the night thumping up the M6 listening to The Bangles, Transvision Vamp, and Sisters Of Mercy cassettes. I'd nearly hit a car in London a few weeks earlier, after seeing a poster for Transvision Vamp. Wendy James looked like a double for my wife Nikki, only much better looking, with a different haircut and far more confidence. In fact, she looked nothing like Nikki but she caught my attention when I really shouldn't have been looking at posters of gorgeous pop stars promoting new albums.

One night I took John along with me to work. John was Helen's sister Nicky's husband. Nicky was living next door to Helen and was now the mother of 3 little boys of her own. Nikki and Nicky spent the night together talking girl's talk, while John and I drove north and talked shit to each other. This was probably the most time I ever spent with John in one sitting, I would usually only see him briefly, or spend a few minutes at a party or other function where our time was demanded by all and sundry. John was weird. He had a morbid fascination with death, beyond even my own dalliances. He talked about toying with suicide, how he may one day inject himself with air to commit suicide. I had lost a friend years before who had done exactly that, the air bubble travelled to his brain and he died, probably very painfully. John also knew strange things, like whenever we passed a fuel tanker he would know what the hazard warning plate numbers related to, he knew the 4 digit numbers for Petroleum, diesel and aviation fuel, yet he had no link to the industry in any way. Nicky was grateful for the break, for me getting him out of the house. He had been in trouble several times for knocking her about, and the kids too. H and I had both wanted to beat the crap out of him when one of the boys accidently fell down the stairs when he was upstairs with him, but without Nicky's say so, we couldn't touch him. One day he'd make a mistake, one day he'd go too far in front of us, but until then we had to wait.

Christina was born in June 1990 and came out with an almost full head of hair. Sian was a year older but was still very thin on top. Our family was complete, we had no desire for a third child, two was plenty enough. I did all I could to help, fed, bathed and dressed the kids, my own needs took second place to them and to my wife, I was tired, always tired, but young enough still to take it. It was hard at times, balancing work, home, a demanding wife and a desire to please everybody. I was there for everyone but myself and I was okay with it, I was happy in the belief that it would all work out in the end.

I got back to the yard in Coventry one morning, tired and ready for bed, only to find that my car had been broken into. A quarterlight window smashed, my car stereo was gone and the glove box had been rifled through. In plain view on the passenger seat was my Haynes workshop manual, nice and shiny, covered in fingerprints. A disinterested policeman arrived about an hour later to take notes.

"If you dust it for prints you should be able to find the little bastard that did it." My comment was met with a wry smile.

"We won't be dusting it, it's not like it's a sixty grand Jag or anything, I mean, what is it worth, £300, £400 ?"

"I paid £600 mate, but what's that got to do with it?"

"So it's not worth our while to do anything about it." I was enraged, how dare he say that, how dare he say that my loss was worth less than the loss from a more expensive car?

"What the fuck are you saying? You're telling me that if I had a fucking sixty grand Jaguar, you'd do something, but because I don't-you won't. If I had a sixty grand fucking Jag I could afford to replace a fucking car stereo and a fucking broken window, but I ain't, I got a £600 car and no fucking money to replace anything, I have to work for what I get!"

"There's no need for that kind of language, Sir. I will have to arrest you if you insist on-"

"Arrest ME? Arrest Me? I'm the victim of a crime here, and you're going to arrest me?" I was livid, absolutely livid. How in anyone's mind any of this could be right I had no idea. If I could be arrested for stealing a penny chew from a store, someone breaking into my car should be arrested too, regardless of the value of the car.

"Look Sir, it's not up to me okay? But if you continue to use that sort of language I will have to arrest you." What the fucking stupid, bollocks, shit arsed upside down, stupid fucking kind of a world did this stupid fucking prick inhabit? Seriously? Arrest me for being a victim of crime, a fucking angry victim of a crime this fucking moron was refusing to investigate? I paid my taxes, I did my time, I tow the line and this fucking idiot tells me I'm not worthy of protection within the law. "Fuck you!"

I jumped into the car and drove to the Police Station at Little Park Street, in town. There were barriers on the entrance and no way I could see of accessing the parking spaces. I didn't actually realise they were for serving officers only, not for the public to park in. Further frustrated by this, I pulled across the barriers and locked the car up, blocking anyone from getting in or out. I was on a mission.

Inside the reception area I demanded to see whoever was in charge, I'd paid my taxes and I had a right to justice and I was damned if I wasn't going to get it. The guy on the desk looked unimpressed.

"I want to see whoever is in charge and I want to see him now."

"He's a little bit busy at the moment Sir, I'll get the duty Sergeant to see you."
Sergeant? Was that all I was worth?

"I want to see someone in authority, not another Muppet."

"I assure you Sir, there are no Muppets working here."

"Is this your car blocking the entrance?" A voice called from behind me.

"Yes it is, and I'm not moving it until I've spoken to someone in a senior position here." I had asserted my position, now let's see them wriggle out of this one, I was willing to put it all over the mornings front pages if need be-'Arrest me, indeed?'

"What's going on here?" Another voice from beside me, and another and another. I was suddenly surrounded by shirt sleeved officers wanting to know what the fuss was.

"I'm not moving the fucking car until someone comes outside and does something about the break in, I want the car dusted and the little fucker that smashed my window, caught." A cacophony of voices all hailing indignation reigned down on me from all sides. For some reason it's a worse crime to swear in front of an officer than it is to break into someones car.

"Come on, then-" said one officer, "let's see what this is all about." He led me back outside the doors and immediately asked me to move the car.

"I told you, I'm not moving the car." I stood next to a drain and held my keys up, threatening to drop them in if he didn't pay attention to me. I needn't have bothered. Right then I was hit from all sides and pulled to the ground, my outstretched arm still held on to the keys, the attack was so swift, so unforeseen, that by the time I let go they were already in someone else's hands. My arms were pulled behind me, my legs pinned and I swear someone sat and farted on my face. I was dragged off to a cell still screaming abuse and threatening to shove their truncheons where the sun don't shine.

For the umpteenth time in my life, I faced the magistrates bench. I'd been told to plead guilty, not say another word.

"For the charge of Obstructing an Officer in the course of his duty, we hereby find you pay a £200 fine and are Bound Over to keep the peace for a year."

Three magistrates, not one of them could possibly understand the ridiculous nature of their findings. They will never get it, these posh twats that live so far removed from the normal, everyday struggles of the working classes. They will NEVER understand our frustrations, as we will never forget.

We were now in the 1990's and the world was pretty dire. The punks were not as they were in the '80s. Glam fashion had been denounced and it was time for dirty clothes to take over. Anarcho Punks now ruled the scene, black clad unwashed squatters blended into rejuvenated hippies, everything was Glastonbury, the Peace Convoy and farmsteads in Wales or Cornwall. My generation had had our time, we hadn't changed the world, we were so busy going to gig's to sing at ourselves that we forgot about the world outside, and it had forgotten about us. There was a new sound in town, Nirvana, Soundgarden and Primal Scream were the new world order. Cocaine was so cheap on the streets of London that nobody wanted amphetamines anymore. Cannabis was readily available in ever increasing strengths, those of us that had survived our own excesses were now being killed off by the clubber's drug of choice Ecstacy. Peace and love, farmyard raves and illegal factory or warehouse parties were what the kids wanted, we were has-been's, the new teddy-boys, archaic and dinosaur like in our new surroundings. Animal rights groups had attracted a lot of punks, swapping their bright outward appearances for camouflage jackets, face masks and balaclavas. Their politics put animals at the fore, a brilliant coup for the government. Skinheads, especially the right wing element, were vanquished, many were in institutions or had hung up their braces, the street fighting men of the 1970's and '80s now undergoing behavioural therapy, anger management training and rehabilitation. It was the end of our era.

I spent the early nineties being a father and husband. I worked my ass off to provide for my family. At weekends we got together with friends and drank ourselves stupid on cheap crap beer. We slept where we fell in the living room or at Helen and H's house. In the morning I would have to look after the kids if Nikki felt too poorly. I seemed to never get any sleep, I was constantly pushed to the limits at work and home. Nikki's post natal depression was worse than ever after Christina's birth. She cried for no reason, swore blind her hips were too wide, her legs too fat, her stomach wobbly. In truth, there was nothing wrong with her but she walked around with a permanent black cloud over her head. I bounced around from job to job, a few months here, a few months there, always giving it up because the money was no good or there were better opportunity's out there. I spent 6 months working for Frederick Allen, nice local work, home just about every night, very rarely did I have to sleep in a truck. I made friends with a couple of drivers on the firm, some I would work with again years later, like Dave French and Jeff Buckler. Dave would go on to have his own truck and I bumped into him again 20 years on in Lille, Northern France, and then again a year or so later we worked side by side going to Bordeaux every week for Atlantic Europe Express. Jeff also had his own truck years later, and when I was in need of work, he got me a job with his mate Julian, who ran John Brindley Ltd, in nearby Sharnford.

I landed myself a job with a firm in Wolverhampton, Hoship. I had my own truck to live in all week and would be home just about every weekend. Most of the work I did was to France, but sometimes I would head out to Belgium, The Netherlands or Germany, even Austria. We didn't go to Switzerland very often and we never went to Italy or Spain. I took my old school mate Mark Norris out to Paris with me one week.

"Is it safe out there?" He asked.

"Of course mate, never have any problems." 2 days later we were being fired at by a Frenchman with a pistol, in a road rage incident on the road around Marne-La Vallee.

I got Lisa a job on the same company, but she left after a few months, it wasn't to her liking and she felt a little at risk, being a female alone at night in the back end of beyond.

John, my old mate from the Rose And Crown, who I'd worked with before, landed a job at Express Freight and kept telling me I should apply too. I was still unsure , I hadn't got enough experience yet to go to Portugal, Italy or anywhere else his boss Malcolm, was likely to send me.

Animal and I met up by chance one day, we buried the past behind us and I took him out with me on a trip to Cannes in southern France. He drank all the way there and all the way back. We sang together, ate together and had as much of a laugh as 2 men in a plastic pig of a truck could have in one week. When we got home we lost touch again, and it was to be another 26 years before we saw each other again.

Another lad I worked with at Dayson's, a lad called Colin, joined Hoship and worked with us for the next couple of years. We had a good team of drivers on Hoship. Everyone helped each other out, we all worked to our own schedules and we all stuck together when we could. We were also a bunch of piss-heads. Two of the older drivers had been banned from working together by the boss Peter Howard. They'd shipped out together but only got as far as Aachen on the German/ Belgian border by the middle of the week. It turned out they'd started drinking on arrival and failed to notice that the sun had gone down, risen and set again before they stopped. When they finally called the office they both gave the same excuse, they'd had a flat tyre and had to walk it for miles to the next garage and pump some air into it. Most Sundays, the Wolverhampton lads would meet in a pub for lunch and a couple of beers before work. They would then go to the yard, pick up their trucks and run to Dover. Once cleared they'd have a pint before catching the ferry to Calais or Zeebrugge. One lad was breathalysed in later years and found to be over the limit before catching the boat and subsequently lost his job. Once on board, we would all have a meal in the freight drivers' lounge washed down with a healthy jug of red wine before a drink or 2 upstairs in the bar. We would pull off the boat in France or Belgium, and go straight to bed.

Derek, a big black doorman from Wolverhampton, Jeff Hansford, another big lad from Stafford, Colin and Myself were all weekended near Munich. Checking my map, I saw were were not far from Dachau and so we all met up and took a walk to the camp. Never in my life had I been so humbled by an experience. The museum was full of the pain and suffering of the many thousands of souls who'd suffered so brutally in this place. The air around it was oppressive, no birds flew overhead and the 'Arbeit Macht Frei' iron sign above the old entrance post, was a chilling reminder of the horror that these people endured. The camp had been destroyed after the 2nd World War, the ovens in the crematorium rebuilt in remembrance of the crimes perpetuated against an entire populace. The horror was real and you could still feel it in the earth we walked on.

Most weeks I would have to drive through the night Friday to get home Saturday, otherwise I would be weekended in Dover which I hated. When that happened I would only be home one night, Monday, before shipping out again Tuesday. I was constantly tired, racing to get home. Late night drinking on Saturday and then having to shop for groceries, wash my clothes and get myself ready to leave again Monday morning. Most weekends I would be in charge of the girls to give Nikki a break. I would always read to them at night whenever I was home, sometimes their voices would squeal for me to "Read it again", and I would. I loved my daughters, and would do anything I could for them, they were my world.

We'd planned a trip to Bournemouth, Decca had a minibus and we went in H's car. Everyone meeting up at the sport's centre car park in Pool Meadow, wet suit, beer and inflatable boat at the ready, we headed off down the A34. We hadn't gone more than an hour down the road when all we could see in the back of the minibus was Brophy blowing up the dinghy, the inflatable boat filling the bus interior and forcing himself and the other passengers against the windows. His little, blonde spiky head was pressed against the glass of the rear window, his face flushed from the effort of blowing the boat up manually, but all was well, he had a beer can in his hand, there was no need to call for help. Brophy had it all covered.

I sat on the sofa one Saturday lunchtime, Nikki had cooked lunch and I was just about to tuck in when there was an almighty boom outside the house. Our windows shook and I nearly dropped a pea from my fork. Along the street there had been a gas explosion, most of the neighbours were coming out of their houses to see what was happening. I looked and saw a woman standing dazed by a house on the other side of the street.

"What's happened?" I called over to her. She looked stunned and I ran over. There were curtains flapping out of the blown out windows, a cloud of smoke billowing from within the building.

"Are you okay? What happened?"

"I was sitting on my doorstep having a fag, and next door just exploded, I don't know why."

"Is anyone in there, who lives there?"

"Just some old guy, lives on his own...." I was already gone. Without thinking I tried the front door but it wouldn't budge.

"Someone call the fire brigade" I shouted, "-and get an ambulance too!" My neighbour, Simon, from over the road came running up to help.

"Come on, give us a hand" and with that I jumped in through the blown out window of the downstairs lounge. Simon followed. The room was a wreck, furniture and fittings blown everywhere. The sofa was blocking the front door, behind it the living room door was off it's hinges and another door protruded through it. We pulled the sofa away from the door and I headed into the back room.

"I'll get the gas," yelled Simon, heading for the under-stair cupboard. I pulled at the doors and made a way through to the back, everything was a mess and the walls were scorched and black, a thick cloud of smoke hung in the air, curtains were burning, the sofa and parts of the carpet. I headed for the kitchen just as the door opened and the old man came out, he was burning, his hair, his clothes, his skin. He seemed dazed and confused, almost unaware of the flames about his head and upper body. I grabbed something, a towel, a curtain, blanket or whatever it was and threw it over his head patting out the fire and working down until there were no more flames on him. Simon appeared in the doorway, between us we took the old man into his lounge where he sat bolt upright on his burned sofa. I returned to the kitchen and pulled down the remaining curtains, throwing the burning materials out into the garden, along with everything else that I could find that was still smouldering or burning. On top of his stove stood a bottle of milk and a dry saucepan. By the time the fire brigade arrived everything was out, we had cleared the house, extinguished the fire and retrieved the old man. An ambulance crew arrived and took him away to hospital for treatment as we were asked for statements. The police had turned up, and the whole street was out in force.

"Well done you two," said the chief fire officer, "-you'll get an award for this."

Sure enough, Simon and I were called to an awards' ceremony in Wolverhampton a few months later, where we were presented with certificates from the Society For The Protection Of Life From Fire, the highest award attainable by members of the public. We were Heroes, officially. The accolade was somewhat tarnished though. After his visit to the hospital the old man was returned to his home, the only place he'd ever lived in was a ruin. The walls were charred and black, the windows had been boarded by Simon and myself when we realised the council would not be able to secure the property until Monday. He was returned home by ambulance just after midnight, left alone on the burnt sofa, in the house he was born in, the same house he was found dead in the following morning.

January 1st, 1992 saw the removal of customs borders throughout Europe. From that date truck drivers no longer had to stop at each and every frontier to clear their freight. Jeff and I shipped out together through Calais. We both had several consignments for Belgium, Holland and Germany. We passed through the dock in record time, no delays, no checking our diesel tanks, no backhanders for the customs officers, it was just like driving off the Woolwich ferry, only more scenic. We refuelled in Calais, collecting our obligatory boxes of beer, and set off to do our deliveries. Having checked our routes, we decided to meet up that night at a quiet little border crossing in northern Holland. Everything went well and as planned, we arrived a short while apart at a parking area on the frontier. There wasn't much on the Dutch side, just a few scattered houses. On the German side we could see some shops and what looked like a bar, so we decided to go there. Inside the bar there appeared to be a celebration of some sort, music blared, plates of food were offered around and beers swiftly placed in front of us. We drank and ate our fill, eventually deciding around midnight, to retire to our bunks. We looked around and could find nobody who understood that we wanted to pay our bill, we gesticulated loudly and spoke in our best pidgin English that we were leaving but no bill was offered. So we left, fed and watered for free. Next day we did the same and arranged to meet at a services in Germany. Jeff arrived after me and explained he'd had a bad day, he'd missed one of his deliveries and rather than go 100 miles back for the sake of a small consignment worth about £50, he signed his paperwork himself and disposed of the goods. We ate supper together, Curry-wurst and chips washed down with a couple of beers each. Somebody came and cleared our table and we ordered another drink each. We chatted some more and then went to retire for the night. There had been a change of shift behind the counter since our arrival and the guy on the till had no idea what we'd had to eat and drink.

"I'll get these Jeff" I offered, and handed the server two empty bottles.

"Das ist alles?"

"Ja, ja , zwei biers danke." I paid for the 2 beers and we quickly made our exit.

Sometimes, things just fall into place like that, other times you're driving along in the sun, windows open, singing along to Killing Joke, when a Bee the size of decent strawberry, bounces off the roof, falls through your window and gestures 'I die you die' by inserting it's sting between your toes. There's a good reason for wearing boots when driving, and getting stung at 58 mph with 38 tons of truck beneath your backside is it.

Back in Coventry, things were going downhill, slowly but surely. Nikki was getting more and more depressed and we were arguing more and more with each other. It was nonsense mostly, usually along the lines of me coming home looking forward to being with my family, only for Nikki to be upset because of something ridiculous, she'd discover a spot on her forehead, or her hair was too curly, her jeans didn't fit anymore, and now she wouldn't leave the bedroom, I wasn't allowed near her and "I just want to die!"

Nothing I said or did would make things better, everything was my fault anyway. It was my fault she'd got pregnant. It was my fault she had no friends. It was my fault she had no life now. It was my fault I was away all the time and probably sleeping with hookers and barmaids, hitch hikers and women truck drivers. If I had had a fraction of the action I'd been accused of, I would never have come home. I wouldn't have had to. I could have been a single guy living in the truck all year round. But I wasn't doing anything. I was doing my job, paying the bills, looking after my family and coming home to a torrent of abuse every time.

"You're never here when I need you...
You do nothing for the girls.....
I can't go out, I haven't got any friends....
I can't go out looking like this.....
Where were you?
Who were you with?
Why were you late?
Who's that woman in the background?
Why can't you come home?"

It was bad enough not seeing the girls all week long, not taking them to the Doctor when they were poorly, not taking them to the park, school -anything. I was missing out on so much, whilst at the same time being accused of doing things I hadn't done.

There was a gig in London. Xray-Spex had reformed and were playing a one-off show at Brixton Academy. Tickets were purchased and I was not missing it for the world. The gig started early on Saturday afternoon, but Friday morning I was still at Nuremburg. I drove like the clappers and was out of Germany, then swapped tacho cards and drove through the night back to Coventry. H drove us all down to London and I nodded off in the backseat. I woke as we arrived in Brixton, queuing for the car park.

"Oh shit!" Said H, "Look at that fucker"

On the pavement beside us, some big fella had another guy held under his arm. His head was trapped in his captor's armpit, his legs wobbling awkwardly alongside, his eyes fixed on the axe in the other man's hand. I didn't think they were playing, but it was none of our business anyway. Inside the venue we wandered round and settled on somewhere to stand near the front. I left Nikki to go to the toilet at one point and bumped into Little Tom. A lot of our friends had come down from Coventry for this gig, but I wasn't expecting to see Tom. I was just about to ask him where Toni (his wife) was, when Tom suddenly lost his smile and made a goofy face.

"Oh mate! I'm so shitfaced, I don't know where I am...."

He knew full well where he was, so did I, and so did the girl I didn't recognise, who was not his wife, but was hiding under his kilt. Tom was away from home, playing away from home while Toni looked after their kids, exactly what I was constantly, and falsely, being accused of.

I quit my job at Hoship after being weekended in Dover for the third week on the trot. I needed to be at home more and Dover was not home, although sometimes it felt like it. Jeff gave me a lift home, putting his own job on the line as I left my truck in the import dock, then took my paperwork home to guarantee getting my wages. I hate being lied to, and I had been lied to badly that week by the staff in our Dover office, the result being me not getting home for the sake of 25 cartons of wine another driver could have collected.

Lisa had a brother called Martin, a plumber. Martin had started coming around our house at weekends for drinks, as had most of our friends, including one guy I never knew who'd always have a bottle of whiskey in his jacket pocket. I saw him many times before I asked H who the hell he was.

"That's Roddy that is, he's got a band, and he used to play for The Specials."

Martin introduced to me to a book he thought I'd like to read, The Holy Blood And The Holy Grail, it was a big, thick book, a real heavyweight full of historical detective work. I spent weeks reading it and debating with Martin over the content. In the end, I believed it was not far from the truth. Jesus was a real man, he lived and died but his bloodline was taken from Israel and given sanctuary in Europe. Rat Scabies made his own quest along the lines of this book, and I was a believer too. The book went on to inspire another, The Da Vinci Code, which later became a film. In return, I taught him the Phonetic Alphabet and Morse Code. I did this by sending him a postcard from all the places I went to, and through, in Europe. I had to find 26 postcards, 1 for each letter of the alphabet. On each card I sent Just the Phonetic word and morse symbol for each letter. A = Alpha .- B = Bravo -... and so on. I dare say somebody, somewhere in Whitehall, has access to a file, a big file, and it has my name on it.

Nikki was getting more unstable and I didn't know what to do with her. She needed time away from the girls, a holiday. We couldn't afford one for all of us, but that wouldn't have helped, she needed time alone to herself. Dave Pep had moved out to America and was now living in Virginia. I made a few calls and arranged for Nikki to go visit for a week or two. John, who I'd worked with at Double D, was now working for Express Freight and promised to get me a job on the firm as soon as one became available. Unfortunately this turned out to be the day I dropped Nikki at the airport.

Nikki rang me most days she was away, she was not enjoying herself. Dave lived in a shared house with a couple of friends and Nikki was sleeping on a sofa. Because they all worked, she was left alone to her own devices most of the time, however, there was one lad she seemed to get along with, they spent some time together, played tennis and talked a lot. Then something went wrong, and I had a pretty good idea what had happened. Nikki wanted to come home, she was crying and back in her self-loathing default mode. A trip to New York made no difference, it took her mind off things for a bit, but overall I don't think she enjoyed being in the States, she had very little good to say about it. Nikki didn't want to talk about what happened between herself and Dave's mate, but I could read between the lines and I had a pretty good idea what it may have been.

Soon after her return I started to work for Malcolm at Express Freight. The money was the best I'd ever earned but I was away from home all week. The bulk of my work was to France, we had a depot at Gennevilliers, near Paris and would often run from Coventry to Gennevilliers and return. Other times, getting to Paris would just be the start of the trip, from there we could go anywhere. The most expensive load I ever carried was for Malcolm, £96,000,000 of analgesic tablets, pain killers, from Leeds to Lyon. Sometimes I would go to Belgium, Holland, Germany, Austria or Spain.

I was in Gennevilliers one Friday night with another driver, 'Shakey'. He was loaded ready to return to England but I had to collect my last consignments from a village near Beauvais, it was a regular job, and I had done it before. This time 'Shakey' said he'd come with me to keep me company. When we arrived at the village, we would always park in the main square, about 200 yards from the depot we were collecting from. The goods were car parts, collected by one of their own drivers and then transshipped onto our trailer, normally around 11 pm on Friday. We arrived early and were told to get a coffee in the bar nearby, they would come and get us when when the goods arrived. 'Shakey' was first into the bar and ordered two beers. I started talking to the barman in French and we were having quite a laugh. Next thing, we're playing pool, all three of us.

"Ho, Chauffeur, votre chargement est arrivé!" A head poked through the doorway. My load had arrived, it was time to load up and go.

"J'arrive!" I replied, saying that I would be out as soon as I had finished my game, and my beer. Almost immediately, more beers were placed on the pool table. The barman told us not to rush. Another little drink wouldn't hurt. We carried on and almost forgot about the truck outside, until the head returned.

"Monsieur, vous-etes chargé, vos papiers sont sur la chaise." The load was on, and my papers on my seat.

"OK, merci!" I called back, and took my next shot. More beer arrived. We retired to the bar, the only people still in the joint, chatting and laughing, chatting, laughing and drinking. Eventually, the barman's wife came downstairs and switched off the lights. It was time to go. I have no recollection of anything after stepping outside into the night air, nothing, until about 10 miles from Boulogne when 'Shakey's brake lights lit up the windscreen in front of me, I jumped on my own brakes and thankfully stopped before hitting the back of his trailer. I was drunk, way too drunk to be driving anything, but in 'Shakey's world, this was an ordinary Friday night run home.

Rich Mulligan had been away from Coventry. He'd been on a round the world back packing trip for a year. On his return we chatted before he left again for a 3 month safari in Africa. He called me again when he got home and asked if he could come on a trip with me, he sounded almost desperate.

"I'm off to Italy tomorrow if you want to come along."

"That's perfect mate, I've got to get away again, my head's shot. I spent a whole year back packing around the world, then bugger off to Africa for 3 months, come home for my first beer in the Rose and some fucker walks in with a bag of records I lent him 3 years ago saying 'I knew you'd be here Rich, sitting on your usual seat at the bar, I brought these back for you.' Cheeky bastard, it's like I've never done anything with my life."

We talked about his travels, the adventures he'd been on since I'd last seen him. I found it fascinating, I loved hearing stories of the outside world, that place beyond the Monday to Friday, beyond the street door. We laughed a lot, drank a lot, and at one point dived into a lake for a swim. We were having an adventure of our own, nobody got mauled by Lions, well, we didn't, but someone on the same safari as Rich had been on- only a week earlier, did get mauled. Attempting to get the perfect photo with a Lion, a Japanese tourist pulled it's tail to get it to look at the camera. The Lion wasn't impressed, but did confirm that Human tastes like Chicken.

Someone I hadn't seen very often the last few years was Adam. I'd known him from my first day in Coventry, way back in 1982 at Rich's flat in Wood End. He was sharing a house with another mate, Naz. They both turned up at our house one night. Adam had split up with his girlfriend and thinking of doing something different work wise.

"So what's the money like driving trucks?" He asked me.

"Depend's on what you're doing mate, and who you work for."

"I'm thinking of doing my HGV test, d'you think it's worth doing?"

"You're already earning some decent money, if you get your licence, get some experience under your belt you'll end up getting back to where you are now mate, you're probably better off staying where you are, unless you want to do it for the lifestyle, but don't think it's all glamorous and shit, it's hard work and and pretty boring most of the time, sometimes you get lucky and get to see some great places, but it is a lonely existence most of the time."

"I get it, yeah, I was just thinking about doing something new, you know, thought it might be something to look at."

A week later, Naz walked into their house and called out to Adam. There was no reply, but as he'd caught a glimpse of him out of the corner of his eye, up on the landing, Naz continued to talk to him from downstairs. It took a while for him to realise Adam was still not responding, so he went to the bottom of the stairs and saw that Adam had hung himself, from a rafter in the loft, above the upstairs landing.

A lot of people turned up for Adam's funeral. He was a gentle giant, and to this day is still remembered as such by all who knew him. I was upset at his death, not because he was gone, but because he didn't say anything to anybody who may have been able to help him, he didn't reach out beyond saying he fancied a change of career, it was a shame, a real shame.

Little Jacqui also took her own life. She overdosed on a cocktail of bathroom medicines. I'd seen her in town a few days before, she told me she was doing okay, was getting her life sorted and things were good. She lied.

I was in Germany after yet another weekend home, another Saturday night lost to cheap french beer and cigarettes, all night stereo sounds and an argument with Nikki. What was I doing wrong? We needed the money but she couldn't handle me being away and being home didn't pay enough to cover the bills. I tried to call several times but was getting no answer. Eventually I called H and asked if he could pop round and see if everything was okay. Later, I called again and he said she had been poorly and that maybe it was best I wait until I get home to talk to her. I tried again the next day and and the next. Eventually she answered and said she'd explain everything when I got home. I knew something was wrong, I just didn't know what. I got to our street door and found the frame was damaged. Inside, Nikki was waiting with the girls. Once I'd put the girl's to bed, I asked what had been going on. It turned out that she'd taken an overdose of paracetamol and aspirin. When H had arrived, two policemen were forcing the door, Nikki was unconscious on the floor, the girl's upstairs in bed. She was taken to hospital and we were within a hair's breadth of having the girl's taken into care.

We decided to go on holiday to Rhodes with Helen and H. Nikki's Mum said she would babysit the girls for us. We needed some time together, in the run up to the holiday I was away for about 3 weeks, Portugal, Spain and Italy. I got home the day before our flight and Nikki wanted nothing to do with me. She was so highly strung I was having doubts about going away. As soon as we got to the airport she hit the vodka and by the time we arrived at our hotel, she was drunk. We were all pretty drunk, to be honest, but Nikki was moody and drunk. She kept me at arm's length and I fell asleep as soon as I hit the hotel bed. I could sleep anywhere, at any time back then. When I was working I'd have at least 1 or 2 nights a week without any sleep, it was a mixture of the job and our socialising at home. I burned candles at both ends and in the middle too, life was for living, you sleep plenty when you're dead.

Next morning I awoke alone in the room. I wandered out to the swimming pool to find Nikki and the others already sunbathing. Nikki was topless, something she had sworn she would never do, I didn't really care, but was frustrated and angry at having had so many petty arguments over it before we left. Breasts are breasts, and having lived in France and been naked on the beach myself, I saw no wrong in it. For Nikki it had been a big deal and she had repeatedly denounced me for being so relaxed about it. Now that she was here, she was showing herself to be a little hypocritical. As the week progressed we argued more and more. One night she stormed off and was gone for several hours. She was drunk. H went to find her, apparently in a field and she came out with some long winded tale about having to hide from a local guy, but something was different, something was very different and I sensed it in both her and H.

Toward the end of the week, things really blew up. I fell asleep near the pool with after drinking a bottle of Ouzo, we'd had an argument and Nikki stormed off again. Helen woke me up to say I needed to come quickly.

Nikki had trashed our bedroom, everything was thrown around the place, clothes, bags, bedding. Empty pill packets were spread around the room and broken glasses peppered the floor. On the mirror of the dressing table in bright red lipstick she'd scrawled ' Fucking Die Whore'.

This was the last straw, this was the end in my mind. We searched around the hotel grounds but she was nowhere to be found. I sat with H on a wall and told him I had had enough.

"I can't do this no more mate, I can't. No matter what I do it's wrong and nothing is ever good enough. When we get back I'm divorcing her, she can have the kids and anything else, but I can't live with her anymore, she's driving me nuts, she just won't believe anything I say."

"Yeah" H slurred, the word trailed off as he looked for more words to add.

"But you know what, mate, you wanna wait and see, y'know, maybe when you get back it'll all be better, maybe she'll calm down a bit."

"I can't mate, I'm going to end up unemployable at this rate, nobody's going to want to give me a job with a record like mine, quitting jobs because she's having a meltdown all the time, and look what she did to that room, for fuck's sake, she's nut's."

"Well...... I don't know, I just.... I love you both.... and y'know...."

"I know mate, and I love you too, but this can't go on."

Helen walked out of the dark somewhere.

"Nikki's back."

I ran to our room and saw her sitting on the bed. Anger rose inside me like a volcano erupting.

"Look at what you've done." I screamed, "Are you happy now, are you?"

Before I knew what I was doing I had her by the throat and was dragging her to the pool. The rage in my head was willing me to drown her there and then, to put an end to her, to stop this continual torture. I knew Rich had been right, I should never have married her, but I did, and this was my punishment. I was ready and willing to take her life there and then, 10 years in a Greek prison would be worth it to stop this torment, but the kids, what about the kids? I saw their faces in my mind's eye and knew right then I couldn't do it. I couldn't hurt them like this, I could not. I threw Nikki's body on the ground and screamed a guttural, anguished scream that should have woken half the island. I could not hurt her, because I could not hurt my daughters.

There is a point in all people where, should they be pushed to it, they snap. The kindest, meekest creature will fight like a rabid fox in a corner, if you push them enough. Never did I ever want to lay a finger on my wife, but when pushed, I snapped. This is not a trait I am proud of, it is not something of which to be boastful, I am saying this because it happens, it really happens. I have a reputation as someone willing to lash out, but that is not something I am particularly happy about. I would much rather be happy, left alone to live and let live, love and let love. Frustration and pent up anger are destructive forces, so destructive they can lead to people to take another's life, to actually kill someone. Think about that for a moment. Taking someone's life because of frustration and anger, when really, all that we needed to do was to talk, openly and honestly, no games, no lies, just truthfully talk and be open with each other.

We arrived home and I called Malcolm, I was about to say I needed some time out to see a solicitor, but he got in there before I could say a word.

"I need you in tomorrow, you're going to Budapest."

I'd never been to Hungary before, suddenly, thoughts of arranging a solicitor, divorce, court etc all seemed too much and it was easier to run away, easier to pack my stuff and go to work than deal with our relationship. So I packed my bags, and went to work as if nothing had changed. There was a difference now though, I was leaving home not as a married man and father, I was leaving as one who felt totally unable to change his lot in life, like I had given up, that this was all there would ever be now. Loneliness, solitude, always departing, never being anywhere, having nobody but myself because nobody else mattered anymore. I had already lost my kids, they would never understand what it felt like to have to walk away, to have to go, because staying was no longer an option. The home was toxic, poisoned by a million little pills, a thousand loud voices and an ocean of tears. My heart was broken, I was broken but still I had to leave, to work, perform my duties and provide for my family. If only they knew, the weight of my load.

Eastern and Central Europe were in transition, the Berlin wall had fallen only a couple of years earlier and whole nations were adjusting to a brand new world. Closed to the west for so many years, the grey concrete cities of the east were now being seen by people like myself for the first time. There was a real pioneering feel to going beyond Austria in those early days of the new Europe. We would transit through Germany and cross the border at Shirnding into the newly partitioned Czech Republic. Immediately on crossing the frontier, I was aware that this was a new world for me. The roads were narrow, often cobble stoned and slippy. Poverty was the norm and everyone seemed oppressed, there was a sense of the heavy weight of communist oppression bearing down on the people, the grey concrete buildings, even the weather. Everything was grey and depressed. I felt very much at home under the black cloud of my failing marriage.

Beyond the Czech Republic lay Slovakia, at times it would feel like the poorer cousin, as broken and worn as it's northern neighbour was, Slovakia seemed even more run down and poverty stricken. We transited through the newly built customs block at Kuty. When I say built, I think I meant to say delivered. The border crossing was no more than a Portacabin dropped onto the central reserve of the motorway between Brno and Bratislava. The queue would stretch for miles in either direction, each truck having to stop and present their papers, one at a time.

Hungary was to become my new favourite destination, after Sicily. I loved the plains, the low flat land between the distant mountains that seemed to surround the country. Budapest was beautiful and darkly dangerous, while Lake Balaton was a haven amidst the mad, mad world that surrounded it.

The UK Intervention Board were emptying the nation's cold stores of their stockpiles of beef. A worldwide ban was coming into force on the sale of British Beef, due to the BSE crisis. Bovine Spongiform Encephalopathy, or Mad Cow Disease which had brought the UK Farming industry to a near halt. We were helping in the export of 120,000 tons of cryogenically frozen beef, some date stamp as far back as 1972/3. It's final destination was meant to be Kenya, we only took it as far as Hungary, after that, who know's what happened to it. My job was to get it to Hungary, after that, to get myself home again.

I took a load of Bicycles out to Holland and was heading back to the yard. The plan was that I would swap trailers and go back again with another load. Someone else would deliver my return load, but I was needed to go back to Holland. Just past Milton Keynes, on the M1, I found myself slip-streaming another truck, sitting so close to his back doors that the wind passed directly around my truck and so therefore I had less wind resistance, used less fuel. It also meant that if the driver in front braked I would get a mouthful of his back doors before even reaching my pedal. I stayed there in the suicide zone for a few miles before deciding to pull out, a gap appeared and as I manoeuvred out an awful sense of impending doom hit me. I felt as though my insides had fallen out my backside, something was horribly wrong. We were approaching the slip road into Rothersthorpe Services and so I swung back into the other lane, and pulled off, straight into the parking area. I caught my breath but couldn't shake the awful feeling, something was wrong. I called home, worried about Nikki and the girls but they were fine. I called my Mum, nothing was wrong there either. I thought I was just being silly, a bit of wind or something, but as I pulled back onto the motorway the traffic was crawling. There had been an accident, about a mile beyond where I'd pulled off. The truck I had been following was on it's side on the embankment, I later heard that the driver had died. If I hadn't pulled off, I would have been in there, somewhere, in amongst the debris.

5 (YOU'RE) READY NOW

"As I love you in anger and bid you sleep in Hell, drown the night with crying eyes so I may sleep as well. The day and night behold me, no peace shall come my way, I'll suffer no more in silence and treasure not this day. So hard to see the ending and to live with it as well, for I loved you as a stranger, but bid you sleep in Hell."

"Istanbul?"

"You're loading in the morning, you'll have to get a visa on the way somewhere, wherever you can find an embassy. Take the Lady Godiva, I don't want to send your truck all the way out there."

Things had not been too good at work, not since 'Black Wednesday', the day when Malcolm's wife dragged him out into the yard by his hair. Just after she'd answered the phone to a French woman demanding to speak privately to Malcolm. Just after he said he didn't know who she was. Just after she rang the fourth time. Just after she rang the third, second and first times. Just after Malcolm had been to Spain in a truck, got into a fight with a van load of Guardia Civil Officers and came home with a black eye, and apparently, a new friend who didn't want to talk to his wife. But that was why I loved working for him, he was just as messy and prone to screwing up as the rest of us. Malc lived the job as much and more, than some of the people he employed. But he never gave up, even when his wife left and the company went bust, he worked some magic and kept a few of us on. Jeff, who I'd got to join after he was sacked from Hoship for taking me home, was laid off, as were many others, but I was offered to stay on, less pay, more work. We were now being bankrolled by the French office in Gennevilliers, although one of the guys, Hafid, left to set up his own company in Bordeaux, Atlantic Europe Express, I still see his trucks on the road today, the only person from the company to come out on top.

Istanbul, the gateway to the East, a city in both Europe and Asia, straddling the Bosporus and laying majestically at the mouth of the Black Sea, twice as far from home as Budapest. I was excited and nervous in equal amounts. Excited to be going on a big adventure, nervous about what may lay ahead, and all that I was leaving behind. There are times when I believe that long distance truck driving is for single people only, that it is not conducive to a stable home life, and other times, when I think that without a family to come home to, there is nothing to come home to, nothing to keep you from your worst excesses, nothing to pull you through the worst days and to keep going when everything is going down the pan. Having a family at home makes you try a little harder, go a bit further and push yourself more, for them, for the kids, the wife, the house.

I loaded at Abingdon, Oxfordshire, a full load of sheepskins, still wet, salted and somewhat unpleasant to the nostrils. I didn't have to touch the load, nor run the fridge so I knew I would sleep well whenever I stopped. I told Nikki I'd be about 2 weeks, a week to get there and a week to get back, but I would call whenever I could. At Dover I took my TIR Carnet to the customs office and filled out the details of my expected journey. Transit from UK to Schirnding, then Kuty, Rajka, Gyula, Ruse, Kapikule and finally clear customs in Errenkoy, Istanbul. My Veterinary papers were stamped, customs receipts proccessed and within a couple of hours, I was on the ferry, watching the white cliffs of Dover disappear once again, behind me.

In the freight driver's restaurant on board the ferry, I got talking to the other lads on my table. It was normal to share a table with your fellow countrymen back then, it was where you swapped knowledge, tips and ideas. Drivers learned from other drivers and we all passed on what we could, the job was hard enough sometimes when you knew what was coming at you, but when you didn't, it could have disastrous results for the driver, his load, and his company. Something else we always did, was to outdo each other, wherever you were going, someone else would normally be going further and it was that person who was the head of the table suddenly. The longer your journey, the higher your status. On this particular crossing to Dunkirk, I held the trump card.

"Off anywhere nice?" I asked.

"Aye, I'm off to Italy" said one lad.

"I got Holland this week" said another.

"Germany for me, where about's in Italy are you going?"

"Milan, tip and reload same place, piece of piss really."

"I was in Prato last week, not a bad run."

"Aye, I like going further south myself, Bologna, Naples, love it."

"I love Sicily myself," I said, "it's a bit wild west down there, but the scenery is great and the locals are always friendly enough, last time I went there, there was four of us together, got the ferry from Genoa, a right piss up it was."

"Where are you to today?"

"Istanbul."

You know when the room goes silent and you don't even have to look up from your plate to know everyone is looking at you, yes, it was that kind of moment.

"Last time I went there was 10 years ago" said Mr Milan, "I fucking hated it then, and it's probably even more of a shit hole now, fuck that shit, you can keep that place, my friend, I don't want to ever go there again."

I was now outranked, not only was I going there for the first time, but I was doing so against the better judgement of my table mate, and he should know, he was there ten years earlier. He hadn't mentioned Sicily, so maybe I hacked him off by trumping him with that one, maybe, but the tone was set now, I was in for a rougher ride that I had expected.

We docked in Dunkirk and I headed across to Lille, joined the A1 briefly and then turned for Valenciennes and Mons. Belgium was only a hop, skip and a jump landing nicely at the German border at Aachen for the night. Congratulating myself on a good day's work, I treated myself to bottle of beer and then pulled the curtains for the night, it had been an interesting first day.

Next day I set off for the Czech border. When I was going to Budapest I would stop at Geiselwind truck stop, it was a good place to stop overnight, but I wanted to press on and get as far as I could as quickly as I could, this was going to be a long trip, right now I wanted to keep it as short as possible in case of delays further up the road. I parked up for the night about an hour short of the border at Schirnding.

German customs were as fast and efficient as always, but crossing the dozen or so metres into the Czech Republic took a whole lot longer. Nothing was ever quick once you left Europe, everyone worked at a slow, suspicious pace whilst intermittently sneering at you through their thick, wiry moustaches and the plexiglass window between you and them. I would always remain nonplussed, I refused to appear intimidated or even bothered, my job was to drive the truck, not worry about upstart little frontiersmen.

Necessary stamps acquired on my Carnet, I pulled the Lady Godiva out of the border crossing and headed off toward's Cheb. My truck was called The Lady Godiva, she was a white 2448 Mercedes, 480 bhp, chrome stack exhausts and in her time was a beauty of a beast. Unfortunately, her time was long passed and she was getting a little rough around the edges. I always loved driving that truck because she was different to the rest of our fleet, they were all green with white roof's, they lacked the appeal of The Lady Godiva.

A few miles in to the journey, the road passes over a level crossing, in a field just beyond this used to lay another British truck, one that had not been warned about the 'Level' crossing. John had warned me about this when I went on my first trip to Budapest, a few months earlier.

"After you get on the road, look out for the level crossing, there's a few of them in Czech, they're everything and anything but level, hit them at more than 20 mph and you will roll over. Slow right down for this one, it's about 3 feet off the fucking ground but you won't know so until you take off, by which time it's adios suspension and hello hospital." John was good like that, he would always forewarn me if I was going anywhere new that he had been to already, we all did the same, helped each other when we could, those were different days, we relied on ourselves and our knowledge to get us through, not computers and technical wizardry, spanners and ratchet straps got us home, and a large helping of pure bravado. I slowed right down at the crossing, the cab of my truck listing one way and then the other, everything in the truck moved, up, down, sideways and back again. My spine twisted and contorted in my seat, a hard backed copy of the London A-Z hit me on the head as it fell from an overhead cupboard, the stereo spluttered and cassette jammed causing a permanent gap halfway through The Penetration song 'Don't Dictate.'

At Cheb I passed the regular queue of prostitutes that lined the TIR transit route to Prague, it was said that many a driver who'd stopped for a quickie here, had been robbed at knife or gunpoint. I didn't fancy either of those and so kept driving past them, out into the countryside and across to the ring road at Prague. Here, we had to be extra vigilant, there was a signpost beside a set of traffic lights that led you onto the ring road, if you missed it you were headed into the city itself, a city of cobbled streets and very low bridges, very old, low bridges. I did it once on an earlier trip, in the rain, I missed the sign and got stuck, very stuck. The top of my trailer connecting with a low bridge and I had to reverse in the dark, in the rain, late at night, about 2 miles to the nearest place I could turn around. Malc didn't like me that week, it wasn't our trailer I'd damaged and it was going to cost a lot to put right.

After Prague, the road south decent motorway again all the way to Brno and Bratislava, the only problem with it was the Czech/Slovak border that had appeared overnight one night, after the former Czechoslovakia split into two very separate states, neither one really liking the other. The queue here could be several miles long and take as much as 24 hours to get through, it could really spoil your day. There wasn't too much of a queue this time, only a couple of hours, and so by the time I made it to Bratislava I decided to call it a day, crack open a beer and pull my curtains. When I say 'pulling my curtains' I do actually mean pulling my curtains closed, it's not a euphemism for anything else, anything I might possibly do on my own, alone, far from home after a frothy warm beer, but if you want think that way you can, just remember that is your filthy imagination there, not mine, I'm a good boy me and I have no idea what it is you're thinking of anyway.

Whenever I went to Budapest, Malc would give me £500 in running money, to pay for cheap diesel, tolls and any bribes that were necessary on route. This time he'd given me £700 but by my reckoning, I would need more than that as Budapest is about half way to Istanbul, and so I would have to be very careful about my expenses. At Raijka there was a weighbridge, unfortunately for me, I was a little overweight on the drive axle of my truck and so had to part with some currency, there and then. I was certain it was a fiddle but you couldn't prove anything when dealing with these people. The head honcho at Raijka was an obnoxious little man who'd regularly throw your paperwork back out of the window at you for no reason, give no explanation, and pull his blind down to signal that he was now on his break. He would often powder his nose behind the screen, his bloodshot eyes and Rudolph like, bulbous red nose were an obvious giveaway, as were his constant sniffing and rubbing his nostrils, the guy had a serious coke problem and chain smoked his way through packet after packet of cheap Turkish cigarettes. No doubt these were acquired from the Turkish drivers as payment following clerical errors or the affecting of turning a blind eye to a certain item not on the load manifest.

Once cleared at Raijka, I headed to Budapest, and the Buda Park on the outskirts of the city. It was a truck stop, in a small wooded area south of the city. I could leave the truck here and go into Buda-Vary, to the Turkish Embassy where I needed to get a visa. I'd been told there were at least three embassies on this route. One in Koln, Bupapest and Bucharest. I didn't want to wait until Bucharest to get the visa, and Koln was too busy a city to park anywhere for any long periods. Budapest felt comfortable, I felt comfortable there, and that made it all the easier to decide. The owner of the Buda Park was as crooked a man as you could meet, a real gangster, but he was straight with his customers, he looked after us in between running a brothel at one end of the building, complete with an armed Romanian guard, the bar and restaurant, as well as all his shifty comings and goings that nobody was ever meant to see or talk about. There was more international trading taking place in the Buda Park than on any given day at the London Stock Exchange. I had a chat with him and he promised to look after my truck, then ordered a taxi for me. A few minutes later I was heading to the embassy.

I knocked on the heavy wooden door, below a sign in Turkish and Hungarian that said either 'Welcome to the 'Turkish Embassy' or 'Doner and chips half price special on Monday night only.' I hoped for the first but when a small window slid open and a pair of very dark eyes stared back at me, I thought I may have found a very private gentleman's club and sauna joint. I lifted my passport and spoke in my best Turkish accent;

"I need a visa, VEEZA, this is the embassy innit? Turkey, veeza?"

The sliding hatch slid shut and a heavy bolt was pulled open, another piece of the door opened and a full face appeared this time.

"Clozed, clo-zed! To Morgen, Morgen Clo-zed!" The hatch closed and I realised that the embassy was closed until the morning. I would have to come back then. I hailed a taxi and told him where I wanted to go, but a few minutes into the journey he took me down a wrong turn and onto the motorway, the M0, he was taking a longer route round the block to get to the Buda Park. By the time we got there, the clock had reached 2,400 HF, it was only 1,000 going into town.

"I'm not paying that" I told the driver, "I'll give you 1,000 the same as I paid to get there, you took me the wrong way, it's not my problem, I'm not paying."

There followed a long, loud slanging match between myself and the taxi driver, I may not be fluent in Hungarian, but if you put enough Z's S's an T's together, you can eventually arrive at something similar to "Fuck off!" and I'm pretty sure we both did in one language or another. Eventually the owner of the Buda Park came over and intervened. It was agreed that I was overcharged and taken the wrong way, but also that the original fare into town was discounted as arranged between the Buda Park and the taxi company. In the end I parted with 1,800 HF and the matter was resolved.

I returned next morning to the embassy, the door was opened and I was allowed in after a full body search. I filled out some paperwork, paid my fee's and was told to come back at 4 pm and my visa would be issued then.

Buda Vary is a medieval area of the old city of Buda, overlooking the River Danube and the Hungarian Parliament building on the north bank in Pest. The twin cities united in the creation of the one, remarkably, named Budapest. I looked out over the old city wall and admired the sprawling city before me, the muddy brown river, no blue anywhere I could see. It was beautiful. Old, charismatic and inviting. I wandered the streets for a few hours, people watching, window shopping, smoking. I treated myself to coffee at a café when my feet grew tired. I felt safe on the streets, safe but aware also that there was danger lurking in the shadows. The city had a reputation for robbery's, pick pockets and gangsters, Mafia groups ran the street walkers and drug peddlers. Counterfeit currency was bought and sold on the streets, along with stolen watches and other personal items. I kept my wits about me, and blended into the background.

At 4 pm I was reunited with my passport, a nice new Turkish visa stamped into one of the pages. My other documents were also returned, and I was free to go on my way again. The excitement of the adventure had returned and I headed back to my truck, with a light step and a smile on my face. I was happy to be on my way again, and once I'd paid for my parking, I headed south on the A5 to Szeged, then Békéscsaba and Gyula, stopping the night in no man's land between Hungary and Romania at the Varsand crossing. Early in the morning I was awoken by a noise outside. A small gang of unwashed children, maybe 7, 8 or 9 years old were standing around my truck holding a bucket of water and some filthy rags. They wanted to wash my windscreen. I declined their offer but still gave them some toothpaste and sweets I had laying around in the cab. Jeff had once told me about a time he was in Romania and a Guard had spent all night walking around his truck while Jeff was eating. On his return, Jeff gave him a tube of toothpaste and later that night, the Guard returned with his daughter as a 'Thank You' for the toothpaste. I didn't want any 'Thank You', I just didn't need my screen washing or my truck damaged if I sent them packing without any offerings.

Once I'd cleared on the Romanian side, I headed off into the country. This was my first time in Romania, I had heard so many stories of this place, I was also a big fan of the Dracula story, Bram Stoker's anti hero, a blood sucking demon who hailed from a castle in the Carpathian mountain range of Romania. Maybe I would see crosses on doors, strings of garlic around the window frames of old houses, maybe, maybe not. What I did see was a nation on it's knees. Poor, under developed and in need of outside help. The roads were atrocious, mud paths and sometimes cobbled streets in better off areas. Houses that were weathered and worn, having survived hundreds of years without so much as a new roof. Chickens and pigs roamed the streets and at every turn there would be a horse and cart in the road. It was like driving through history, through a time long since passed in the west. As I drove through the little towns and villages, people would turn the heads, their faces sun burned and ravaged with months of dirt and dust. Every where I looked I saw rusty cars, tractors and machinery laying dead where they'd finally coughed their last black cloud of exhaust fumes. This was a bitterly poor country, it's president, Nikolai Ciaucescu had been toppled and executed after a short revolution a few years earlier. This was a country in transition, from dictatorship to a new European democracy, and it had a lot of catching up to do in a very short time.

My route took me from Varsand to Chisnieu-Cris on the A79, along to Deva, Sebes, Sibiu, Ramnicu Valcea, Pitesti and Bucharest. At Pitesti the road crossed a railway line and it was here that I had heard of drivers having their fuel tanks shot at by a rifleman. The story was that the red light was controlled by a watchman who would stop any foreign trucks coming through, a gang of kids would appear by the truck demanding money or gifts, if none was paid, they'd disperse and before the lights changed, someone would take pot shots at the truck's fuel tank. I'd heard of this, but thankfully, as I crossed the railway lines there was not a child in sight and no bullet holes on The Lady Godiva.

Each of the larger towns that I passed through, had an archway across the road with the name of the town written in huge letters as a welcome sign. The reverse side stated 'Drum Bun' which I took to mean Farewell, or Drive safely.

Bucharest ring road was next on my list of new experiences. My maps showed something like a miniature M25 encircling the Romanian capital. The reality of it was totally different. Concrete sections, about 13 metres long, had been laid end to end on the ground and called a road. There couldn't have been any foundations laid as each time the trucks weight transferred to the next slab it would drop at one end, creating a kind of seesaw effect as you drove along. Jets of brown water would be pushed out from where puddles had formed beneath the slabs, slowly eroding the soil beneath even further. Maximum speed was posted as being 40 kph but I struggled to get beyond 15, it really was that bad. Once I'd mastered the seasickness inducing ring road, my next challenge was finding the exit. As I had been warned, the exit was no more than a gap in the hedge that fringed the road. There was a signpost, literally a sign post, the sign itself having been knocked off, had been laying in the ditch behind it for many years. I took the sharp turn between the trees and drove down a cobbled roadway, under a railway bridge and followed the road south to the Bulgarian border at Ruse. By the time I reached Ruse I had been driving for about 13 hours, I was well over my legal drive times, but paid no attention to this, the only people who would want to see my Tachograph cards were the German Polizei when I got back to Schirnding or Waidhaus on my return journey. So long as I produced 3 legal cards, they would let me through.

It was late when I reached Ruse and there was only a short queue, so rather than pulling my curtains before passing through customs, I transited through, crossing the Danube again, for the umpteenth time on this journey, over the bridge and into Bulgaria. Formalities done, I pulled into a parking area and prepared to sleep.

There was a knock on my door, 3 to be precise, not exactly urgent but somebody wanted my attention. I thought maybe I needed to pay for the parking or another Brit wanted to say hello, but in both cases I was wrong. It was a prostitute vying for business. I shut my curtain and and ignored her.

Bang, bang, bang.

"Go away, I'm not interested!" I called out.

Bang, bang, bang.

"Fuck off! I'm trying to get some sleep."

Bang, bang, bang.

"For fuck sake!" I pulled the curtain back a second time, "Will you just fuck off and let me sleep?"

"Kalt, Kalt!" The chubby young woman with long black hair feigned a shiver, she was wearing track suit bottoms and a t-shirt, she may well have been cold, but that was not my problem.

"I don't care if you're cold, go away and leave me alone." I shut my curtain again and again, she knocked the door.

"For fuck...." I pulled the curtain open and began to open my window, trying to get it through to her I was not interested. Just as I put my head out into the cool night, she jumped up and put her arm in through the window, opening the door. I almost fell out on top of her, but instead, grabbed a handle and steadied myself. I was not a happy bunny at this point.

"Funfzig mark!" She exclaimed, offering me her personal services.

"I don't care, English, nichts Deutsche, English, but I ain't interested!, now fuck off and leave me alone."

I became aware of another person in the dark outside, and climbed down from the truck to try to put an end to this situation. A thin, dark haired man stepped up and I took him to be someone working for the truckstop.

"Tell her to get away from here, I'm trying to sleep and she won't leave me alone, I've had a long day and I've got another long day tomorrow, I don't need this shit, I'm trying to sleep."

"You must pay" he said, "You must pay her 20 Deutschmarks."

"What. 20 DM, for what?"

"You take her time, she could be earning, you must pay."

"Fuck you, I ain't paying no-one mate" I turned to get back in the truck but as I did, he dipped down and I turned back to see him pick up a rock from the ground. He motioned towards my windscreen, threatening to smash it if I didn't hand over the money. As quick as a flash, I pulled out my trusty wheel brace, swung round and smacked him in the side of his head with the steel bar. There was a scream, and the prostitute ran off in one direction, her pimp picked himself up from the dusty ground, with one hand on his head he ran off back into the dark night, still clutching the rock.

"Fuck it!" I thought, "Time to get out of Dodge."

I was now a target for a very rude awakening, and so decided to put some miles between us. I found a lay-by some 20-25 miles away and pulled up for what was left of the night. It was only an hour or so later the sun rose, and again there was a knock at the door. I had parked on the pitch of another prostitute, her pimp, a younger man than the elder gent I'd had word's with in Ruse, came across as very polite but a little exasperated that I was disrupting their business. Time to move again.

As poor a country as Romania was, Bulgaria seemed to be it's poorer cousin. The roads were in an even worse condition, pot holes littered the roads, everywhere seemed barren and sunburned, dry fields spread across the land with barely a crop in sight. The Lady Godiva bounced and bumped her way through the long empty roads. Everything shook and rattled in the truck. At one point there was a loud bang, followed by a constant rattle and bang behind the cab. I thought I'd blown an air bag on the suspension, but thankfully not, there was no leaking of air anywhere but instead, what I found was one of the brackets holding the air tanks to the chassis has snapped and the tank was holding on by it's pipework. I took a ratchet strap from a locker and secured the tank to the chassis again, disaster averted.

I followed the TIR route through Bulgaria arriving at Svilengrad in the afternoon, a short while later I pulled up to back of the queue at Kapikule, the border post into Turkey. I was here, one foot in Europe, one foot in Asia. This was the point through which all my earlier ambitions and dreams of driving to the middle east had passed. I was on the doorstep of the world beyond, the entrance to Persia and Arabia. The little Essex boy who couldn't sing, who'd been told on more than one occasion that my life would amount to nothing, that I would go nowhere. Well I was here, I was somewhere, somewhere the haters, the drunks with their threats and punches, the skinheads with their hatred and bile, townies with their hidden knives, they'd never see this, they'd never make this journey, but I had, I made it and in my mind, that meant I'd won. I'd beaten all of them, every kick, punch, cuss or spiteful word amounted to nothing now. O' ye of little faith.

I pulled up to the barrier for the Veterinary declarations, and took my paperwork into the office building beside the border. A guard escorted me inside and proceeded to introduce me to every man and his dog, I wasn't sure if I was being introduced or shown off. 'Hey guys, look what I found!'

The Chef of the Turkish side sat back in his seat like a lord looking down upon a farm hand. He asked me some questions about my trip, had I been to his great country before and did I know Paul Gascoygne?

"Paul who?"

"Paul Gascoygne, Gazza, you know Gazza?"

"The footballer? No, I don't know him personally, I know of him but I don't follow the football myself."

I guessed I was meant to be leaving a little thank you note in each office I was paraded to, but my money was running short enough as it was, I could ill afford giving out 'Backsheesh' to anybody, however, the Vet was a practised master and he knew who held the power, and the rubber stamp, in this relationship. He insisted he was tired and ready to go home to his family, I said I was grateful and at the insistence of the guard place a note in amongst my papers, 20 DM was the going rate, the Vet feigned a yawn, the note vanished and I stood firm, reluctantly he lifted the rubber stamp and slowly brought it down on my documents. I was now free to go.

There was one final hurdle, one final back-hander to be paid. The guard at the barrier. I pulled up and innocently handed over my papers, he took them and after a cursory glance looked at me.

"Magazine?"

"Magazine?" I thought, and then I remembered something I had heard in the past about having to hand over porno mags or the guy on the barrier will keep you waiting for hours. I scrambled around the cab and came across an old Sunday Times Colour Supplement, lots of gardening tips, and adverts for pensioner's holidays, wills and the very latest in home baking. The gardening section was full of lovely photo's guaranteed to get his blossoms up and blooming, or so it said. I rolled the magazine up and quickly handed it to him, he snatched it from my hand and gave me back my papers, the magazine having been stashed under his desk. The barrier was probably the only thing he managed to raise that evening, but I didn't care, I was gone already.

It was another 100 miles yet to Istanbul, and too late in the day to be clearing customs. I drove toward the airport and turned off just in time for the Londra Park. It was here I would get the air tanks welded back on, by one of the little mechanic's stores that littered the truck stop.

My instructions were simple, stop at the Londra Park, call the local agent and he would come get me and my paperwork. I waited until the next morning to call the agent.

"You are at the Londra Park?" He asked.

"Yes mate, I am."

"Wait there, I will be with you shortly."

I bought myself a coffee and an Istanbul road map from the cafe at the park, sat outside in the sun and waited to be collected by someone I had never met before. When he turned up, I gave him my papers and he said I had to go to the office with him. He grabbed my hand and walked me to the taxi. Once again I felt as if I were being 'Owned' by someone, maybe I was, and maybe, it was for my own protection.

We rode taxi through heavily congested streets, people beeped horns and squeezed past using every last inch of the road as we crawled along, it was shambolic chaos at it's best. What should have been about a 15 minute drive turned into an hour of hot, dusty, arm waving and shouting by our driver. These were roads I had no desire to negotiate in my truck. The visit to the office was brief, followed by a quick coffee and then I was given directions to get to Errenkoy TIR park, for final customs clearance. It was Friday lunchtime, I would not clear now until Monday, and in the Taxi back to the Londra Park, I stared out the window at this strange, bustling, exotic city, knowing full well I would not get to see very much of it, not on this trip anyway, I was running out of money and needed to call Malc.

I crossed over the Bosporus bridge and revelled not only in the beautiful view all around me, the deep blue sea, the wonderfully clear sky and the Blue Mosque standing out against this amazing background, but also in the fact that I was now, truly, in Asia. I was in the Middle East for the first time in my life. A world of fables, Ali Baba, Aladdin, and the real life T E Lawrence. The lands of the Sultans, the Ottoman Empire and Saladin. Where the sun burned brightly, and sand blanketed the earth like water filled it's oceans. I was home, in my heart, I was home. Throughout my childhood, I had dreamed of coming here, to see for myself the palms and oases, camel and bedouin.

The weekend passed slowly, there was only myself and a Czech driver weekended in the customs park. We shared some beers together, ate camion stew, and swapped cigarettes. It was all we could do. We were both strangers here, far from home and penniless. I'd made a point of calling home everyday that I could, I always did. Everything was fine back home but not so good in Istanbul, my money was almost gone.

Once cleared Monday afternoon, I drove out to a village on the outskirts of the city, as instructed, I passed by a phone box, took the next dusty turning and arrived at an unmarked warehouse. It was an old stone building and looked like nothing more than a semi constructed ruin left over from the days of the empire. Within minutes, a team of labourers was gathered behind the truck and they manhandled every skin off my trailer. The men wore nothing to protect themselves, no gloves, no hats, no overalls. Instead, the blood and platelets that still oozed from the skins, stained their jackets and shirts, these were the same clothes they would wear tomorrow, and the day after. The only clothes each man owned. I passed round a box of beers, a bonus for the workers, they drank and carried on unloading the skins unperturbed by my not helping out. Here, the driver was king, a mighty traveller who didn't need to get his hands and clothes dirty. Here, the driver did the driving, others did the work of loading and unloading. Labour was cheap, drivers were valued.

I went back to the Londra Park and washed out my trailer. It was too late to do anything and so I waited until morning to call Malc. There was another British Truck here now, one I recognised from an earlier trip to Hungary. Paul was an Owner-driver I had met at Schirnding. He'd had a problem and needed some cash but I had nothing to give him, now the tables had turned, although I would manage, I'd get a Sub from the Agent once I've spoken to Malc in the morning. I said nothing to him about being skint, just shared a beer as the sun set over the Bosporus, then wished him a safe trip.

"Start heading back to Bulgaria, I might have a load for you from Sofia."

"OK Malc, but I'm running low on cash, I'm going to need some soon."

"Have you got enough to get to Sofia? If you can get to Sofia I will get some from the agent for you." I felt reassured hearing Malc say that, all I needed to do was cash in my Turkish Lire, and the Romanian Lei that I had left over, that should pay for my Bulgarian Visa. I had enough diesel, but I would fill up again before leaving Turkey, I had a fuel card I could use here and in Germany, but it was no good in between.

Back at Kapikule, I found nobody would change my Romanian Lei, it was worthless. I was able to get out of Turkey, but not into Bulgaria, I didn't know before, that a Transit Visa for Bulgaria, which I had coming out, was cheaper than a loading visa, even if I could change my Lei, I still didn't have enough cash to get into the country. I was stuck, literally stuck in no man's land. My Turkish Visa was gone, used, I could not return, and no Bulgarian Visa to go forward, I was in the proverbial shit stream without a paddle, somewhere I tended to be reside quite a lot in my lifetime, only this was different, this was somewhere I couldn't walk away from, I was stranded. I could do nothing but wait for another British driver to come through and bail me out, this was international trucking at it's most real, stuck in no man's land, skint, no way to contact the outside world, not a lot of water left and food enough for one more day. It's such a glamorous life. I sat and waited, watching everyone else pass by, free to move on, free to go about their day, free because they had money. I watched the number plates, Turk's, Bulgarian's, Romanian's, no Dutch, Italian, or German's, no French and definitely no British. I decided to call home and used the last of my money to rush out a garbled message to Nikki, she had no idea what was happening, but knew it wasn't good.

"Call Malcolm, tell him I'm stuck at Kapikule in no man's land, run out of money, I can't get in to Bulgy and can't go back into Turkey, tell him to get someone out to me, the embassy, an agent, someone, but do it quick, I'm running out of food too!" That was it, my last coins, my last contact.

For supper I ate the last of the stale bread I had left over from a loaf I'd bought in Hungary. Dry and crisp around the edge almost to the centre, it was hard to swallow without taking a mouthful of water with it, and my water bottle was running low too. I should have topped up before leaving the Buda Park but thought I had enough to get through. Rule 1 of long distance driving, stop thinking about it, just do it.

It was a long day and evening, an even longer night. The flow of trucks eased to a trickle and I was finding it hard to stay awake, my eyes were closing when all of a sudden Paul appeared at the Turkish barrier. I rushed over to see him. Without so much as a pause, he pulled out a 20 DM note and handed it over. "Here, give me your address, I'll send it to you as soon as I get home." I've never seen Paul since, but I did send him 50 DM as a thank you.

Once I got through the border I headed toward Sofia and parked up for the night. Next morning I called Malc and he asked how I was getting on.

"I knew you were stuck but there was fuck all I could do, anyway you're out of there now, get yourself to the collection point, don't say anything to anyone, but I'll get the agent to sort you out once you're loaded."

I found the place I was loading at, Kostenets Cold Store, in the village of Kostenets, at the foot of Rila Mountain, maybe 70 KM from Sofia. Only problem was the 12' bridge between the entrance and myself. I locked the truck up and went inside the Cold Store. A young lad was sent out to direct me around the bridge, about 10 miles around the block to go 20 yards up the road, I guess they didn't have big trucks back when this place was built. I was to load in the morning, but tonight, I was to be taken out for a meal, and put up in a hotel, compliments of the management. I could hardly believe my luck, 24 hours earlier I thought I was going to starve to death, left to rot in no man's land at Kapikule, now I was being fed, watered and given a hotel bed for the night.I thought I'd won the lottery. Sometimes, you just gotta roll with the punches and let life work it's magic around you, it's good like that-innit?

Next morning I was picked up by the boss of the cold store. His black Mercedes made light work of the drive back, we seemed to miss most of the pot holes even though we were travelling at breakneck speeds, the car bump and bounced over the cobbled streets. About us, the houses looked like they belonged elsewhere, unfinished buildings sat quietly behind unfinished gardens and pathways, next to the unfinished road. There were broken cars, chickens and dirty faced little children in some of the gardens, others were empty and almost eerily so. It struck me that this was more than just a poor country, this was a country that had been made poor. There were oil fields out in the countryside, farms where crops survived the heat of the summer and the bitter cold of winter. There were opportunities here, but corruption was rife, everyone had their hand's in someone else's pie. Everything, and everyone had a price, nothing was impossible, if you had the money and the contacts.

Once loaded, I was given my paperwork and was again accompanied by a young lad who directed me all the way to the TIR Customs Park in Sofia. Once there, he showed me to the Agent's office and then bid me farewell, he left to get the train back to Kostenets, while I hung around waiting to clear customs.

The TIR Park in Sofia was as bad as you'd imagine it. The drivers toilet was a pit in the ground,to use it was a bit like having to use the French 'Hole in the Ground' toilets, place one foot either side, bend and flush, but without the flush, and lights, and toilet paper, and the steps you put your feet on to help you attain the perfect 'Hole in One'. The one thing it did have was flies, lots and lots of flies, as well as an overpowering aroma of rotting human waste. It was a septic tank with no cleaner, no water, just a mass of septic waste.

I didn't clear customs until the following day, the Agent gave me 50 DM to get me through after a fax arrived saying I was to meet another driver up the road that night. At the barrier, trying to get out of the Park, I got into an argument with the guy I was meant to pay for the parking. I only had the one note and he refused to change it, someone came up behind me and before I knew it, we were swapping punches. My lip was split and I had a black eye starting to come through. Thankfully I still had had my money and after threatening him with my wheelbrace, the barrier was lifted and I was freed to go, without paying. I headed off and before I knew it was back in Ruse the following day, I hadn't seen the other driver anywhere on route, even though he was supposed to be waiting for me. If there's one plan that is always guaranteed to fail, it's the one where someone is going to wait for you somewhere you've never been, when he just wants to get himself home too. I sat at Ruse all day, finally receiving a fax to say the other driver was now in Romania, he'd gone to Calafat and not Ruse, it was no good trying to chase him, he was homeward bound and I was out of sight- out of mind. It was Saturday, I was once again without funds, and unable to do anything now until Monday.

I spent the weekend looking out for other Brit's, none came through until Sunday evening. A couple of lad's working for Denholm Shipping bought me supper and a couple of beers, but more than that, they gave me hope.

"Chuck all your gear in my truck if you want, I'll take you home, leave the truck here, if your boss wants it- he can come and get it!"

"Thanks, but no, I can't do that, I'll never be able to work again if I do that, and besides, Malc's alright really, we're just struggling a bit at the minute." I didn't want to ditch the truck, but it did give me an idea. I wrote out a fax and sent it back to the office, saying "I would leave with them tomorrow night if I hadn't heard and had not received a guarantee that some money would be coming to me." The bluff worked, Monday morning I got a fax back saying the Agent would be with me later that day with £500 to get me home. By the time he turned up it was Tuesday afternoon and the last thing I'd eaten was a tub of Margarine, it was all I had. I ate it with a spoon and told myself it was blueberry yogurt.

The Agent arrived and gave me an envelope, he was gone as soon as I took it, smiling and wishing me well. I tore open the top of the envelope and was rewarded with 2200 DM. 2 x 1,000 notes, 2 x 100. What the fuck did he think I was going to do with a 1,000 DM note- let alone 2 of them. I could buy half of Romania with this much money and get most of Bulgaria thrown in as a sweetener. These were the sort of notes that could get people killed, he must have known that, surely? The only place I could dare show a note of that size was on the bridge, to pay the toll into Romania, and I had to get change to get diesel once I was able to do so. I broke into one of the 100 DM notes to pay a fine for having exceeded the time limit on my Bulgarian Visa, apparently I was meant to only spend 3 days in the country, hardly conducive to a warm welcome, let alone a cheery goodbye. I joined the queue and paid the bridge toll. I pulled up to the next window and my passport was confiscated.

"Problem!" Was the only English these people seemed to know.

"What problem? What is wrong now?" I asked.

"You must pay" came the reply, without explanation. He didn't need to explain, this little, unimportant, human parasite didn't need to explain to me, or anyone else for that matter. It was obvious what was wrong from the blow I felt on my kidney. I'd been jabbed from behind by another guard, hidden from view behind me, unseen by anyone else because of the angle of my trailer blocking any potential witnesses from seeing what was going on ahead. I felt the sharp pain behind, and then the other side too, I felt winded and vulnerable, I couldn't fight back, I had to give in to them.

"Okay, Okay! Enough." I put my hands up and stepped back. The guard who'd struck me took a side step and seeing me concede, went round to a rear door into the cabin where my passport was still being held.

"I can see there's a problem Okay, how much of a problem is there?" Now we were talking numbers, the price of my freedom, the size of their bung.

"Zwei hundert Deutschmark!" Bastards, that's a month's salary here. I put a 50 DM note on the window, in plain sight.

"That's your fucking lot, no more, I have no more!" I lied. The note was whisked out of sight as quickly as I 'd been set upon, my passport thrown at me through the open window. I picked it up and almost ran to my cab.

"Bastards!" I thought to myself, holding my sides as I drove through the mud of No Man's Land and into Romania.

I had heard some drivers say that it's not a good idea to drive at night in Romania, I'm not known for being particularly afraid of the dark, or Vampires even, so to me it seemed perfectly reasonable to drive through the night, despite there being no street lights, no road markings, potholes the size of Mancunian Housing Estate, Vampires and other monsters at every turn. It had just got dark as I hit Bucharest and I missed the Ring Road, there was a coach in front of me and I missed it, I didn't see the 'slip road', so I followed the bus up to town and drove around the inner ring road, despite the signs saying there was a 7.5 Ton weight limit. The bus shot through a red light just as it had changed and disappeared round a corner. I waited for the green light and then pulled round to see the bus stopped, a Policeman had pulled him over. He saw me and at first waved me on, but when I passed him he saw I was sat on the right, that it was a British truck and he blew his whistle. Blowing a whistle when I'm listening to Sham 69 at full blast, with the windows shut, watching the road ahead, is not going to stop me. Pulling your police car (even if it is a Skoda) across the front of my truck at the next set of lights, will get my full attention.

"Problem!"

"Here we go again" I tutted, "what problem?"

"Hurdy gurdy, gurdy gurdy hurdy gur de gur, hurdy hurd de hurd!" He said inflating his chest and pointing at his whistle and the badge on his shirt. I kinda got the impression this meant parting with money, again, but seeing as he was all alone, I didn't think I was going to get slapped again. If anything, one punch on his rum filled belly would probably have sent him into the next life had I chosen to do so.

"Receipt!" I demanded, handing over the 18 DM he was demanding. I had tried haggling, but it didn't work, he just kept 'Hurdy gurgling' and I was keen to get out of Bucharest as soon as I could. He tore some receipts from a pad, a total of 18 DM I gave him the cash and he ripped the receipts up, throwing them in the air like confetti.

"Hurdy fucking gurdy receipts!" he jumped into his car and returned to the Bus Driver, still waiting for his grilling.

Once out of Bucharest I realised I was on the road to Craiova, a slight detour from intended return back the way I had originally come, so many days earlier. I came around a corner at Alexandria and almost ran into the back of an Iranian truck. It had stopped, in the dark, around a bend, with no lights on. Luckily my reactions were swift enough to get The Lady Godiva around it without hitting the bloody thing. As I pulled forward, slowly, I saw the reason he'd stopped. Another Iranian truck in front of him had run over a horse and cart. Literally over it. There were bundles of straw, pieces of wooden cart, scythes and a dead horse under the truck and all over the road. An entire family of Romanians had been on the cart and were lucky to be alive, and as I am sure, is exactly what they were telling the unfortunate driver. It wasn't my circus, so I kept moving and eventually made it to Craiova. I stopped outside a truck stop and had a short break, drank some water and pulled back onto the road in time to be stopped by another Policeman. I wound down my window.

"Disc!" He wanted to see my tacho, I had barely handed it to him when he used the 'P' word.

"What fucking problem? That's legal and you know it."

"Hurdy gurdy Deutschmarks gurdy hurdy English!" I tell you what, I shan't transcribe the entire conversation but it went along the lines of -"Hurdy."

"No, no pay!"

"Hurdy!"

Eventually cop No.2 comes along and pushes cop No.1 out of the way. He snatched my tacho and gave it back to me, neither one of them had even looked at it.

"Eengleesh?"

"Yes boss, Marlboro?"

He smiled up at me and gladly took a packet from my hand.

"And one for your friend, but next time he get's none, ok? You tell him I said that, no hurdy gurdy, just Marlboro!" I think he understood what I was saying, because he let me go and I chucked in the towel for the night, pulling my curtains at the first place I could park, a few miles away, outside of the town.

Next morning I headed off to Timisoara, the birthplace of the revolt that lead to the downfall of the Communist state. I thought it would be a good place to take a photo of the sign at the entrance of the city. I stepped down from my cab, straight into the remains of a dead dog, my feet covered in decaying body matter, became a major attraction for every flying insect East of Brussels.

Other than a couple of dodgy speeding tickets and a fine for having too many cigarettes when entering Germany, the rest of the trip went relatively well and I even managed to get home, a little bruised, and slightly lighter than when I'd left, 28 days earlier.

In my absence, H had had an accident, he'd been lifting some glass sheets and his grip failed, the glass slipped and ripped a gash about an inch and a half wide right down his wrist and forearm. He underwent many hours of microsurgery to reattach the tendons and repair the damage done. For months his arm was useless, the tendons sewn onto hooks, glued to his finger nails, his arm protected in a cast. For a while it wasn't certain he would ever get his hand and fingers to work again, but he was determined to do so. As soon as he was able, he picked up his guitar and played with a renewed passion, he wanted to become the best he could, because he wanted to overcome his injury. Roddy, the little fella with a taste for whiskey, became an evermore important figure in H's life. He'd played for The Specials, and some other less well known bands, and H was keen to learn from him. Eventually, he recovered from his accident so well, that Roddy invited him to play in his new band The Skabilly Rebels. H was made up, it was all he'd ever wanted from life, to be a rock star. He was like a young Sid Vicious, not particularly talented but had the right face for the job, and he loved every minute. I helped out a couple of times, driving them to gigs, moving equipment, listening to the same old stories night after night. It was fun, Roddy even sold me a Teddy Boy style Drape jacket, it was black and had blue trim, beautiful.

Craig's little sister Sam was married now, she and Little Rich had been busy making little people. Nikki and I popped round one night to visit only to find they were in the middle of a domestic. The insults flew both ways but Sam somehow managed to still make a decent cup of tea. Rich was being really arsey, not to us, just Sam. I wanted to intervene but couldn't, it was between them but I really felt like slapping Rich, he was out of order and the whole experience reminded me of why some people just don't gel, their marriage was every bit the sham mine was, and I didn't appreciate the reminder.

Nikki and I continued to live badly together, our marriage was falling apart, not helped by my job, but not because of it either. Most weekends I would end up at Helen's or Nicky's trying to work out what was wrong, they were the best friends I could ever have wished for, even though they had enough problems of their own.

Nicky and John split up eventually, he went to live with his parents but one day attached a hosepipe to his car exhaust, closed all the windows and died. In doing so, he left the kids with unanswered questions, insecurities and problems that would continue well into their adult lives. I saw in John's death the ignorant arrogance of suicide, the 'Screw you, I'm alright Jack' exit that it truly was. There was no grieving for him, only shock that it had happened, relief that he could no longer threaten, intimidate or abuse anyone any more. His last act had been one that yet again, we would not be able to punish him for, the only people to suffer, were the innocent.

Nikki managed to get herself a job with a local courier company, Phoenix. All was going well for a while, she had something to concentrate on other than her downfalls and our girls. She would drop the girls at school, then go to work for a few hours, finishing in time to collect them afterwards. Everything was going well until a few months in she hit a low. Depression was back and she couldn't get out of bed. She had broken out in a rash of spot's on her face and refused to go into the outside world. I took some time off work to look after her, and had to go see her boss, to beg him to keep her job open.

"You're a driver yourself, I hear." Said her boss, Mark Williams. He'd been a van driver, bought his own and built up a small company employing a dozen or so other drivers. For that, I had a lot of respect for him, respect that grew the more I got to know him.

"Yes, I drive an artic, for Express Freight." I replied, "I've been around a bit."

"Why don't you come and work for me? I'll give you a good job and you could be home more with your family."

"You couldn't afford me" I joked, testing the water.

"Tell me what you want and I'll let you know."

I couldn't believe it, I'd come in to save my wife's job and been offered one myself, one that meant I'd get the same money Malc was paying me, but I'd be home every night. No being away for weeks on end, no running out of cash, no more bullshit at the frontiers, lack of sleep, driving through Eastern Europe in the dark listening to Elton John's Rocket Man and thinking it was about me and my fucked up life. I was back home, back with my family. I had missed the bedtime stories, the baths, the games, jokes and play. I'd missed Sian sucking her thumb while watching telly, Christina crying because she thought Sian was being rotten to her. I'd missed being a Dad, the one thing I'd always wanted to do properly.

Leaving Express Freight was easy, it was harder to leave the road though. I had diesel in my blood, I was certain of that much. Within a couple of weeks of changing jobs, I was asked if I'd go to Germany, and I did. I took a load of shoes to Mainz and came back empty, something unheard of when I worked for Malc.

It was coming up to Christmas and there was a work's do at Coombe Abbey. A medieval feast and lot's of drinking. On our way there, we were taken in a minibus, Mark spent most of the time on his phone with a client in London.

"I'm sorry but the driver left this morning about 11.30, I know it's Christmas and that, so she's probably stuck in traffic somewhere."

A female owner-driver had gone missing for a few hours with a very urgent consignment, and the recipient was giving Mark a hard time. During our meal, his phone rang again, the same scenario, she still hadn't arrived. After eating, we retired to the bar and the drinks began to flow. I had an idea. A friend of mine, Steve Guest, worked at the abbey and I got him to call Mark, pretending to be the customer in London. We'd already heard that the consignment had been delivered but couldn't resist winding up the boss. We stood in the corridor outside the bar as Mark answered his phone.

"Where's my Parcel?" asked Steve angrily into the phone. "Where's my parcel? I still haven't had it arrive yet, your company are an absolute disgrace-" this was good stuff, I mean really good. From our viewpoint in the hallway we could see Mark physically slump at the table. His spare hand rose to hold his head, the man was distraught.

"I'm going to make sure you never get this work again." Continued Steve, into the mobile phone we'd given him. We opened the door into the bar and slowly walked up behind Mark, still slumped on his elbow, apologising profusely to this absolutely apoplectic customer on his mobile. We stood right behind him, as he begged for forgiveness and just another few minutes while he called the driver to see what had gone wrong. Just then, Steve leaned forward, the phone still in his hand next to his ear, his other hand reached out to Mark and tapped him on the shoulder.

"Where's my parcel?" He asked calmly.

"Not now mate, I'm on the phone........." Marks face dropped to the floor. "You bastards!"

There was a disco on too, just the usual pop and chart stuff mostly. I sat at a table talking to one of my workmates when my arm was tapped.

"Come on you, get up." It was one of of the office staff, Julie. She'd been dancing with her husband and now she was demanding I dance with her.

"What?"

"You're getting up and dancing and I won't take no for an answer." She lead me to the dance floor and I shuffled nervously and uncomfortably around. I had no idea what I was doing, I never danced to slow music and certainly not with another woman. I have no idea what made her do it, she was petite and elegant, beautifully dressed with a green basque and long hair down beyond her shoulders. Right there and then, when we danced, it was like she knew the turmoil inside me, as if she could see in my eyes, all the hurt and sadness I felt inside myself. She held me gently without saying a word, and for about two minutes I felt at ease, uneasy on my feet, uncomfortable in the surroundings, but my heart and soul felt at ease. It was the kindest, most spiritual and the most humane thing I'd felt for the longest time, such a simple act, but it meant so much. When people say they miss 'That human touch' it is exactly this they miss. The kindness of others when you need it the most.

Nikki eventually lost her job. She kept having too much time off and Mark had to let her go, he needed to know she would be there when she was meant to, not keep calling in sick, depressed or just unhappy with life. I'm probably coming across very cold and callous here, but this is now, at the time I gave all I had and I was there for her all I could be. No matter what I did though, it wasn't enough and the atmosphere in the house was wrong for the kids. Then came the news that Tracy, a friend who'd been quite close to Nikki, had terminal cancer. This was awful. She was such a lovely person, energetic, vibrant and full of life. She'd recently split from her husband Tom, and lived alone with her daughters. I was talking to her one night when she asked me why I was still with Nikki. I was shocked, this was her friend.

"Don't get me wrong, I've known her for a long while" she said. "I just don't know why you put up with her, I don't even like her, and she's my friend, I can say that, I can say it because it's true, you deserve better."

I wondered myself, I asked myself a lot of questions but never found any definitive answers. Maybe I was a glutton for punishment, maybe I was loyal, maybe I was too scared to go forward, too scared to take the plunge into the unknown. I knew I loved my kids, I knew that if I left them they'd survive, I'd be devastated, but they'd survive, they would have to. I had spent so much time away from them already, it would be just as if I had started a new job.

I'm not sure where I was when I first heard the news, but it took time to sink in fully, and for me to process everything.

There had been a demonstration at Coventry airport, it was ongoing, and had been getting more violent as time went by. Animal Right's Activists had been trying to stop the export of live animals in Veal crates from Coventry airport. Jill Phipps had been a regular protester at the site, she was also someone I'd known from my earliest days in Coventry. Little Tom had been married to her for a while before he left and went on to live with another friend, Toni. Coventry was a small city, we all seemed to date each other's cast off's at some point or other. Jill was a vehement advocate for Animal Rights. She was a practising Vegan long before I even knew that it meant. On the 1st February 1995, Jill died beneath the wheels of a livestock truck attempting to deliver animals to the airport. Her death brought about a change in the law. Her funeral was held in Coventry Cathedral, with dignitaries and the rich and the famous all turning up to be noticed. Jill made history, but lost her life. I wasn't too sure how to take this in. I was a committed meat lover, a pig killing blood on my hands kind of guy with a life long love of bacon, and nobody was going to stop that. But I knew Jill and understood her passion, I knew how much it meant to her, and as a punk, I knew that if I had been there, I would have probably been even more reckless than her. I avoid protests because I know, I will be the one to lose out, I know it. Isn't that how it always works out though, the nicest folk get the worst deal.

I spent the next few months in some kind of dazed state, I was able to function normally but my head was foggy. I was constantly otherwise engaged in my mind, my thoughts were consumed with my own survival. In a very short time, I had lost Adam, Jacqui, John (who wasn't really much of a loss, but his passing still had an effect.) Even Shakey, who I'd worked with at Express Freight, had died in the last couple of months. Tracy was dying of cancer and moved into a hospice in Rugby, her new boyfriend Paul was taking care of her kids, and now Jill was gone. Even Nikki's 94 year old Grandfather had recently died following a fall in the city centre. There was too much death in my life all of a sudden. I sometimes believe that I was living with undiagnosed PTSD (Post Traumatic Stress Disorder). My trip to Turkey had been a bit of an ordeal, Nikki's suicide attempt, her behaviour and mine in Rhodes all weighed very heavily on my mind. Then one day it snapped.

I knew I couldn't take Nikki's life, nor could I stop her depression and extreme behaviour, I wasn't equipped to do any of that, and if I did, I would be the one to lose out. I would lose my kids and anyway, they'd hate me, forever. If I left them though, there was a chance that one day they might forgive, they might understand, that Nikki might even wake herself from this state that was so destructive. I had to leave, because there were no other options I could see other than my own death, and had there not been enough of those already? Was I next, was I? Not this time, not me, not now, I had to leave. I had to get away, for everybody's sake.

I got up one morning, Nikki had taken the kids to school and I packed my bag and left, with just a rucksack, the clothes on my back and my passport.

6 CHANGE

"Fear not the wings of angels, fear not the tongues of men, fear not for life when life is gone and whatever happens then. Fear not the sons of Satan, fear not the whores of God, fear not the words nor anxious cries of one mans love of God. The piety of preaching, the silent kiss of fright, when all that's left of reasoning is sex shared in the night..."

I stayed with Brophy for a few days, got drunk a lot and tried to avoid running into Nikki. I was done with her and wanted to rebuild my life somehow. This wouldn't be easy, the government's Child Support Agency were sure to be taking every penny I earned, it had been all over the press at the time, absent fathers committing suicide, unable to cope with the high demands and the fact that the law was very much against them. I couldn't avoid seeing her forever though, once she had time to understand this really was it, it was over, we bumped into each other.

"You were right," she confessed, "I did cheat on you." I laughed, I laughed long and loud, I had been right all along, I had been punished for her own sins. The who, when and why are immaterial now, the lesson was simple, 'Let he who is without sin cast the first stone.'

I headed south, to Romford and stayed at my Mum's new flat. My parents were divorced now, or well on the way to it. She was staying at a 'friend's house' in Harold Hill, so I had the place to myself for the most part. It was only when I finally sat down, my bag unpacked, that the enormity of everything hit me. I broke down and cried. I barely left the flat for day's on end, venturing only as far as the corner shop. I didn't want to be seen, I hated the world and I hated people. I didn't know what I wanted or who to trust anymore. I just wanted to get away, to be alone. I wanted to forget everything that had ever happened in my life. I wanted peace and quiet, but couldn't bear the silence, I wanted to curl up and die. What had I become, what had happened to me to make me hide away like this? I went in to Romford one day and had to get a taxi straight home again, I was having panic attacks in broad daylight. I was scared of everything that moved and I had no control it. I started on a course of Prozac, and was able to function a little better after a few days. Lisa invited me to visit her stay with her in Wales. She had long since given up truck driving and was living near Aberystwyth. I accepted the offer and spent some time in the country. The peace and solitude worked wonders, I spent most of the time alone as she was working. Her house stood alone in a field, sheep wandered right up to her back door. Near where she worked was a hill which I climbed and sat upon. for the first time in as long as I could remember, I actually felt the wind on my face, on my body. I felt life and the universe all around me, I felt alive and ready to move on. Before I knew it I was heading back to England, refreshed and feeling better about life.

I stopped taking the Prozac, I didn't need the crutch it provided anymore, and I hadn't enjoyed the totally devoid of emotion feeling that it induced. I wanted to feel, I wanted to know I was alive and so desperately wanted to live.

Listening to Rich and his stories of travelling around the world, as well as my own itchy feet and sense of adventure I began to plan a getaway. I'd heard about people finding themselves, rekindling their love for life by travelling to Israel and staying on Kibbutzim. It made sense, to go and meet people from all over the world, use it as a stepping stone to somewhere else. If I ended up dead in a shop doorway in Thailand nobody would care, just as nobody would care if I died in England. But if I survived and lived to tell the tale, one day I would see my girls again, one day.

I had bought a book a couple of years previously, 'How to work your way around the world.' In it were many contacts and tips for getting out and living the life of a migrant worker, anywhere in the world. In this day and age, there is so much intolerance and hatred for migrants that options have been limited, international travel and adventure are seen as hazardous and even dangerous in many parts of the world, mostly fuelled by terrorism, racism and religious fanaticism. The world is a changed place to how it was in 1995. I used the book to get an idea of what I could do, and through the contacts inside, was able to apply for a position on a Kibbutz in Israel.

While waiting to hear back from the Kibbutz Representatives, I applied for a job with Encounter Overland, a company that specialised in overland adventures to the Middle East, Africa, South America and Asia.I had been very keen to become a driver for them, I would have loved to have been an expedition driver but the world was changing and unknown to me, Encounter Overland were forced to close. Along with Guerba and a couple of other small companies, independently minded travellers could spend weeks, months even, travelling around the world in specially converted ex-army trucks. The driver would be fully responsible for his passengers on route, sourcing local foods, water, fuel and all other necessities. To me, that sounded like a dream job. Travelling the world and getting paid for it. Unfortunately, I never got the job, and settled for the comparative safety of having a few months in Israel instead. Israel and the Palestinian Authority had brokered a peace agreement, Gaza and the West Bank were now controlled by the PA and peace had come to Israel, it was said, somewhere.

Once I had got my head around the fact I was going, I found things falling into place and my emotional and mental state improving. I stayed away from Coventry, I tried to contact my daughters whenever I could which was stressful for them and hurt me too. I knew they would be okay without me, because they had been without me, for so much of their young lives, already. I found it hard to be without them, knowing I had no idea what lay ahead. I even wrote a will, just in case. I had to do this though, there was no future in my marriage to Nikki, it was done, forever.

An interview was arranged in Golders Green, but I had to have a medical first, which I arranged with my GP. I passed the medical but decided to have myself tested for HIV, just in case. I went along to the Royal Free Hospital in London, HIV testing was anonymous there at this time, anyone could be tested without anybody else knowing. My friend, or ex-girlfriend Fiona, came along with me for support. I saw her a few times after my split from Nikki, the last time was just after I'd sent her a 'Thank You' gift. She had been there for me a lot at this time, she felt and knew my relief when the result came back Negative, and I wanted to thank her for it all. A courier knocked her door one morning with a parcel labelled as Fragile. It had been sent priority, urgent and had to be signed for. Not expecting anything, Fiona still signed for the delivery, it was for her and her mind raced as to what it could be. She recognised the handwritten label and immediately thought "Chocolates!" Tearing open the outer package revealed a layer or three of bubble wrap, inside which was another box. When she finally got inside this, she sat silently in shock having found a house brick, painted bright red, with the words 'Fraggle's Rock' on the top of it. She described it as the most surreal and wonderful gift she'd ever received, probably the most unique door-stop in London.

The interview was held in a building around the back of some shops. An anonymous entrance was protected by CCTV cameras, there was razor wire around parts of the roof and the heavy, blast proof steel door, had a sliding hatch which opened only once you had been approved entry by the security staff. The atmosphere inside the offices was one of heightened security, almost blatant suspicion. It felt as though everything was being scrutinised, that one false move and someone would pull out a gun and start shooting. Everyone seemed either on edge or in serious need of a laxative.

The meeting went well and I was told I would have to come back to meet other members of the group I would be travelling with, find out where we would be going, and what to expect there. I was excited, but nervous. A little piece of doubt lingered in the back of my mind, was this really going to happen or was I going to fail at the last hurdle, join the ever growing 'Would have, Should have, Could have' group of 'Never did anythings'. Those people constantly wanting to do something, but never making the effort to make anything happen. Those people that sit on their arse all day moaning but never make change happen.

I started to collect things I would need, sleeping bag, water purification tablets, water bottle, sunscreen with a Sun Protection Factor equivalent to a nuclear detonation, mosquito repellent and anti-malaria pills. I read as much as I could about where I was going, pawed over my atlas and made rudimentary plans for visits to Egypt and Jordan. I remembered a conversation I had with 'Big nosed' Dave one night in the Courtyard pub. He was asking me about a trip he was planning.

"I'm planning on taking the Mrs to Africa," he said "and was thinking of doing some travelling while we're there."

"Yes, whereabouts are you thinking?"

"Ideally we wanted to start off in South Africa, you know, maybe by the ocean and move up, take in a couple of Safari Parks 'cos the Mrs wants to see some animals and that out in the wild, would be great to see some Gorilla's too and maybe Egypt, do the Valley of the kings and the Pyramids."

"Wow, that's some adventure, when are you going?"

"Nothing's booked yet but thinking of going next year, you know, what do you think?"

"I think it sounds great, I'd love to do it myself mate."

"So how long d'you think it would take?"

"I don't know, depends how long you spend in each place, you'd want about 3-6 months to do it properly."

"Really?" Dave seemed shocked. "Oh, I was hoping we could do it in 2 weeks."

I'd read Ffyona Campbell's book about walking from Cape Town to Tangiers and revelled in the descriptions of the beauty of the country, the people. It was a great inspiration, marred only by the revelation that she had cheated on some sections of the journey and travelled by car, the reasons for which were actually understandable, in some cases. Nobody wants to die, chased out of town or raped on an expedition, self-preservation has to kick in at some point and her achievement was non the less admirable, in my opinion.

I had thought about walking to Israel, or maybe walking the length of the country when I got there, it seemed like something I could aspire to, to walk, and keep walking, go where the air is clean and the wind blows gently on my skin, without rippling through my underpants first.

Mark Norris invited me out to see Peter And The Test Tube Babies at Fulham one night. The Greyhound was half empty but the audience were keen. Bouncing around like it was 1982 still, I felt detached and didn't really enjoy it that much, I had other things on my mind apart from the fact that they were not my favourite band in the world, but Mark loved them and we had a good night out regardless. I was glad of getting out of the flat. I was spending too much time alone in there, sleep was fitful, boredom total, and every morning the same noise of the tipper trucks in the recycling yard next door to our block of flats.

I received a letter one day, saying I had to attend a group meeting at the Kibbutz Rep's office. There would be other volunteers there and we would find out when we would be travelling, and where to. This meant everything to me now, it was a lifeline out of a world that eating at my heart and soul. I was running away, I knew that I was, but I had somewhere to run to now, not just an uncertain ending. This was a chance to find another life, somewhere. I had been pushed from my home and family, rejected and dismantled, word by word, by the woman I had thought I could rebuild, the fragile woman I'd wanted to protect and care for. Now I was homeless, directionless and had only one thought to maintain myself, the resolve to stay alive long enough to see my girls once again. Israel would be my sanctuary, somewhere to sort myself out and move forward once again, just as I'd done so many times before, it was my safety net.

There were about eight or nine of us at the meeting. I was just about the oldest volunteer present, the rest were either late teens or in their twenties. I could see immediately some of the ways the group would bond, pair off and segregate, the guys looking at the girls for possible mates, looking at each other for possible contenders, competition. There were two Stuarts, both with military affiliations, one had just left the army following an injury, a broken leg bone, the other a cadet waiting nervously for the confidence to commit himself to a life in the service. Both men would go on to compete with each other for the attention of Rebecca. She was the youngest and quietest of the group. She stood out with her short curly hair, bright red lipstick, youthful looks and her voluptuous figure. She barely spoke, but scribbled keenly with her pen on her notebook, the only person to have the presence of mind to bring one to the meeting. I thought she may have been a journalist but later found out she had barely left college. While the rest of us appeared uncomfortable, overly under-dressed for the occasion, she was graceful, clean and bright. She had everyone's attention. She was going to break someone's heart, that was for sure, but I felt a vulnerability in her, she too would hurt.

We were greeted and welcomed into a class like room, a small screen on the wall projected images of a lifestyle we all aspired to, temporarily. Working, playing and uniting with other volunteers from around the country and the world at large, all members of the same team, helping to make the kibbutz experience a success. To bond, learn and find ourselves, before stepping out into this crazy world ahead of us.

It seemed we were all destined for one of two kibbutzim, either Kibbutz Dafna, or Kibbutz Kfar Hannasi, both in an area called 'The Upper Galilee'. I could relate to this, it was somewhere I had heard of, The Galilee, or at least, the Sea of Galilee had been drummed into our imaginations at junior school, a beautiful place where you could walk on the water and the fish were so big Captain Bird's Eye could feed 5,000 people with just one fish finger and a pitta bread. My attention was was full on as we were shown photos of sunbathing volunteers holding cans of beer, a swimming pool, river and dairy cows. There was a larger pool at Kfar Hannasi, the kibbutz was a functioning hotel where volunteers were expected to work as housekeepers, kitchen and laundry staff. I didn't really fancy that as much as Dafna, which had a commercial boot factory on site, as well as a dairy, farmland and it's own nightclub. I fancied the sound of that much more, an industrial and agricultural workplace with a nightclub for relaxation. Sounds good to me, where do I sign up?

We were also given a talk on the politics and history of the country, what to expect from our time on the kibbutz and the various organised field trips. If we wanted to, we could take part in a 6 day desert trek for an extra £100 or so. This included a camel trek, a dip in the Dead Sea, and a boat ride on the Red Sea from the resort town of Eilat, Israel's most southerly point. The more I listened the more I wanted to jump on that plane and go, to leave all the heartache behind. There had always been a pull to the Middle East, something in me knew that it was important, it was somewhere I would have to go one day, somehow. I thought it would have been as a truck driver, eating dust and feeding mosquito's through sweltering hot days and nights on my own, always moving forward, one corrupt and filthy border after another. Yet here it was, a summer camp for the weary, the abused and those in need of something other than Club Med 18-30.

I signed up for the desert trek, paid my fee's and all the disclaimers sent my way, there was nothing more to do than await my departure.

When we left the building, some of us stopped for a social drink together, and the chance to get more familiar with each other, have a few laughs before heading home. One of the Stuarts had come from Norfolk and was unsure of how to get to the airport in time for our flight, which was at the same time every day, 0945 from Heathrow. We had to check in at least 2 hours before departure but his connections wouldn't get him there in time.

"I'll have to find a cheap hotel in London and come down the day before."

"That might be expensive, but if you want, come down the day before and stop at my place, we'll have a pint somewhere and my Brother-in-law is taking me to the airport in the morning, so you're more than welcome to come and crash at mine if you want." I offered.

"If you're sure, yes, that'll save me a few quid and I can get a train straight to Romford from my place. Thanks, that's brilliant."

Stuart was very grateful, we swapped numbers and made plans to meet up the day before our flight, Tuesday June 6th, 1995.

I had a couple of weeks to kill and popped back to Coventry to say goodbye to my friends, and the girls. It was hard to tell them I was going away for a while, and that I didn't know when I'd be back. Christina was fine, she turned to her mother and said that everything would be okay, that she would look after her. Sian clung on to me, she would be the one to feel this the most, not I, not her mother. Nikki had by this time shaved all her hair off, a sign that she was not happy with herself, she had imitated Sinead O'Connor, screaming to the world that it was fucked up, but the world continued regardless. It took no notice of her before, and continued to be a fucked up place, it always was, always will be, the world doesn't care for the sensitivities of man. Ignoring her lack of hair, her almost androgenous appearance did little to make me want to change my mind. All I could see in her now, was the spoiled little rich kid who'd wanted to play with the dirty little street kids from the council estate. She was not one of us, she never would be.

Alone in the flat, I cried a lot over the weeks that I was in Romford. I was grieving the life I'd known. Feeling sorry for myself and hating myself in equal measures. Sleep eluded me. I couldn't settle. My only friends in the quiet night hours came in glass bottles, white rum and coconut, or schnapps. The sickly sugary drinks masking the bitterness of my tears. Harking back to my childhood,to the books I'd read as a kid, I was imitating the characters from the Sven Hassel stories, pulling slugs of schnapps from dirty bottles in dust filled bomb craters, then diving back into the bloody affray. There were no battles here, no bullets flying around me. As lonely as I felt, I was not the last man standing at Stalingrad, or Monte Casino, I was a washed up punk rocker, a truck driver who no longer trusted himself to get behind the wheel. A sad, useless runaway, anything and everything you wanted to throw at me, I was it. But the one label that hurt the most, was absent father. It felt like punch to the stomach. It hurt more breaking my hand, having my toenail cut out or denying my body the alcohol and drugs I had become so dependent upon at times of need. This was a pain that would ache throughout my body for the rest of my days. I would never shake the empty feeling in my heart. Not then, not ever. This was my punishment, my eternal sentence for having hoped for more than I could achieve. For being naive enough to think I could make someone happy, only to find they were happier without me. I didn't want to die, but life was doing a good job of making it hard to live. I prayed that one day I would see my daughters again, that they may understand, even forgive me.

I did have some days when I was able to get out, I managed to get to Brentwood even, to The Castle pub. It was the new hangout for the local alternative crowd. Most of the old Rez crew now drank at The Castle, and they had live bands play from time to time. At some point I bumped into Rags, I hadn't seen him for years. He never really had a lot to say for himself and seemed to cling to me a little too closely sometimes. He was probably lonely, or in need of a friend to hang around with. One day we arranged to go for a drink together. He turned up in an old banger, a car he'd probably rescued from the scap yard my uncle Mick owned, or fished it from a watery grave in the Thames somewhere. Rags drove just like he'd stolen it too, loud, fast and dangerous. He wanted to go to Dagenham first, collect some money from someone that owed him a few quid. He didn't get his money, his mate didn't have any and Rags seemed a little pissed off, so much so, that when we got back in his car, he put it in reverse and hit a telephone pole behind it. The impact jolted us both forward in our seats, dented the back of the car, tilting the telephone pole at the same time. It was not a smart move. Rags was really pissed off now, he put the car into first gear and floored the accelerator, by the time we got to the traffic lights at the bottom of Heathway, he was doing nearly 100 mph. The lights changed to red and as hard as he braked there was no stopping us from bumping the car already stopped at the white line in front of us.

"For fuck sake Rags, I'm off to Israel in a couple of days, don't you be killing me now!"

Stuart arrived on schedule at Romford station, I was waiting in the entrance lobby for him. As always, I was early and had to hang around for a while for his train to arrive.

"Wahey! Great to see you mate, did you have a good journey down?"
"Not too bad really," he replied, pulling his backpack around his side and back over his shoulder. "Took me ages to pack all my gear, but I think I got everything I'm meant to bring."

"Did you remember your passport?" I asked.

"Got it here, in my pocket, I've been looking at it all day, reminding myself we're on our way at last. I was never like this going away before, this is different, this is pretty exciting stuff, I don't know if I'll be able to sleep later."

"Don't worry about it mate, you'll be fine. We'll just go back to the flat, have a bite to eat and pop round the pub for a pint, it'll be good, help us both sleep, tomorrow is going to be a long day."

We walked the mile or two back to the flat. Stuart was keen to walk as he wanted the exercise, he was treating the whole thing as a military training course. He was going to Israel to hone desert skills, to carry his pack in the heat and march endlessly through the wilderness. I wondered to myself if he had only ever been a cadet, he was a pretty big youth, fit, strong and of excellent build for a life in the army. He wanted to fight too, he was about as alpha as an alpha male could get, whilst wearing khaki shorts and ankle boots. Stuart was an infantryman in waiting, it was obvious where his heart was, in the centre of his chest, it pumped furiously, propelling him onward and upwards, his pack on his back and a smile on his face.

We ate some supper together and were just getting ready to go for a drink when the phone rang.

"Hello!"

"Hello, is that mister..." A heavily accented voice trailed away to check his notes. "-Mr Reid?"

"Yes, speaking."

"I am sorry to trouble you Mr Reid, but I am talking to Mr Wayne Reid?"

"Yes, that's me, who is this?" I asked.

"My name is Mr Shalom, and I am calling from the Kibbutz Representatives." I wasn't expecting any calls, let alone from them. Not now.

"Hello, how can I help you?"

"Well, Mr Reid, I understand you are preparing to visit my beautiful country of Israel in the near future."

"Yes, I am flying out tomorrow, why, is everything okay?"

"I am very sorry to have to tell you that I have some bad news for you Mr Reid, I am sorry to call you like this -so close to your departure." I felt a sudden weight on my shoulders and my face must have drained of all it's blood. I looked to Stuart and he looked at me, stunned but not entirely sure why. He couldn't hear Mr Shalom but he could see my face.

"Wait, hang on, what is going on? What are you saying?"

"Mr Reid, I am sorry to have to tell you that you can no longer go to Israel."

"Can't go-what do you mean, I can't go, why?" I was in a bit of a panic. Stuart shuffled nervously, not sure where to look or how to react.

"Mr Reid," the strange little voice continued, "- I'm afraid that we have finally had all your references, your application has been declined and you cannot now come to Israel."

"My references-what's wrong with my references? My references were fine, there was nothing wrong with them."

"I'm sorry, Mr Reid, but it seems you have been a very naughty boy, and you cannot come to Israel, you are very naughty."

"I what?" I was furious, gutted, distraught. I didn't know what was wrong with my references, but surely they couldn't cancel my visit at this late notice, they couldn't just.... Wait, did he just say I was a naughty boy?

"You can't just call me now, this is wrong, there must be a mistake."

"There's no mistake Ribs."

"There must be.... Wait, what?"

"Hi Ribs, it's Jules..."

I hadn't seen Jules since just before I moved to France. I knew he was living in London now but hadn't spoken to him for a while. The bugger got me hook, line and sinker. I fell for his phoney accent, he seemed to know enough to fool me and for a few moments, I was absolutely petrified.

"You bastard Jules, you utter bastard! Hahaha, you got me going there, how the devil are you?"

"I'm good mate, look, me and my girlfriend are coming over to Ilford, it would be great to have a drink with you before you go."

Seeing Jules was a great boost, he'd been to Israel on holiday a year or so earlier and told me of things I had to do and see. It was the best send off I could have hoped for, good friends, laughs and a belly full of Caffrey's beer, by the time we got home again, we managed a couple of hours sleep before my brother-in-law Trevor, called to take Stuart and I to the airport, tired and hungover but excited all the same. Life was about to change, ahead of me lay a whole new world and adventures. What they would lead to, where I would go, I had no idea. Israel was to be a stepping stone, I had up to a year to sort myself out and move forward to the next phase, what that would be was anybody's guess, maybe travelling to another country, another continent, nothing was set in stone, I was but a leaf in the breeze.

Travelling to Israel means having to go through more stringent security checks than most other destinations. Searches, scans and queuing, more queues and more questions, the world keeps turning but my head was already sore. I was tired and in need of a decent meal and sleep, neither of which I would get, so instead, I mixed with the other volunteers and started to make friends. In the weeks leading up to our departure, we received notice of our destinations, and I was going to Dafna. I was pleased about this, it seemed like a good choice, being situated in the north of the country it wouldn't get too hot and in time I could get acclimatised. Stuart was going to Kfar Hannasi and began to mix with other volunteers heading there too. By the time we boarded the plane, we had pretty much split into two groups, the Dafna Volunteers and those headed to Kfar Hannasi. Until we reached our minibus at the arrivals area of Ben Gurion Airport, I was team leader,(*Me?*) in charge because I was the oldest and most responsible (*that sound in the background just then? That was me falling off my bar stool*).

I sat by one of the emergency exits, just to be safe, but also for the extra leg room, I had heard that long flights could cause Deep Vein Thrombosis if you didn't get up and stretch your legs, and seeing as the flight took about six hours and I wanted to be comfortable. The other volunteers were seated all around me, there were about 20 of us in all, maybe more, some heading to other Kibbutzim alone or in small groups. I sat with Andy, a Scottish lad from Edinburgh, a few years younger than myself with a thick accent even I found hard to negotiate at times. Andy was on his way to Israel because he needed to get out of town pretty quickly, he'd been caught out by his landlord, apparently in the act with his landlady. We all had our demons, our reasons for being on this flight, for going to Israel. For the other Stuart, it was a sporting injury that had cut his military career short, he was planning on taking a year off and then going back to the army. Rebecca was taking a year out too. Her father was a high ranking officer in the metropolitan police, a strict disciplinarian, that much I could tell from the sadness in her eyes, that sort of curtain to the soul that some people choose to draw closed, because it hurts too much to keep it open. Anne and Eve, were travelling together. They'd met working in a sweet factory in Scotland. They were polar opposites in appearance, Anne looked as if she hadn't eaten for months, Eve looked as if she knew why. Anne was 6 stone in the rain with a wet sleeping bag, Eve was not. Eve also had the misfortune of having a lazy eye, sometimes giving you the impression she was talking to the person behind you. Little Katie was from Belfast, that in itself seemed reason enough to come along.

The Alps rolled by beneath us, such a beautiful sight with their snow capped peaks and green valleys. I'd driven across these mountains many times in my truck. I knew the country beneath us so well, I'd lived in my own metal prison for so long, away from home, alone fending for myself and trying to provide for my family. But not anymore. I had turned my last wheel and would never step foot in a truck again, I would never do a lot of things again, I was going forwards, not backwards.

Another volunteer in our group was Phil, a big soft bear of a man. He was the type of guy who looked like he'd swallowed a whiskey barrel and it was stuck in his chest. If he lost his temper, he could be dangerous just because of his size. Phil had had an awful hand in life, both his parents had died within a few months of each other when he was little, and now his Nan had died too. Phil was trying to get through life, having had to raise his younger brother, without the support of their parents, an elder brother running their farm even though he too, was too young to be left in such a position. Phil was grieving, through his laughter, his sorrow clung, always there, always present.

We all had our demons, we all had our reasons, we all wanted something, and whether we'd find it, only time could tell.

7 ISRAEL

"What can you do with 3 months? I had nowhere to go but the rest of my life to get there......."

I

3 Months. It was 3 months since Jill had been buried. 3 months after Adam, then Jacqui. 3 Months since my wife slapped my face in public because it wasn't her funeral, her party. 3 Months of endless arguments and fights. 3 Months was no time at all, but it was the only time that counted. Sian was 3 months old when I took her and her mother to Spain with me. Christina was 3 months old when we moved into our new home. It had been 3 months since Tracy was moved into a hospice, never to return. 3 Months is no time at all, unless it is these times, these days when the drugs don't work, when the nights bring only the same dream again and again. Night after night, until it is so real that it becomes a memory with tastes and smells, sensations so strong as to blur the subconscious into the conscious, reality into dream, fact into fiction. *The unseen entity behind the cubicle door was stirring.*

As we reached the eastern shore of the Mediterranean, I peered out of the window to see rows of small houses, yellowed earth, just as I'd seen on the news. The hot, arid landscape stretched out beneath us, it was beautiful, just as I had hoped it would be.

We made our way through the intrusive immigration procedure, the prying questions, so many questions that I didn't think they'd ever end.

"Who are you, Where are you from, What are you carrying, Are you a terrorist, Do you know Manchester United?"

I shepherded everyone through immigration and bag reclamation, then outside into the heat of the day. I have always loved that feeling of stepping out from an airport, that moment when you leave the comfort of the air conditioned concourse, pick up your bag and step outside into the heat and noise of the outside world. The air hits you immediately, like the opening of an oven door, the dry air, full with the noise of hustle and bustle, the traffic, the people and the smells of a new country. It lasts only a few seconds, and then is gone, until the next time.

Our minibus was a 12 seat Toyota van, designed and built for 12 persons of oriental build, not 12 over-indulged Lilly white Europeans. Our ride to Dafna was a 4 hour slog with an Arab driver who spoke no English. We left Tel Aviv along a flower lined dual carriageway, there were billboards and signs everywhere, the Hebrew characters enforcing the sense of far away, 'other worldliness'. Tel Aviv was like a close cousin to Madrid, hot and dusty but with a wholly indecipherable language. The streets were busy, bustling, noisy but a little less crowded than Istanbul had been. As the city passed behind us, I looked out the window at the landscape around us. Crickets hummed in short, sharp leaved bushes, hills rose and steadily grew into mountain ranges behind which set the sun, turning the bright blue sky into a dark blanket pitted with stars, many, many stars.

As the group leader, I sat in the front seat next to the driver. The hot summer air was having a wilting effect on him, and he drifted occasionally, his eyes momentarily closing. I coughed, I nudged him, I talked as much as I could in order to keep him awake, keep his attention going. In the distance I saw the unmistakable arches of a McDonald's restaurant and demanded he pulled in. I find it funny now, that my first taste of Israel was a bloody Big Mac at Golani Junction.

"Do you want cheese with your burger?"

"Sorry?"

"Cheese, do you want cheese with your burger?"

"It's a Big Mac mate, of course it has cheese." Was this guy for real, it's a Big Mac, you know. 2 burgers, special sauce, lettuce, CHEESE, pickles and onion. I remembered the advert even if he'd never seen it.

"No Sir, do you want your cheese in your burger?"

"Of course I want it in my burger, it's a fucking Big Mac, it has fucking cheese in it, of course I want it in there, what is this?"

I looked at the guy at the next till, a tall man with a wide brimmed hat an long beard. Despite the heat, he still wore a long black jacket. In front of him were 2 plates, a burger on one, a slice of cheese on the other. The confused look that washed over my face must have been pretty obvious, as he turned to say "It's Kosher, we don't mix meat with dairy, not even in a cheeseburger." I smiled back, enlightened, and just a little bit stupid.

I bought an extra coke, for the driver, I didn't want him falling asleep in the dark, we still had a long way to go, in the dark. We climbed back into the van, our driver refreshed and more awake than he had been previously. I looked around at our group, we were all here, Stuart the elder, the ex military man was telling Steve, a volunteer I had only briefly chatted with, about how he knew Andy McNabb, the ex-SAS soldier turned writer. In return Steve told Stuart about why he was in Israel, that his girlfriend had wanted to start a family and that he wasn't ready. Not yet. Steve was running away, like I was, but I already had a family, I had 2 little girls that I'd left behind, that I was trying my hardest to forget because remembering was too painful. Steve reminded me of my girls, my little babies. He shouldn't be here, he should be home making that family, being the man I was running away from, because he wouldn't like to feel what I felt, nobody should feel what I felt.

We stopped briefly at HaGoshrim, a Kibbutz Hotel near to our destination. We dropped off a couple of other volunteers who'd come with us and then continued up the road a short distance to Dafna.

Kibbutz Dafna is situated about 3 miles from Qiryat Shmona, the most northerly town in Israel and it's name translates as the Town of Seven, honouring seven martyrs who'd died in the town during the war for Israeli independence. The road from Qiryat Shmona continues to Metulla, the military crossing point into Lebanon. HaGoshrim is between Qiryat Shmona and Dafna, both lay in the Hula Valley beneath Mount Hebron, and the Golan Heights, beyond which lies Syria. To our north and west was the Lebanon, the warm air tasted exquisite in my lungs, I hated the British weather, cold damp air, I hated Britain, it's hypocrisy and the daily rat race, I hated it all. Here, in this far off strange land, I was happy. I had no idea what lay ahead, but the warm, sweet air, kissed by the sun and clear sky, tasted so good, so clean and full of life.

The Kibbutz itself is a small village of little buildings, mostly concrete sections, built to a predetermined design. I say it's a village because it has all the functionality of a village, houses, a shop, a sports facility, doctor's surgery, a dairy, small factory and farmland, it even has it's own 'post office'. Surrounded by razor wire and fencing, interrupted only by the front and rear gates. The front gate has a guard room and the Israeli Defence Force guard the site 24/7. At first glance it looks more like a prison than holiday destination or somewhere you would choose to visit, arriving at night, we were saved the worst of any bad first impressions.

We alighted the van, thanked our driver and collected our bags from the rear of the vehicle, by which time our reception committee had arrived to greet us.

There was a strange noise in the distance, like the continual reverberating sound of a heavy steel door being slammed somewhere down a long corridor. Craig and Dave introduced themselves to us, they were from Southend, a town near to where I'd been brought up. When I was little, it was our 'go to ' seaside town. Jack appeared as if from nowhere, slipping in between where the lights shone and shadows fell, a place he seemed to know well.

"What's that noise?" I asked, addressing the elephant in the room.

"That's the war dear boy," replied Jack, his accent rich with the Valleys of South Wales and an old Etonian education. Jack had never studied at Eton, but his voice was beautifully British, the sort of sound that could easily force his way to the front of the queue at any East European border. I wondered briefly if he'd been in the RAF, or the Diplomatic Corps, judging by his Adidas shorts and pale blue t-shirt, I doubted it somehow.

"That's the sound of katyusha rockets, a gift to the people of Israel from their friends, the Hezbollah, over in the Lebanon there. Iran supplies them in the hope that Israel will fall-and that sound, that is is the sound of the Israeli Defence Force saying Thank You, here, try one of ours!"

We had landed in a war-zone, the demilitarised area between Israel and her enemies lay only a few hundred yards beyond the back fence of Dafna, and was anything but demilitarised.

Jack's cigar, almost ever-present after work hours, barely twitched as he spoke, he rarely lit the bloody thing, but it was an integral part of his appearance.

"So what about the peace accord, how come this isn't on the news back home?" I asked, suddenly wondering what on earth I'd let myself in for.

"It's a daily occurrence old boy, not important enough to get upset about. So, welcome to Dafna, here, I'll take you through to see Shlomo."

Shlomo was the Volunteer's supervisor, administrator and general dictator. A grey, humourless, bespectacled man, tall, thin and very abrupt. Our presence seemed to be a constant source of irritation to him, even though it was his job to deal with us. It seemed a more formal meeting was to be held in the canteen the following morning, for tonight we were told to choose a bed and familiarise ourselves with the other volunteers.

Volunteer accommodation was pretty basic, a bed, a cupboard each and a shared bathroom. There were several rooms, maybe 20 or so, either side of the open walkway known as Death Row. The guys were housed in the buildings on one side, 3 to each concrete hut, the girls on the other side, their rooms were slightly smaller and they were only 2 to a room. The rooms were meant to be bomb proof, but I doubted it, the roof tiles wouldn't stop anything stronger than a good fart, let alone an errant ballistic device, it was nice to know the walls would be okay though.

I found myself in a room with Andy and Phil and immediately chose the single bunk, if we were going to get hit in our sleep, I didn't fancy the idea of the top bunk collapsing down on me, no matter who was in it. Jack reappeared in the doorway.

"Sorry chaps, but the volunteer's bar is not opening tonight, you'll have to wait until tomorrow." Having spent all day travelling and recovering from the previous night's excesses, I was ready for a beer, even though I had hoped to avoid getting into the habit, I was on limited funds and wanted my money to last, at least until such time that I could get some work somewhere. I'd been drinking a lot in England, trying to knock myself out at nights but still sitting in bed watching TV as the sun came up. I know I was not alone, not the only person ever to struggle with sleep, but now I was making a new start, and hoping that sleep would become a close friend, not a distant memory.

My bed was comfortable enough and I was tired after the journey, but still I could not sleep. The explosions in the near distance were an alien sound to me, too alien and real to ignore, but also there was Phil.

"I'm gonna apologise to you now," he warned us in his best Geordie accent. "I have a problem with my airwaves and it makes me snore, very loudly. I'm waiting to have an operation when I get back to England, but until then it's a nightmare, I can't even sleep through it some nights."

It's one thing to say you snore, and he did say it, but it's another thing when your snoring rattles the window frames, when your lungs expand so far that the space time continuum bends out of shape as you inhale. Phil didn't snore. Phil broke the laws of physics, the sonic booms emanating from him set off car alarms in Beirut. Sleeping in the same room as Phil, meant no sleeping at all, it just wasn't possible.

Breakfast was a lavish affair, all you can eat buffet of fresh peppers, onions, salad, fruits, bread, yogurts, eggs, fish and cereals. I cleared my plate and then went for more.

"If this is how they feed us, I'm definitely staying."

As the Kibbutzniks and other volunteers filed out of the canteen, we- the new arrivals, stayed in our seats, watching the canteen volunteers as they cleaned up, and then began to prepare for lunch. A water fight broke out and for a few minutes there was mayhem until Shlomo re-appeared and the atmosphere calmed. I swear that man carried a black cloud around with him wherever he went, he was dull, grey without any trace of humour, and did I say he was grey already, grey, inside and out, grey hair, grey eyes, grey skin, and I'd bet my last dollar his shit came out the colour of cigarette ash. Surveying the scene before him, he was probably calculating the cost to the budget of all that lost water, every last Shekel, every single one.

Shlomo's welcome speech was a long monologue of all the 'Do's and Don'ts' of Kibbutz life. Everything had a price apparently, and everyone of us had to remember, we could lose our deposits if we misbehaved, stole or damaged anything. As if we would, us, misbehave? By the time he finally shut up, I'd calculated I'd probably lose my deposit a dozen times over.

After the meeting, we were free to do as we pleased, today was a day off for the new arrivals, a chance to find our feet and get settled in. I headed into Qiryat Shmona, with Anne, Eve and a couple of volunteers who'd offered to show us where the bank was. I needed to cash a traveller's cheque, I thought it might be a good idea to have some more cash, seeing as there was a bar on site, if it was ever going to open that is. Michael and Maria were madly in love with each other, it was obvious and very sweet. Michael was English, Maria from Denmark. There were many such couplings at Dafna, it was like an episode of The Love Boat at times, but without the water.

I found the bank and joined the short queue inside, it was nice to get indoors, out of the heat, even though it was still only late morning the temperature was rising and the air conditioned bank felt refreshing after the short walk from our drop-off point. In front of me in the queue was a well-groomed, smartly dressed man, probably in his late 30's, his hair was short and black, his clothes were spotless and clean, his black shirt tucked neatly into the belt of his black trousers which created the ideal background for the big silver handgun tucked neatly behind the back of his belt. I stepped backwards and took in a sharp breath of air. I'd never been in a bank heist before, and I don't recall ever seeing such a shiny, silver pistol either. Surely someone else must have seen it too? In this, of all places, there should be a camera pointing straight at this guy. Any moment now, the alarm will go off. Bullet proof screens will shoot up from the desks in front of the tellers, doors will lock, tear gas and smoke bombs will be fired into the foyer as a SWAT team come crashing through the windows on ropes, all guns blazing. I'd seen Point Break, I knew how these things went down. How did I get into this position? The guy stepped forward, his turn was next as I stayed where I was, not wishing to get too close, I didn't want to be taken hostage, nor did I want to die here, not on my first fucking day in Israel, Jesus Christ what the fuck had I done to deserve this ending? Was this it, really, I came all this way to become a hostage in a bank raid?

The guy stepped up to the counter and took a slip of paper from his pocket. This is it, that's the 'I have a gun, give me your money' note, should I jump on him now, while he's talking to the cashier? Go down fighting, don't just accept your fate, create it, do it, go for it and die like a hero. I took a deep breath and steadied myself, taking a moment for the adrenaline to kick in and fill my body with it's wonderful analgesic power, I felt a rush of power just as the cashier handed over some cash. The gun was still in the man's belt as he picked it up and walked away. Wait. Was that it? Is it over? The cashier signalled for me to come over, I stood open mouthed still ready to pounce. Someone behind me coughed and I nearly fell over. I half ran to the counter, my mouth still open and my eyes wide in disbelief.

"You are English, yes? In Israel, everybody has a gun!" said the young lady behind the desk, counting out my shekels.

"Big shiny ones?" I asked. She smiled then replied,

"You'll get used to it, Shalom!"

Redfaced, I smiled and wished her 'Peace' too. A strange greeting in a land so famed for it's lack of peace.

Back at Dafna, lunch was being served in the canteen. I sat next to Craig and David on the long table we shared with the other volunteers. Jack was close by analysing the Jerusalem Post, predicting a fresh wave of bombing attacks in the Upper Galilee.

"Things have been too quiet for too long, we can't have that-can we boys?"
Across the table, Maria and a South African volunteer, Carmel, were noisily
flicking food at each other. Michael was splattered with sauce and stood up in
mock protest, accidentally upsetting a glass of fruit cordial which Maria tried
to catch but only managed to cover Carmel's t-shirt with sticky red liquid. Her
mouth wide open and eyes bulging, Carmel emptied the contents of her own
glass over Maria's head. The table was in in uproar, everyone laughing at the
high jinks as Maria then reached for a jug of water to retaliate with, but
Carmel was gone, she'd left the table and was running around the dining
room, Maria, hot on her heels, pulled her arm back to throw the water at
Carmel but was already too late, Carmel had side stepped her and was now
heading for the exit. Maria skipped around the end of a table filled with ageing
Kibbutzniks and was catching up with Carmel as she disappeared out through
the glass door, the door swung back in as Maria put her arm out and there was
an almighty crash. Maria went through the shattering glass and fell to the
floor, still holding the jug of water. Her face and arm were lacerated and
blood poured from her open wounds. Michael ran to help her, followed by
many of the Kibbutzniks and a handful of volunteers. Towels were wrapped
around her wounds and blood still poured out the folds as she was carried off
to the medical room, and then via ambulance to the hospital in Qiryat
Shmona.
Shlomo used this accident to warn us of the dangers of tomfoolery Maria
would be unable to work for many weeks now and this would cost the
kibbutz a lot of money. There were many things that were looked upon in a
negative way at the kibbutz, theft, damage and Toga Parties with our bed
sheets were the highest of the sins. Any volunteer caught in the act would lose
their deposit and be evicted from the site immediately. Shlomo was a very
grey man, humourless and devoid of any sense of fun, he hated us volunteers,
rich, spoiled westerners who only wanted to have fun. But also himself, I was
convinced he hated his own status on the kibbutz, Volunteer Manager, with
no control over anything but the money for our food and our deposits. He
hated that we could travel the world without care, drink cheap vodka and hold
toga parties all night long. Such frivolity was destructive and obscene, but to
us, it was therapy, escapism and the only way we could deal with the issues in
life which had sent us all here in the first place, we were all screw-ups, one
way or another.
We spent the afternoon tanning ourselves by the communal pool. The water
was refreshing but highly chlorinated, my eyes stung and reddened almost as
much as my pale whit skin in the middle eastern sunshine. Much of our time
was spent getting to know each other still, couples began pairing off. Steve
was all over Rebecca like a rash. We took turns in rubbing sunscreen into each
other's skin. The afternoon sun was strong but not as searing as I'd expected
and looking out for each other was a good way of marking one's territory,

staking a claim in one or other of the opposite sex. I had no such desires, but instead, became an observer as Steve paired up with Rebecca, Stuart the ex-squaddie paired up with the Katie,the little Catholic girl from Belfast, leaving Phil and Andy with Anne and Eve, none of which, would ever be happening. Phil was so obviously gay that he had no interest, and Andy would get nowhere with the girls, they could see straight through any of that nonsense. He had his eye elsewhere though, he was already sniffing around Karen, another Scottish volunteer who, at 34, was possibly the oldest volunteer already on site. Karen had already been at Dafna for a month, she had come straight from Africa where she'd been volunteering for the Volunteer Service Overseas. She was a slip of a woman with a pretty face and long straight hair. Her thin body looked out of perspective with her large toothy grin. She smiled a lot and genuinely seemed to care about people. She worked in the Dairy, herding and milking the cows, but because she started at 4 AM, her workday was over at lunchtime and she was now free to do her own thing, like bathe at the pool. She gave us the run down on what to look forward to at Dafna, day trips to Haifa, Tiberias and the Sea of Galilee. The ultimate experience would be the Eilat trip, a 4 day journey to Eilat, similar to the desert trek I had already booked, but free.

"Have you been to the river yet?" She asked.

"No," Andy replied, "what river's that then?"

"The one over the back there, near the orchards. C'mon, I'll show you's."

We collected our bits up, towels, cremes etc and followed Karen away from the pool, beyond the boot factory and out of the back gate of the kibbutz. There was a path that took us through the orchards and away closer and closer to the fence, the border fence to the Lebanon.

"Don't ever come out here at night, and during the day, watch out for the wild boar, they can kill you too!" Snakes and scorpions I'd expected, but wild boar only ever lived in the Asterix books my father had bought home for me when I was little.

Karen led us through some more trees, we could hear the rushing river, and then the trees opened out onto the river bank. There was an old bed frame set into the ground on top of which were a couple of old wooden pallets, it was an ideal spot to sunbathe or jump into the fast flowing waters. We were only a few yards from the Lebanese border, but we were in paradise. The cold water was straight from the springs beneath Mount Hermon, clean enough to drink, deep enough to swim in. These waters were the lifeblood of Israel, one of three tributaries that joined to form the river Jordan. The moment I entered the river I had a realisation. I could almost feel the power and energy of the water, how it controlled and commanded our lives. It was the one thing that had the power to both give life, and take life. Without water we all die, too much water and we drown. Our very existence depended on our ability to obtain just enough of this precious resource. For the first time in my life, I felt truly refreshed and invigorated. There was something magical about this place, something good.

Jack had invited us to climb the water tower. It was a concrete structure overlooking the dairy and had panoramic views across the Hula Valley and into Lebanon. It was a place for reflection, to appreciate the scenery around us and also to watch the war. Climbing the metal ladder to the top of the tower was a challenge for me. I had always had a strange dislike of heights. I could stand on top of mountains and feel perfectly safe, well I was on the ground wasn't I? You can't fall off the ground. But ladders and man made constructions gave me the heebee-geebee's. I didn't trust the ladder not to peel away from the concrete structure, or the rusty metal rungs to give way under my weight, not that I'm a fat bastard, but because it's me, and sod's law say's it would only happen to me. It was falling that I feared most, the bone crushing thud as you hit the ground and splatter across the pavement, I could live with that. It was the useless flapping in mid air, trying to swim through the sky and failing miserably that I hated. In my childhood, I dreamt I could fly. It was easy, I just swam through the air, gently drifting like a fish in the ocean. In reality I could do no such thing, and that bothered me, a lot. The thought of air rushing through me as I fall to the ground sickened me, when I die, it will be in my bed, no flapping, no gasping for breath, no last look down, well, not if I'm alone anyway.

"And over there, Ladies and Gentlemen," Said Jack, "Is the Lebanon." Jack knew this shit, he knew it too well be just a tourist.

"There is a civil war going on at the moment, between the Arabs in the North, and the Christians in the South. The Israeli army is engaged in the South to assist the Lebanese army and to protect it's own border." I was sensing MI5 or SAS Intelligence, but the cigar? That kind of spoiled the picture, nobody would wish to be given away by a scent of cigar smoke, maybe he wasn't on active duties. Stuart, Katie, Andy and myself were new to this speech, Craig and David looked bored enough to have heard it a dozen times before.

"You see, the Hezbollah use southern Lebanon to launch attacks against Israel. They're funded by Iran and Iraq, together with the Palestinians, to bring an end to the Jewish State. Syria used to control the Golan Heights, but these were taken by Israel in the 10 day war of 1967. Snipers used to sit in those mountains and take pot shots at the farmers down below. Then of course, there is the water. A few years ago, Syria began tunnelling under the Golan Heights in order to divert the waters from supplying the River Jordan. Naturally, that was a step too far and would have turned this valley into a desert, so now the UN police a 30 km zone in both the Lebanon and Syria."

Jack thrived on his 'Welcome to the Middle East' speech. None of us were fully aware when we'd signed on for our Kibbutz experience, especially the younger ones. We'd already had the Gulf War (the first one) and as far as we knew, the Israeli conflict was settled, The Holy Land was at peace, innit?

"And I thought I was leaving all that shit behind me!" Said Katie. "I thought it was going to be all olive trees and a wailing wall."

"So how do you get into Lebanon?" I asked.

"You don't, not unless you join the IDF."

"You wouldn't want to," said Craig. "Dave and I were there at Metula getting our photo's taken with John, just a couple of weeks ago. A bus full of American tourists turned up and a load of mortar bombs started coming down on us. The Americans were back on the bus and gone before Dave could even get his camera back off one of them."

We stayed a while before climbing back down to the ground, then headed to the Volunteer's canteen, where we ate our evening meal. The main canteen was reserved for the Kibbutzniks at night, we had a separate building near Death Row, with a tiny kitchen, a few tables and chess sets. We were supposed to entertain ourselves here, but once we'd eaten we usually sat outside in the late sun. Our room would only be used for changing clothes and sleeping, that is, on the rare occasions we could sleep. If it wasn't Phil's snoring keeping us awake, it was the telephone on the wall outside, ringing at all hours for either the Israeli soldiers billeted at the far end of Death Row, or some concerned relative embarrassing one of the volunteers.

"Are you eating properly, are you washing your knickers regularly? Don't forget to take your pill, and please don't come home pregnant..."

Word came round that the bar was open tonight, not only that but we had to use it as we were going to be attacked. Israeli Intelligence knew what was happening before even Yasser Arafat was briefed.

The volunteer bar was also our underground bomb shelter, it was where we were meant to hide from the rockets due to fall upon us. But we had other ideas.

The last rocket fired from the unlit helicopter hit it's target. A large fireball, burst upwards, silencing the ground to air missiles. Someone had just been killed. An Arab was dead. From our viewpoint high up on the kibbutz water tower, we continued watching across the orchards, beyond the razor wire and the fence, off into southern Lebanon, where a tiny village lay invisible in the night, but for the flames, a fire here, a burning vehicle there. Invisible but for the death and destruction indelibly printed on our memories.

I took a cigarette packet from my shirt pocket, a soft pack of Israeli made Noblesse, took one from the pack and lit it, dragging the noxious smoke deep into my lungs, savouring it's taste before washing it away with a mouthful of cheap Israeli vodka. Overhead, rotor blades echoed throughout the Hula valley, filling the void between the dark night sky above, and the budding cotton fields beneath the first of 3 helicopter gunships now returning to their base, flying low between the Golan Heights and Qiryat Shmona, the town of 7 martyrs, it's guns still warm.

No one says "Cut!" or "It's a wrap!" Instead, we shuffled uneasily, shaking off guilt and fear, gratification and horror. We were kibbutz volunteers not soldiers, not men of war. We'd only offered ourselves as cheap labour, for the fun and experience. We were hungry for travel and knowledge, world weary wannabes, the been there done it brigade that came in search of our own peace, only there was no peace here, we had landed in a war zone, someone else's war in which our presence made us legitimate targets in a continuing struggle for peace, freedom and survival. By day and night the air boomed with shellfire. The mountains around us giving up clouds of dust and rock as the Israeli Defence Force retaliated to the katyusha rockets raining from the sky above. The Hezbollah determined to finish off what the Nazi's could not, to kill the unwanted Jews, these men and women that toiled quietly in Dafna, who in other countries would be retired to the coast, cared for in homes or hospitals, not working still on production lines, their concentration camp numbers tattooed on their forearms. 50 years on, still living the horror, in a state of war surrounded by barbed and razor wire fence, with enemies at their door. The old man who'd sat with us at lunch earlier today, Zelik, he'd had to watch his wife and children enter the gas chamber in a concentration camp. His job had been to greet the new arrivals from the transportation trains, offer them stones instead of soap and tell them that all would be well, they were going to be deloused and showered, knowing full well what was really happening to them, hearing day after day their screams as Zyklon B gas pellets were released into the chambers, day after day, year after year his memories taunted him. Why would anyone wish him harm, had he not suffered enough for all of mankind, not just one lifetime. did he not deserve some peace or respect?

I questioned my own self pity. How could I have anything to complain about compared to what was going on around me, I was free and able to move on, the Kibbutzniks of Dafna were here to stay, always living within the razor wire, always within the sights of someone's gun. Being at Dafna was the closest I would ever get to being back at Dachau, not as a truck driving tourist with a weekend pass, but as a witness to all the horrors these kibbutznik's had survived. Could I ever have survived the images hidden behind their eyes? Could I have gone on, day after day with that weight upon me? The truth had to be told, someone had to survive and tell the story, it must never be forgotten and never, ever, repeated.

When Phil and I hitch hiked to Metula the following evening, the border crossing was quiet, as was the town itself, about a mile or so from the 'Look out post', an army observation point overlooking the border and the valley beyond. We took photo's of each other beneath the crossed flags of Israel and Lebanon. As the sun faded, we walked back along the dust track to Qiryat Shmona. It was our first time seeing the Israeli army on the move, a convoy of tanks and trucks of all shapes and sizes were slowly crossing the border.

Jeeps laden with men and equipment passed by on their way to an uncertain future in the Lebanon. Young soldiers and battle hardened veterans sat side by side looking down at us.

"Bloody tourists!"

The centre point of Kibbutz Dafna is the boot factory. Container loads of rubber boots, shoes and snow boots manufactured in the Middle East, beneath the blazing sun. We had travelled thousands of miles to work in a bloody boot factory, it was almost comical. The boots were trucked in from a factory at Metula. When they arrived at Dafna they came on metal racks, covered in dust. Our first job was to clean them, and that was my first job, wiping and cleaning dust off rubber boots, with a tiny cloth and a bottle of the Israeli Wodka (Vodka) I'd been drinking the night before. It seemed the Wodka was cheaper but no less effective than industrial solvent, and we drank that shit.

Once cleaned, the boots were sorted into pairs, one left, one right according to size and style. They would then have plastic soles glued on, before being spray painted and moved along the line. The air in this little corner of the factory was thick with the fumes of paint, glue and vodka, as well as the soup of chemicals into which the boots were dipped, we believed, in order to stiffen the soft rubber uppers.

Fortunately for me, I couldn't keep up with the onslaught of rack after rack of boots coming at me, mostly because I had no real idea of what I was meant to be doing. Eve was working alongside me and fared little better. We only managed to clean and wipe a fraction of the boots before us, the toxic air around us taking me back to my days in the little room over Oxford Street, making silly hats, inhaling glue and listening to The Psychedelic Furs. The morning passed pretty quickly though, even though we both felt pretty nauseous. The fumes and the constant banging, whirring and whistling of the aged machinery was doing my head in. We went for a break, 15 minutes on the grass, in the fresh air, with coffee and biscuits, or the sickly sweet red or purple squash like drink we consumed with vigour. We sat on the grass outside, in the sunshine and quizzed each other about the various jobs we were given. Katie, Anne and Rebecca had been placed further down the line, stapling labels into the finished boots, while Andy and Stuart prepared cardboard boxes on an upstairs mezzanine. Steve had been packing and Phil had been busy sorting pairs onto the conveyor track from the drying area

After the break, some of us changed roles as David, our foreman, tested our abilities to suit the jobs available. I was moved from the stink tank and given the pairing job. After lunch, we changed roles again, by this time I had a much better idea of what we were doing, and how the process worked. The end result was meant to be a pair of equal sized boots, one left, one right, lined, labelled, wrapped and packed in the correct box, ready to ship to the shops in Scandinavia. The Danes were making boots, to sell to themselves back home,

I guess the change of scenery made it all worthwhile. The flow of production depended on everyone working efficiently and quickly, sometimes the wrong number of boxes or boots would create a backlog, but on the whole, everything ran pretty smoothly and a long line of boxes disappeared through a hole in the wall, into the warehouse, where Jack, and Zelik, the old Kibbutznik with the tattooed forearm would stack them into rows according to size, colour and style. Once enough were ready, orders were loaded into a container and shipped out to Haifa. Zelik was now in his 80's. He lived in Qiryat Shmona and cycled into Dafna each day to work, something Jack took some level of pride in, like a son for his elderly father, still able to look after himself, despite his small stature and permanently hunched back.

There were 2 bars at Dafna, the Vol (Volunteer's) bar, and Domino's the kibbutz nightclub. Domino's was open to all at weekends, whereas the Vol bar was ours, it was for us, the volunteers, and it was run by us, or at least, by one of us. The bar was underground, accessed by a thick steel door above ground and a steep staircase leading to another door that led into the underground bunker. The whole place was meant to be bomb proof, but I didn't fancy being there when it was tested, I'd rather meet my end upstairs, not suffocating under a ton of steel, concrete and mud. The doors were bullet proof and the stairway only dimly lit. Occasionally, someone would get a little too drunk and fall back down the steep stairs, taking whoever was behind down with them.

We had been at Dafna only a few days when Michael, Rob and John invited us to a tequila party in their room. We'd had a few beers in the Vol Bar before they came down and were more than happy to make up numbers with them. John was a short stocky guy from London, but lived in Belfast. Until he spoke, he looked like a football hooligan, tattoos, close cropped hair and a cheeky grin that could lead to a pat on the back or a smack in the face, either would do. When he spoke, he had the quietest voice I'd ever heard. He was calm, relaxed and wise. I began to call him John 'The Baptist', it seemed to suit him. John was a good influence on me, I found myself learning to 'chill-out' in his presence. He may have looked like a thug, but John was a good man, a peaceful man who'd seen enough violence in his lifetime. He chose the path of peace and was the most chilled out person I have ever met, despite, like most volunteers, being a pretty heavy drinker.

The room was full of smoke when we walked in, about a dozen volunteers had filled an equal number of ashtrays to the point that they were overflowing. There were empty bottles on the floor between those that sat cross legged on the tiles, and the legs and feet of those sitting on the beds. We joined in a drinking game, unaware of the rules or how to play, we just followed the lead of those around us. For some undetermined reason, we were required to swallow a mouthful of tequila. Michael seemed untouched by the amount of alcohol he'd already consumed. Carmel, Karen and Maria and roared with laughter from time to time, Maria doing her best not to knock her bandaged arm, and then it happened. I lost consciousness.

I woke the next morning in my bed, having slept the whole night without being woken up by either Phil's snoring, or the volunteer's phone ringing outside our room. Since our arrival, a group of Israeli soldiers, all young girls, had been billeted in the spare rooms near to our own. At night, one call would follow another, irrespective of the time of night. It had made it impossible to get any sleep, with Phil snoring, the phone ringing again and again, then all the cries of;

"Betty, telephone!"

Andy and I were beginning to fray around the edges. I would take my sleeping bag outside and sleep by the campfire or on the roof of the volunteers kitchen, looking up at the stars and thinking of my daughters. Even though I had a stinking hangover, I felt much better for having slept the whole night, that was until I stepped outside and felt the strangest feeling that something was missing, 4 small holes marked the spot where the phone should be. What made it feel even more wrong, was that Andy, Phil and myself had asked Shlomo if we could have the phone moved, just the day before, his reply was an emphatic "No!" Something was wrong, but I didn't know what.

We were off on our first Kibbutz day out, a coach full of Volunteers climbing aboard like the oversized school kids we really were. Naturally I sat near the back with the cool kids-I mean, the older (more time served) Volunteers. We stopped at HaGoshrim to pick up the dozen or so Volunteers from there, among them were a couple of Danes and a South African girl called Pete. Yes, you read it right, if my Mother-in-law could live with a man called Lynn, why shouldn't a girl be called Pete, even in South Africa?

Pete was an attractive girl in her early 20's. Clever and confident, pretty in a girl next door way, and she was Craig's heartthrob. He would often disappear from Dafna to go and hang around with Pete and her friends. Unfortunately for Craig, he lacked the confidence to follow his desire, he had just come out of a long-term relationship, a bit like I had. He also had a son, back home in Southend, and he suffered from Crohn's Disease, a condition that affected everything he did. Craig spent many days in Dafna, in intense pain and discomfort, usually he would soldier on but some days he could be bedridden all day long.

Once everyone was on-board and seated, we headed off toward Tiberias. We were going to see all the famous places around the Sea of Galilee. I was sat next to Kelly, a nervous young woman from New Zealand. Her only fellow countryman at Dafna, was a guy called Louie, whom she avoided like the plague.

"He's a wanker!" Craig explained to me one day. Kelly felt the same.

"He's full of shit!" She said. I had yet to make up my mind, I hadn't really met him properly yet, so I reserved my judgement on whether or not he was either, none, or all of the above. His stories of being a member of the Australian Special Forces, seemed a little far fetched and didn't endear him to me, especially when his whole personality and character were so 'Not' killer material. If he'd ever fought his way out of a bus shelter I'd have been surprised, Louie might have been able to fart his way out of crowd, but he couldn't fight his way out of a wet paper bag, honestly.

Kelly was distracted. I'd spoken to her before this trip, in the Vol Bar a couple of times, and generally around the Kibbutz, I'd even bought her a couple of beers in the bar the previous night, before the tequila party.

"So tell me about New Zealand then," I demanded.

"Oh it's, you know, it's okay. My folks have a Hotel in Nelson if you ever wanted to visit, that would be cool!"

"Yeah, I'd love to. There's so much of the world I want to see. I don't know when I'll get there, but one day I will." There was a short pause, and I asked "Where are you going next?"

"I don't know" Kelly sighed looking out the window as we pulled out to overtake a car. "I don't know what I'm doing, I'm not really together at the moment and- well, you know, I just don't know yet, I can't seem to get my act together. What about you, where you going next?"

I thought about it briefly, then replied.

"At the moment I've got no idea," I replied, "I want to stop here for a bit and sort my head out before I go anywhere, I've got all my life to go anywhere I want, but home."

Outside the bus, the familiar golden arches flashed by as we passed the lights at Golani Junction. I laughed at the absurdity of coming all the way to the Middle East, only to have a bloody McDonalds for our first meal. Kelly half grinned, it was a sad attempt at a smile, but the best she'd made all morning.

"What's wrong with home?" She asked.

"It's a long story."

"They usually are, but I'm listening."

"I can't go home because I left my wife and our daughters. If I go back the government will make my life, and theirs, a misery. They'd strip me of everything and give half of it to her so she'd lose out, I'd lose out and the kids would be made homeless when the bank takes back the house. Being out of the country, she get's all her benefits and the mortgage paid."

"What made you leave if you have kids together?" She looked puzzled.

"It would be easy to say she cheated on me with my best mate, but there was more to it than that. A lot more. I could have forgiven her if that was all it was, but no." I told her about my frustration at Adam for not giving me the chance to help him, or anyone else. That he didn't even confide in Naz, his housemate and best friend, someone he left to have to find him, to clean up the mess he'd left behind. And Jill, John, Jacqui, and now Tracey. How I thought I was next if I hadn't got out, if I hadn't walked away.

"If I hadn't got out, one of us would have been dead by now." I told her about the suicide attempt Nikki had pulled when I was in Germany, that we could have lost the girls because of her selfish actions. About when she slapped me at Adam's funeral because I didn't want to leave early, because she barely knew him. He was my friend, I wanted to stay and celebrate his life.

"I couldn't spend my life trying to explain to the girls that Mummy was dead, that she'd done it to herself, I'd let it happen or whatever, you know?"

I looked out the window, my mind repeating the words 'One of us had to go, and I am not ready to die yet, not for her.'

The road outside twisted and turned, as we passed through more and more sharp bends on the descent down towards Tiberias. Kelly half smiled and then turned away, her words stuck at the back of her mouth. She had wanted to say something but thought better of it.

We dismounted the bus at a place called Mount Arbel, a few miles outside of Tiberias. We had no idea of where we were or what we were going to be doing.

Our chief tour guide for the day was Yitzhak, one of the foremen from the boot factory. He told us to get in pairs.

"Stick to the path and be careful, it get's narrow and steep."

I teamed up with Kenny, a Danish volunteer who arrived the day after me. He spoke English like a true viking, with lots of grunts and growls, a rippling top lip and a fist of iron. Kenny was small but powerfully built, a 'metalhead' who despised all things 'Pop', we were a perfect match, and from our first meeting, we did nothing but compete with each other, it was like living with Animal's Danish cousin. The mighty Brit and the Viking Warrior, we were big kids, boys being boys.

The path was indeed, steep and narrow, all the more so the further we went. A long line of multi-national volunteers clumsily lumbering along the mountainside. We stopped at a rockface where once again, Yitzhak warned us to be careful.

"There are some handles" he said, "and ropes, hang on properly, we don't to lose anyone."

"Not even Kenny?" I called. Kenny slapped my chest.

"Motherfucker!"

"Not even Kenny" smiled Yitzhak.

I felt a touch nauseous at the thought of all this mountaineering lark, I hadn't signed up for this. I thought it was going to be all churches and statues, a plate of fish and chips at the seaside maybe, but mountains? Who's idea was this?

Foot holes had been cut in the rock at regular spaces, handles and ropes set into the cliff to give us something to hold onto. Maria, with her arm still in bandage, struggled more than the rest of us. Michael, Kenny and I helped her when we had to and without losing anybody to the mountain, we soon stood victorious at the top. I admit, Mount Arbel is not the tallest mountain I've ever seen, but it was tall enough, our view was breathtaking. Below us lay the Sea of Galilee, a beautiful blue lake spreading out before us. We could see Tiberias too, and in the distance, on the opposite shore, Syria. There is another name for the Galilee, the Kinneret, some people even call it Lake Tiberias. I prefer to call it by the name I had been taught as a child, The Sea Of Galilee. Lake is too small a word for somewhere of such biblical importance, this is where Jesus walked on water, he walked on it. Not a fucking lake or paddling pool, he walked on the SEA. It was special, and deserved a bit of recognition, I mean, let's face it, anyone can walk on a lake, right? it's a big puddle, no problem, but the sea, that's a different kettle of fish, that's like proper legend making stuff. And talking of fish, it was here that he fed the 5,000. This was exciting stuff, somewhere near here must be a really old fish and chip shop, and I was just about starving.

The mountains we could see beyond the water, ran northwards, through Lebanon and into southern Turkey. To the south, they continued deep into Africa, where they form part of the Great Rift Valley. To our left, was an almost identical cliff to that we had just climbed, pockmarked with caves.

"These caves," Yitzhak explained, "were the homes of the early natives of Israel, they were Zealots and earned their living from the valley below. The valley was part of the great silk route, the road to Damascus. A toll would be levied on the travellers and traders passing through here, anyone not wishing to pay would be attacked and stoned from up here, few would escape alive, unless they paid the toll."

Beneath where we stood, was another network of caves. Having taken all the photo's we could ever want of the view from the top, we walked down to check out what we found to be an entire little citadel, cut into the rock. Some of the chambers were interlinked, and there was evidence of ovens, baths and crude water channels for toilets and showers. They may have been primitive, and lived rough compared to modern people, but these Zealots had been great engineers, everything was catered for here, storage, medication, schooling. It had all been done in these very caves, thousands of years earlier. How it must have looked in it's time we could only guess at, but these were undoubtedly people's homes, this was real history, not cathedrals and statues, stained glass windows and empty fields, this is where people washed, bathed, ate and cooked. It was where they slept, had families and lives, this was where they lived, and it was beautiful. The scenery was spectacular, all that was wrong was our presence, we didn't belong here. These caves belonged to an age, and a people, so far removed from ourselves. There was no instant, hi-tech gratification in their world, no telephone, no television, they didn't even have Taco Bell.

I wanted to travel back to their time, to experience their lives for even just a short time. Just to be free of the bonds of modern life, free to forage, to fight, to starve. Free to die of septicaemia, dysentery, smallpox or gangrene. Where I could be stoned to death, shot with an arrow or bludgeoned with a club. I wanted to travel back and see what beauty there was in a world without plastic and neon. A world without electricity. This was a city carved in the stone, it's memories transposed in the rocks themselves. Could I live here forever, be part of this. In thousands of years from now, would people stare in awe at my antiquated credit cards, my shattered old television set, would they know even, what it was? Would they know who I was, what life I'd lived, would they have read my book? Probably not. (Kindle, maybe....)

It's funny how we look back at antiquity and burden it with modern values. Equally so, how we look back at ourselves and see only that which pleases us. We forget the bad days, and especially our own sins. We filter out the uncomfortable truths and leave false accounts of the memories we make.

Taking our lives in our hands, Kenny and I raced down the track that wound it's way across the front of the mountain, down the steep incline, faster and faster. The faster we went, the more gravity pulled us and momentum built to the point of imbalance, where either of us could stumble and fall because our top halves were travelling faster than our legs could move. One wrong turn or twist, one wrong foot and it would have been game over. I bounced from one footstep to the next, like a hill runner, or a goat bounding gleefully along a cliff edge, totally unnerved- except I was shitting myself. Adrenaline was pumping through me, I felt charged and invincible, I was breathless other than the great whoops of excitement I was screaming out. This is life, this is what it is all about, freedom and simplicity. I fell in love with Mount Arbel, and I hoped she loved me too.

By the time I reached the bottom of the hill I was spent. Kenny, the viking, had already plundered the coach, disembowelled the driver and had sex with 3 goats and cross-dresser from Wolverhampton. Even more incredulous, was that Craig and Dave, the Essex boys, had beaten him down.

"Nice one geezer" said Craig, "-but you'll have to do better if you want to beat our record at Masada." I fell to my knees, panting.

"What's Masada?" I asked.

"It's a town on top of a mountain, down in the Negev Desert. It overlooks the Dead Sea, a bit like this, only bigger, better. You'll see it on the Eilat trip, you'll love it. There was a film made about it. Thousands of people committed suicide there after 10 years of siege by the Roman Army. Me and Dave, we ran up the snake pass, in 32 minutes, that's the record."

The Snake Pass is a long winding pathway that leads to the ruins of Masada. The challenge had been made, it was up to Kenny and myself to take it up and accept. We had no idea what we were letting ourselves in for, but it seemed like a plan at the time. We knew Dave and Craig would be long gone before we went to Masada, so we promised to write to them in England, to let them know we'd beaten their record.

In true Dafna tradition, the old ways and knowledge were being passed down to the newcomers, it would be up to us now to teach the next generation of volunteers.

Our next stop was the 'Kenneret', The Sea Of Galilee. A huge wooden table with benches either side and shaded from the midday sun by an even bigger gazebo with trailing vines, had been reserved for our use. Cool boxes and insulated food bags were unloaded from the coach's luggage compartment and emptied out along the table. Sandwiches, hot and cold meats, vegetables and gallons of the ever present purple syrup drink, were shared out and hungrily consumed before we were marched off to the beach.

There were no 'Jesus fished here' signs, no roller coasters or banks of ATM's to feed the slot machines and video games I'd expected to see here. Only row upon row of perfectly bronzed Israeli bodies, bathing in the sunshine, enjoying their Shabbat, (Sabbath) and tons of litter abandoned, strewn along the water's edge. If Jesus had been here today he'd have been giving out bin liners, not fish and bread.

The cold clean water we bathed in at Dafna, was now warm and polluted. Sun kissed after centuries of lying in the cold, dark rocks beneath Mount Hermon. We played and swam in the warm water, until Rebecca challenged us all to swim out to a bouy, about 500 yards away from the beach. Steve, Stuart, Rebecca, Baz, John and myself were the first to head off. Of the 20 or so volunteers who'd set out, only 5 or 6 of us made it, the rest had turned around and gone back. Breathless and tired, I kicked water for a few minutes before heading back to the shore, my legs cramping and my body drained by the time I returned.

"Who wants to ride the Banana?" Asked Yitzhak. Was this a trick question, 'ride the banana?' What the man did in his spare time was up to him, but it seemed a bit odd to be putting it out there in public like this, I mean, really, we're British, we don't do that sort of thing.

It turned out that the Banana was an inflatable raft dragged along by a tow rope behind a speedboat. I'd never done this before and so was definitely up for it, once I knew what it was, that is. We were also given rides on the 'Donuts', large rubber rings with grab handles, enough for up to four of us at a time, to be dragged across the surface of the water, it was like flying but much wetter. Again, I'd never tried this before but once I had my first go, I wanted more, this was way too much fun not to make the most of. The rings bounced at high speed across the surface of the water, carrying us as they went. We had to hold on tight or be thrown into the air only to hit the water with a jolt. The sensation of travelling low, at high speed across the water was incredible, it was like flying through the air as a bouncing would, dipping into the water's skin before ricocheting once more into the air, fast and furious until that final slip and the ultimate explosion. Each bounce of the 'donut' was like a hammer blow to the chest, as our hands gripped desperately to the handles and we flew through the air, screaming, whooping and swallowing mouthfuls of the water as we went. I could not think of a greater thrill in all my life, all those rites of passage, my first orgasm, fatherhood, my first gig, all the milestones that had led me to this place, nothing compared to the sheer thrill of a ride on a 'donut.'

Jesus himself may have frowned at the sheer selfish indulgence of it all, but by heck it was fun. Life was good, and it couldn't get much better than this.

In the days following our trip to Tiberias, Michael and Maria left to go to Egypt. Taking the well worn trail from Dafna to Dahab, a coastal town in the Sinai peninsula, it was a favourite destination for people on the backpacking trail. It was said, that in Dahab, you could buy a carrier bag full of cannabis for as little as £5 sterling, or £25 Egyptian. Although illegal, nobody in Dahab cared, and cannabis was smoked openly in the streets and on the beach. Attempting to smuggle it out of the country, however, that could get you a death sentence or life in prison.

Kelly left too. The night of the Tiberias trip she had a breakdown and was taken to the hospital in Safed, about an hour away from Dafna. A couple of weeks later, we received a postcard from her. She was in Fiji, resting before her last flight home to New Zealand. She hoped we would stay in touch and promised to make good on the beers she owed me.

Steve also left. He'd been dating Rebecca but received a phone call from a girlfriend in England. She was pregnant, and he left Dafna, and Rebecca, the very next day. Rebecca sought refuge with Baz, who'd been running the Vol bar with Rob, sharing the profits and drinking the rest. They'd have made more money if they'd actually opened it more often, but they couldn't be bothered. Without notice, they sold the running of the bar to Louie who immediately began to run it like a proper business. This didn't go down too well with the majority of volunteers, but it was our only bar, and if we wanted to use it, we had to pay Louie's inflated prices.

Andy, Phil and myself were summoned to Benny's office. Benny was Shlomo's boss, he had ultimate power over the volunteers and the running of the Kibbutz. He was head honcho, a big strapping guy who liked to hunt out in the fields at night. Bouncing around on a land rover and firing his shot gun at wild boar was his favourite past time. He was a square jawed alpha male who commanded respect with just his presence. You didn't want to argue with Benny, not if you were sensible.

"The telephone is gone from outside your room." Benny wanted a confession. Shlomo wanted us all removed from Dafna immediately, no messing around, no notice, no taxi, no deposit, gone. We told him we knew nothing about the missing telephone, which we didn't, did we? Our plea fell on deaf ears but a compromise was reached.

"Return the telephone, and I will let you stay. You have 24 hours." And with that we were dismissed from his office.

"This is pesh man!" Said Andy. "I canny remember what happened to the phone, I was steamin' fer christ's sake, I did'ny know what I was doing."

"I know mate, but Shlomo wants our blood and there's no way out of this one." I told him.

"But I didn't do anything" said Phil, his eyes watering with the injustice of the situation. "It's so unfair, I didn't do anything, they can't throw me off like this!"

"They can, and they will," I said, "if we can't talk our way out of this, we're all going. Now what do you remember? I want the truth, if we can return the phone, we at least have a chance."

"Jeez man! I just dunno. I was ratted on that tequila shite, man it was rough, but I remember something flying- it went right over there, over the top of the Vol bar somewhere." Andy was beginning to remember what he'd tried so hard to forget. "Shit man, what'll I do? It was me, I did it, I pulled the phone off the wall and launched it over there. I was pissed off with it ringing all night." The realisation of his guilt began to hit him, he knew he'd be kicked off Dafna for this.

"Look, I know Louie gets on with Benny, and I have been getting on with Louie. I might be able able to strike a deal if we can find the phone, after all, that's the most important thing in their eyes right now."

The telephone was still where it had landed, where Andy had thrown it a few days earlier, in a flowerbed beyond the Vol bar. Louie took the the phone to Benny, with strict instructions, no names.

"Remember mate, no names, we found it, the guilty party is deeply remorseful and it will never happen again, but you have to fight our corner, nobody wants to go home, okay?"

Louie had agreed to act as a go-between but refused to make any promises. I had agreed to help him run the Vol bar if he helped us out, it was enough to get him on side and so when he went to see Benny, I waited in the bar, cleaning up from the night before, chain smoking and feeling more than just a little bit anxious as the heavy steel door slammed and Louie returned.

"I'm sorry mate," Louie looked at me sheepishly, "you and Phil can stay, But Andy has to go, tomorrow."

"I said no names Louie, what did you tell him?"

"Nothing mate, just like I said, I mentioned no names, but they already knew, and they reckon nobody in the factory likes him, which is the real reason behind it, they don't like him. Taking the phone of the wall was just one step too far."

Benny had known who did it, he just wanted the phone back and to be able to tell the Kibbutz council that someone had been sent packing. Now it was up to me to tell Andy, but he knew what was coming and had decided to leave, he was going to Dahab, with Rob and Rebecca.

I felt sorry Andy had to go, I had wanted to stand by him but it was a lost cause, after all, he'd done it and he had to go, even though we were pretty good friends now, and in the coming weeks he wrote a few letters back to us, from Tel Aviv, Dahab and Eilat. 'You have to come down here, there's plenty of work and money' he wrote. It was tempting, but I wasn't ready to leave Dafna yet, whatever cure I was hoping to find, had not yet appeared. I was still afraid of the outside world.

I am back once again in that sandy brown building of my youthful dreams, listening to the drip, drip, drip of the taps. Three cubicle doors face me, but only one draws my attention. The door to the right begins to bow and strain, the laminated coating splits and fear grips me again, once more I am in it's icy grip. Again the chase, running as fast as I can, I am scared, scared stiff of something that I don't know, some fear of something that is after me. I am hunted and losing ground. I leap over a grassy mound and stumble, roll on the floor and then it hits me. My eyes open and I wonder if I am dead yet. Above me is a clear blue sky. Sweat clings to me as I turn in my sleeping bag. The log fire has long since gone out, it's morning, and I am laying on the grass behind Jack's room.

"You!" David, the boot factory foreman, points at me. "Here." I am gestured to the end of the production line, my job today, is wrapping and packing the finished boots. I am working with Carmel and her sister, they were from the Transvaal, South Africa. I could barely talk to them because we were right by the speaker of the factory's radio. All day long it played British and American music, Israeli DJ's butting in between songs of the bands of the day, Oasis, Blur, Pulp and others. Every time I heard 'Common People' I thought of Rebecca and my own Nikki, both of whom were out of place, chasing the rough when they could have had much easier lives.

I danced and sang along to the music, after all, it was just a laugh, we weren't here to take anything seriously, were we? The factory may have held us captive, but it would never break our spirits, not mine anyway.

At break time I took my coffee and biscuits outside and sat on the grass. Jack and Stuart were talking about a Syrian woman who worked on the production line. Her name was Jaffa and she wore the tightest fitting clothes she could squeeze into, despite the heat. Her make up was always perfect, even though there would be enough to decorate a 3 bed apartment in Walthamstow. She was certainly pretty, and she knew it, but she was also untouchable. There was a coldness about her and she was not to be messed with.

"Are you missing your girls?" Anne looked straight into my eyes as she said it.

"Yes, this business with Andy and the phone kinda knocked me off track a bit."

"How old are they again?" She asked as she sipped her purple drink.

"5 and 6, Sian is the eldest, Christina's the cheeky one, you know, always pushing that little bit more. They're beautiful and I love them dearly."
"It must be hard for you to be away from them for so long, don't you want to go back?" *Bang, right between the eyes.*
"It's not so hard being here, this is easy really. I got used to being away when I was driving around Eastern Europe. You get into a mindset with it, y'know, you have a job to do and you have to do it, you're away until you can get home. Being here is a distraction from everything, what hurts is knowing I had to leave to make things better, I will always be seen as having walked away when the truth is I'd tried the best I could to make it work, I can't win, I will never win. If I'd stayed, one of us would have been dead, I'm certain of that, and I couldn't look into their eye's and say Mummy is gone. Anyway, they're used to me being away, and one day, if I live long enough, I'll get to see them again, but I tried, heaven knows I tried to make it work."
I looked over at the other Volunteers, sitting and chatting idly, not a care in the world. Some were on extended holidays or gap years, wasting time before diving back into the cesspool of modern society. A society that see's every mistake but never the good things you do. I'd made mistakes and was paying a heavy price, everyday. Everyday the nightmares, the longing, the anger and the suppression of it. The guilt was meant to wash away with the vodka, it was meant to cleanse my soul like it cleaned the rubber boots in the factory, but it didn't. It didn't clean me. It kept me company, night after night as I looked up at the stars, the myriad of clean bright lights in the night sky. How I wished I could smell my children next to me, to feel their hands in mine, to hear their voices. All I had were tears, bottled tears for sleepless nights under the stars.
"They're very lucky," Anne was looking straight at me still. "To have a father like you. Most men would have stayed and prolonged the agony, spent their lives being horrible bastards, but not you."
For a moment we paused. She had seen right inside my heart, right into my soul, damn, she read me and knew me better than I knew myself, she could see the pain I was hiding, she could see something. Maybe she saw something of her own upbringing in reverse, maybe she was the child in a loveless marriage, a victim of parental abuse or was an unloved child. Maybe, maybe not. She never said, and I will never know. It was time to get back to work.
"Thank you" I said, holding back the urge to squeeze her and burst into tears, this was not the place, nor the time to breakdown.
Back at the line, I felt radiated, something in me had been rekindled. I danced and sang with renewed vigour, much to the irritation of some of the Kibbutzniks. I was sweating like the proverbial pig, the beads running down my face and dripping off my chin, nose and eyebrows. I worked like a man possessed, pairing, wrapping and boxing everything that came at me but still able to pick out the odd pairs and return them to Jaffa, with a smile. Her stern cold face hardly acknowledging my presence.

Craig caught me in the dinner line at lunchtime.

"Benny wants to see you when you've got a minute."

"What, not again, what have I done now?" I threw my arms out.

"Nothing mate, he wants to take you out hunting with him, he's going to hunt wild Boar tomorrow night and you're invited."

"Wild Boar, me?"

"Yes, but don't fall off the land rover, he shoots at anything that moves."

Benny was meant to pick me up at 8 pm but was late. I jumped aboard the Land Rover and took my place in the back, standing with 2 Israeli guys clinging on for dear life. There was just enough room for the 3 of us to stand across the back of the cab, we seemed to hit every pot hole, ridge and bump on the road and tracks we took. I had no idea where we were or where we were going, only that if I slipped or let go, I would be flung into the air like a half cooked pancake. Benny was laughing at us, and we were laughing too, I hadn't had so much fun since I threw up my lunch getting off the roller-coaster at the amusement park in Margate.

"Okay!" Said Benny once we stopped. "This is what I want you to do. I want you to scan the field with this lamp. When I say 'ON' try to pick out the Boar, they will freeze and I will shoot them."

"How will you know it's a Boar ?" I asked.

"Because their eye's reflect the light in the dark, it is pink, not white like humans." Benny seemed to know what he was looking for, but I doubt he'd have cared if he shot a human by mistake, so long as he shot something, he would be happy.

We drove around slowly, me manning the big lamp, Benny with the shotgun ready to burst my ear drums. The other guys just seemed to be along for the ride. We turned a corner and Benny yelped, I switched the light on and half a field of corn lit up in front of us. Two little pink dots reflected back and there was a bang from the rifle beside me, almost immediately another shot rang out and all I heard was a dull buzz. Benny reloaded, his shots had missed but the temptation and the smell of the kill was enough to warrant 2 more shots into the corn rows. We replayed this scenario half a dozen times, at one point Benny jumped off the vehicle and ran into the dark pulling a sheath knife from his belt, he was ready for the fight but too far behind to catch whatever he'd seen. We returned to Dafna a couple of hours later, empty handed but with a trail of dead corn in our wake.

"Hey, we will do this again soon," Benny said, "Shalom."

"Ken, (yes) Shalom." I replied, waving back to him.

I walked past my room and over to the Volunteer's kitchen. There was no food to be had, only coffee, which I took up onto the roof of the building. The stars shone brightly in the clear sky above as I lay on the coarse concrete, sipping at my coffee. I looked up and wondered if Sian and Christina were looking at the stars too. Could they see them from their bedroom window, would they even be looking, wondering about me as I thought about them? I doubted it, it was late back home and they would be sleeping, the whole world was sleeping, except me.

My journey to Dafna was a long one, and I wasn't alone in that respect. There were many tortured souls, runaways and basket cases on the kibbutz. There were holiday makers too, people in search of something different than 2 weeks in Ibiza, and surprisingly few Jewish Volunteers. Religion was unimportant to the Kibbutz Representatives. As a Gnostic, I fell in well with most other peoples' faith, that is to say, that I was open to debate but felt there were enough real demons on Earth as it is, without creating any more. Since I couldn't prove the existence, or non-existence of Demons and Gods, I was quite happy to sit on the fence. There were no bibles at Dafna, no prayer meetings or structured worship, crosses or candles. I saw no Rabbi, no Synagogue. Here in the holiest of lands, religion was being ignored. I lay on the roof of the Volunteer's kitchen, staring up at the stars, alone with my thoughts. The stars looked down, and it was quiet.

Living at Dafna was like being resident in a bus station. People were constantly coming and going, on their way to somewhere else, or they'd just arrived and were already weary. Everyone is on a journey of some description, everyone is a little bit lost and confused. Since my arrival, I had been in a state of constant fatigue, unable to sleep because of the turmoil in my head. Even the cheap alcohol did little to help, I was drowning in my own thirst, unable to quench the sadness within. I spent many nights alone, on the roof, watching the stars and hearing the comings and goings below. The voices that didn't know I could hear. I lay on the roof alone, always alone.

In the weeks that followed Andy's departure, I tried my utmost to stop drinking. I avoided the bar as often as I could, spending my time on the water tower to watch the sunsets and the constant military activities over the border. The boot factory was my greatest distraction, that and my constant need to put pen to paper. I was writing songs and poems at every opportunity. Words would just come into my head and I had to write them down. So much of it was shit, just constant words and half meanings, waffle and dross, but in amongst the crap were some good ideas, good songs, lyrics and prose. Afternoons were spent by the pool or the river, sometimes playing football, despite the heat. Volunteers came and went on an almost daily basis.

Anne-Marie was part Canadian and Indian. She introduced herself to me when she arrived, we were outside Shlomo's office when I saw her. I asked her what tribe she was from and immediately regretted it.

"No, not that Indian. My father is from India" She smiled. As a native of Quebec, her first language was French, and so we were able sometimes to speak together in her native tongue, my second language. When Anne-Marie had settled, I invited her to visit Castle Nimrod, a fortress ruin between Dafna and Mount Hermon. We sat upon the upturned rocks of Nimrod and chatted for hours, the wind about us was warm and gentle. We both behaved impeccably, I was a gentleman and she was a Lady, both enjoying the company of the other amidst the beauty of our surroundings. As the evening drew in, we returned to Dafna and agreed to go to a music festival together at Jaffa. It wasn't a date, we were not intimate, but we had connected in some way, like good friends meeting for the first time.

Anne-Marie moved in with Ruth and Sheila, They'd only just arrived a day or two earlier. Ruth was English, she was head girl at the school she'd been to and still carried some of that authority around with her. She was a lovely girl, but still, very much a student. Sheila was Scottish and very grounded, even if a little innocent to the outside world. Kenny had invited Sheila to the festival at Jaffa, so it made sense that we all travelled together. Kenny was smitten with Anne-Marie, Anne-Marie had her eye on Jack and Jack's eyes were pretty much all over the place. Me, I was doing my best to stay celibate and not get caught up in a relationship.

Once we finished work on Friday, we set off for Jaffa, an ancient town on the coast, north of Haifa. We struggled to get lifts, the event was popular and most vehicles heading that way were already full. By the time we reached Jaffa it was late and we headed for the beach, we had missed the festival but weren't bothered, it was fun just getting out and about. Sitting on the beach we could see the lights of the old town a short distance away, the sound of Arabian music drifted over to us between the waves, the coffee shops were rocking as we sat with our cheap vodka and cheap Israeli cigarettes.

Sheila delved into her bag and produced a packet of Marlboro, gold dust to our eyes. Kenny was there in a flash.

"Marlboro! I must have one, my lungs are dying from these cheap Israeli shit sticks."

"Your lungs are dying alright mate, from all that shit heavy metal crap you keep listening to!"

"Goddamn motherfucker!" He yelled, diving on top of me. We rolled around in the sand, wrestling like little cousins on a hot summer day. Eventually I gave in and the little Dane sat astride my chest with his arms raised flexing his muscles.

"Viking Power!" He yelled into the night. Despite his small size, Kenny was always willing to bust his gut in order to prove his might, he was a true Viking, unafraid and dauntless. "Goddamn English pussies, where's my vodka?"

"Would you like some of mine?" Anne-Marie produced a bottle of Smirnoff from her bag.

"You can't give him that, he'll go crazy and want to rape and pillage, he'll set your sleeping bag alight and everything, you mark my words"

"English Mother...." I dived on top of Kenny and we rolled around in the sand a little longer.

"Don't you two ever stop?" Asked Sheila.

"I am invincible" proclaimed Kenny, standing above me.

"Oh fuck it!" I replied, "let's have a drink-to the great god of Iron Maiden."

It wasn't long before the girls were asleep, Kenny was semi-comatose and I was finishing off a cigarette, listening to the waves crashing on the beach. Suddenly there was a noise behind me, I looked round and saw a man approaching.

"Erevtov" *(good evening)*, he announced.

"Erevtov" I replied.

"What are you doing here?" He asked, crouching down on the sand.

"We're just taking it easy, we were heading for the music festival but didn't get there. Thought we'd stop here for a bit."

Our conversation had woken the girls, they seemed a little uneasy, Kenny shuffled in his sleeping bag, half awake, half viking.

"May I?" The stranger picked picked a Noblesse from my packet of cigarettes. "Do you have a light?" His English was very good, I couldn't tell if he was Israeli or Arab, his curly black hair too long to be a policeman or a soldier.

"Sometimes, you know, it can be dangerous, with women on the beach, you have to be very careful, you know?"

The only danger I'd felt all evening was this man's presence, until he crept up on us we felt very safe and comfortable. My hand was already on the handle of the knife I'd hidden in my sleeping bag, I'd borrowed it from the kitchen, in case it were to come in handy, for a time like this, maybe. I looked him straight in the eyes, friendly, but unafraid.

"Isn't it a little late to be walking alone on the beach, that too could be dangerous, especially in the dark here." I had invited him to leave, his next move would determine whether he meant us harm or was genuinely interested in who we were.

"Yes my friend, it is time I went home." Our gazes met in the darkness, there was a short pause and then he stood up. "Shalom my friend, and Todaraba." He thanked me for the cigarette and faded back into the darkness, the red tip slowly disappeared into the distance. Just one more sleepless night, waiting for the sun to rise.

8 WE GOTTA GET OUTTA THIS PLACE

"Endless conversations repeating lives we lived, heads bowed lowly, furrowed brows, the loves we cannot give.
Campfire, lonely campfire, you've heard it all before, crackling embers crying out, tears falling to the floor.
I've seen the silhouettes at night dark clouds that cross the moon,
I heard the tears and fears, the pains of your self doubt, then swore with every passing breath at lovers walking out.
Still, I am just the campfire, my tears you never see, I am the burning light at night, the answer that you seek.
Campfire, lonely campfire, I've heard it all before, crackling embers crying out, tears falling to the floor.

It was official, Louie was dating Ruth, the Capitalist Kiwi and the Head Girl were an item. Ruth stopped me on the way to the kitchen.
"What d'you think?" She asked.
"I don't know, he seems okay but what matters is not what I or anyone else thinks, it's your relationship, you and Louie's, not anyone else's business who either of you are dating."
"Well the thing is," She said, "Louie and I want to go away next weekend, we were wondering if you and John would look after the bar for us."
The Volunteer's bar, me and John, was she on drugs or something?
"Of course, yes, no problem, me and John will do it for you, gives you two a break and we get a free drink or two out of it too."
"We'll pay you!"
"Even better," I said, "I'll look forward to it."
What could possibly go wrong?
 I was already helping Louie with the running of the bar, so preparing for the weekend was just a continuation of the status quo, work, buy supplies, deliver

to Vol Bar, work, clean Vol Bar after previous night, work, open Vol Bar. There was a slight difference now in that John and I were going to have a bloody good weekend. Louie had been bragging about the amount of money he'd been making from the bar, from us, the volunteers. It struck me that this opportunistic capitalism didn't fit well with either the Kibbutz ethic, nor the fact that we were all poor folk with limited funds, except Jack, Jack could afford chips and cigars, I'm sure he was getting government money from somewhere, his accent was a giveaway.

Craig and Dave were due to leave the day after our weekend at the bar, so we organised a little going away party. Louie had given us strict instructions on how much to charge for drinks, he was buying a bottle of Vodka for 5 NIS (New Israeli Shekels) and charging 1 NIS per shot, averaging about 20 shots per bottle. In the few weeks since he took over the bar, Louie had already put the prices up and made enough money to buy himself a car. He must have been the only Volunteer in the whole of Israel to have a car, and that was a piss take, seriously. I wasn't jealous, I just felt it was against the whole spirit of the Kibbutz experience, so given the opportunity to do something about it, John and I made sure that nobody got ripped off that weekend. Shots were still 1 NIS but we were pouring only 5 or 6 per bottle. Everybody, including the soldiers who came down to the bar, having heard what was happening, got absolutely rat arsed. The money kept coming in, the drink flowed, I was Tom Cruise, John was Brian Brown, this was Cocktail in a bomb shelter in Israel, only we broke more bottles. We sang and danced, behind and on the bar. The drinks kept flowing, the money kept coming in, the shots got bigger. The Damned, Pogues and Rolling Stones squeaked loudly from our cassette player (for cassette player description, see Antiques, or ask your parents...)

Craig and Dave arrived and were promptly taped back to back on a couple of chairs in the middle of the floor. Beer, Vodka and Tequila were poured with total abandon, nobody ever died from too much drink, did they? Their clothes were adorned with messages, bold scrawling words written in permanent marker pen. A make-up kit appeared and both men were made up before being finally released. Dave and Eve kissed, someone threw up and by the time everyone left, the bar was dry. It had been a total success. We locked up and headed back up the steep steps to see the sun coming up. Dafna was asleep, the world was asleep, everyone it seemed, was asleep except me.

I walked round to where our campfire burned and rekindled it's flames. I sat for a while and then decided to have a walk.

Next to the bus stop, by the little roundabout outside Benny's office, was a bike shed. I hadn't ridden a bike since having done my HGV licence a few years earlier. Despite it not being allowed for volunteers to use them, I took one of the bikes and headed off around the kibbutz perimeter fence. I passed the factory, the maintenance sheds and the back gate. Past the kibbutznik's houses, the pool, the creche, and back around to 'Death Row', the name given to our row of little homes. I carried on down to the gatehouse. The Israeli guards looked bemused as I passed them, peddling furiously and singing 'Keep on rocking in the free world!' as I went. I completed another lap and one more for the hell of it. I put the bike up on the roof of Benny's office, certain I would be thrown off the kibbutz for such an act of sedition. As I walked back to my room, I gathered up all the dirty washing that had been put outside the rooms for collection by laundry staff and built one big pile outside the door to Shlomo's office, before settling down by the fire and catching a short sleep before breakfast.

We'd made arrangements to visit Banias, a nature reserve that is home to the largest waterfall in Israel, and happened to be just a few miles east of Dafna. Karen led the way and the rest of us followed, some trying to hitch lifts, the rest of us deciding to just walk anyway, and by the time the walkers got there, the hitchers had only just arrived. We split into 2 groups and sneaked in through the exit gate at the rear of the park, Jack had been before so I followed his group, attempting to look like regular tourists but walking the wrong way around the site. It wasn't long before we were spotted by a park ranger who escorted us back out of the park and told us to use the front gate, which meant paying 10 NIS each to get in, I told him I doubted there was that much money in the whole world, but he didn't get the joke. Instead, he smiled and firmly locked the gate behind us.

We were 13 in number and believe me, 13 is a very lucky number. We decided to walk back to Dafna, but instead of going the long way round following the road, some bright spark came up with the idea of going across the fields and taking the straight line back, thus cutting off about a mile. Seemed like a good idea, Jack took pole position and we followed.

"Goddamn motherfucker piece of shit!" cursed Kenny. Jack was now seeing Anne-Marie and Kenny wasn't very happy about losing his girl.

"Don't let it get to you mate, getting all fired up and Viking-like isn't going to help anything, it won't win her back."

"But that little cock sucker....Look at him, he's all over her and she should be with me. I'm gonna teach that son of a bitch a goddamn motherfucking lesson." Kenny's Heavy Metal lessons in the use and execution of the English language usually served him well, but on this occasion, I thought some tact and diplomacy may have been preferable. Slugging it out with with Jack over the affections of Anne-Marie was not going to get her back, not that he ever had her in the first place. Kenny was stubborn and the friction continued, despite my pleading with him.

We found ourselves up against a metal chain fence surrounding a field.

"We'll have to go around it," Jack said, "the girls aren't going to want to climb over this."

"Hey Jack! There's a gate here behind these bushes." Stuart and his new American girlfriend Tree, had found a way in. Stuart went first, then Tree and the rest of us followed. The field went on for several hundreds of meters, it was overgrown but there was no discernible crop to be seen, just long grass and scrub.

"I'm gonna beat his little ass to a pulp!"

"No Kenny, let it go, you're sounding a little repetitive and boring now mate."

"I swear, I'm gonna..."

"Do nothing mate, leave it. You're starting in the dairy tomorrow, just think of all the fun you can have with the cows when nobody's looking, you'll even get to wear your own pair of wellies" I laughed, but Kenny was still seething. Jack had a charm about him, he could have had any of the girls he wanted, he was suave, he was good looking, he was Welsh, and if he wants any more compliments it's gonna cost him more than a couple of pints and a bag of pork scratching's, I'm talking big money now boyo!

Soon enough, we'd reached the other side of the field but there was no gate, no way out. We had to climb over. Karen and Katie were first over the top, then Stuart and the rest of us, all clambering over the wobbly wired fence.

"Hey guys, I think you'd better look at this." Katie had found an old rusty sign on the outside of the fence. It was a metal plaque, painted yellow and had a message on it in 3 languages, Arabic, Hebrew and English.

'Danger....Minefield.....Do Not Enter......'

"Mother fucker.....!"

Louie was waiting for me in the Vol bar. The place was still a mess from the previous night.

"Streuth matey! Looks like a Katyusha came down the stairway."

"Sorry mate, I was gonna clean it up this morning, but we kind of got sidetracked, we've just been to Banias, couldn't get in though, so we came back through a minefield."

"A fucking minefield?"

"A real fucking minefield mate, didn't know until we got across it, mind. It was a bit of an eye opener. How was your break?"

"Me and Ruthie stayed in a Hotel in Haifa, it was cool, you know, really cool."

"Good, glad you enjoyed it mate. I've got your money here. I paid John and took my 10 sheks, so that's all yours."

Louie looked at the handful of notes and coins on the upturned oil drum that we used as a table, his face contorted a little.

"Where's the rest of it mate? I mean, the pub's dry and that's less than I take on a week night."

"Mate, those shots you measure, that's taking the piss, honestly, we didn't come here to be make money and we certainly don't deserve to be ripped off mate. We're all volunteers, all on limited budgets."

"But this is my living, this is all I've got, it's got to last me forever."

"And the same for me mate, and everyone else. Look, you wanted a break, we wanted a good night, you made a profit and everyone's happy, just don't be greedy with it."

Louie was furious, but there was nothing he could do. He knew I was right, but he had hoped I'd play his game and make him lot's of money while he went off with his girlfriend. He was still up on his investment, just not as much as he'd hoped for. I left him with the clean up, he didn't want me around anymore, so I got a bottle of punch from my room, it was left over from an earlier party, then went to see Kenny.

"Come on mate, we're off to Barhash."

Barhash was an open air night club, about halfway between Dafna and Qiryat Shmona. Volunteers and clubbers would come from as far away as Haifa and even Tel Aviv, to attend Barhash club nights. The music was 'banging', so they told me, it was 'proper good club sounds, you know, real house and electro with a bit of garage thrown in, yeah?' I was trying to imagine the sound of a house with a garage thrown into it, it probably would bang about a bit, at least until it settled down and the dust cleared. The club was hidden behind a wall of bamboo and sloped down to a small waterfall and river. From time to time, revellers would plunge into the water and be escorted off the premises by security. It wasn't the best place in town, just the only one.

We hadn't been seated long when a group of soldiers entered the bar. The music was switched off and an announcement made in Hebrew, some people gathered up their possessions and friends before leaving. We had no idea what was happening until Jack stepped up to one of the officers and asked what the fuss was. The officer took the DJ's microphone and made another announcement in English.

"We are about to be bombed, you must go home!" We headed outside, some managed to get lifts, the rest of us walked back to Dafna and were herded into the Vol bar, our underground air raid shelter. There was nothing to drink, the shop had not opened and so Louie had nothing to sell. I sneaked out and climbed the water tower, if I was to get hit, I wanted to see it coming. There were several explosions in the night, mostly towards Qiryat Shmona. The Jerusalem Post reported next day that a French Volunteer had been killed farther down the valley, he'd been hit by a rocket whilst walking back to his Kibbutz.

I started a new job, taking over from Craig who'd now gone home. I was to be working out in the fields with Haim, a kibbutznik who'd been born in Manchester. He spoke excellent English and so we were able to talk freely. Jim started at the same time as me, taking over from Craig's mate Dave. Jim and I started getting on well, and in time would become as close as I had with Kenny, who now was spending time with a new love interest, another Danish volunteer called Trina, Stina, Lina or Tina, they were all using the same name and it puzzled the hell out of me trying to remember who was which.

Jim and I got on well, we were both game for a laugh, hard working, hard playing guys who would do absolutely anything. Our first day at work in the fields consisted of walking along row after row of Sunflowers, checking for splits in the drip pipes that kept them watered. After breakfast, we walked through a field of onions, what for, I still don't know to this day, but the exercise was good. Eventually, Haim returned and took us to the river in the works van.

"We have to check the filters in the water inlet, make sure everything is clear, no dead animals, no branches, no bodies....." Anywhere else in the world and this would have sounded like a joke, here it had probably already happened.

At the back of the Kibbutz was a water pumping station. Fed by the river, water was pumped up into the water tower, when gravity then fed it down into the factory, kitchen and houses all over Dafna. From time to time, the filters could get blocked, so it was part of our job to get in the water and manually clear anything that was stuck.

"In you get" Haim pushed me from behind and I hit the water flapping like a goose on take off. The water was up to my chest but there was no current here, just a slow swirl feeding into the pumping station. Another splash and a shriek, just behind me, told me Jim had come to join in, Haim stood laughing on the bank. Once I'd hit the water, I felt a little sting on my legs and just above my ankles, I thought I must have some tiny scratches on my legs and the water has got into them. Nothing to worry about. Jim and I checked the filters, apart from some natural debris, leaves, twigs and a bit of moss, everything seemed fine. As it was almost lunchtime, this was our last job of the day, so we played about in the river, the cool water shielding us from the hot sun, it felt so good to be alive. The little scratches on my legs turned out to be Leeches. When we got out of the water, both of us were covered in blood, Haim was laughing his head off, he'd done this before which is why he'd pushed us in, he knew the little jelly like creatures were waiting for a feed.

Back in the canteen, Jim and I squelched over to our seats, our clothes still dripping. We'd taken our boots off and left them outside, it didn't seem right to be wearing muddy boots in the canteen, soggy clothes were probably not appreciated either, but nobody said anything. Most of the talk was about the previous night's bombing raids. Qiryat Shmona had been hit and some of the volunteers were not happy about being so close to the action.

"So have you guys heard? Karen's left." This was a bit of a surprise. She wasn't due to leave for another month. "Someone moved her washing the other night, and has been hanging around outside her room, she got scared and left this morning." The washing was a silly prank, a joke, nothing serious. I had no idea she was scared of anyone but had definitely not been hanging around outside her, or anybody's door. Word soon got round that I was the one that put the bike on the roof and piled the washing outside Shlomo's office, my summons to his office was swift and not too sweet. The little grey bureaucrat took great joy in tearing me apart, as did Ruth and Louie who just happened to be there in his office. Shlomo told me I had 24 hours to get out of Dafna.

"This is ridiculous!" I protested, "Yes I rode the bike and moved the washing, it was a joke, you know, a laugh. But I had nothing to do with scaring Karen away, I liked her, she was a lovely girl and I wouldn't do anything to scare her. If I do something, I put my hands up and yes, it's a fair cop innit? But you've got it so wrong about this, it's got nothing to do with me." With that, I left the room and went straight to see Benny. He wasn't in his office but I bumped into Haim and apologised that I'd no longer be working with him because of what had happened.

"Don't do anything, leave it with me. I will see you at work in the morning." Haim worked some magic and I was reinstated but barred from the Vol Bar, except for during air raid warnings. Everything was back to normal.

I was invited to go Boar hunting again. Benny sent a message to meet him same place and time as before. I waited and waited, Benny didn't show and I was left jilted at the altar. The following afternoon I was to get my own back. Benny was going hunting again that night, without me so I set up a few surprises for him. Stuart left a few sheets of cardboard behind the factory, along with a marker pen, some reflective stickers and a box cutter knife. I drew a life sized pig on each sheet of cardboard, cut out the shape and used the reflective stickers as eyes, they were perfect and would have looked like the real thing in the dark. I took my cardboard pigs out into the fields and set them up where I thought Benny would be most likely to see them.

"Tonight, I get the last laugh."

Volunteers were coming and going at a pretty fast rate. When our group arrived there was a total of 30 volunteers at Dafna. Most of these came from the UK, with a couple of South Africans, Danes and Kiwi's. We were soon joined by a Dutchman called Phil, who'd cycled all the way from Holland. Dom from Australia, Juan Carlos from Colombia and Pirri from Guatemala. There was a large group from Scandinavia too, Danes and Swedes all called Christine, which we adapted to Trina, Stina, Tina, Kristina and Lina, not forgetting my favourite, Jette, whom I took to calling my "Wife" just for the fun of it. She was a good laugh, and we got on well together, nothing romantic, just fun company. Our numbers were rising, and we soon topped the 50 mark, 50 plus volunteers being catered for on the same budget as when we were only 30. Ruth, our Volunteer leader, received a daily budget from Shlomo. The money was to buy food and drink for the volunteers for our evening meals which were taken in the volunteer's kitchen. I had helped Ruth previously, when she first started as Volunteer leader. I helped her with the shopping and knew how tight the budget was then, so when the numbers kept rising I knew she was struggling to feed everyone. Some volunteers would go to Hagoshrim or Qiryat Shmona, where they would treat themselves with falafel and fries, or kebabs, whatever they could afford. The poorest of us, would join the end of the queue and hope there would be enough food to feed us all. Bread, cheese, crackers, meat, salad, fruit and drinks were laid out on a table for us to help ourselves, leaving those behind with less choice and less food as the queue moved along, the last in the queue usually finding nothing left by the time they reached the table. After several hungry nights at the back of the queue, I began to forage at night. Instead of laying awake on top of the Volunteer's kitchen, I sneaked off out into the fields, returning later with a bin bag full of onions, sweetcorn, sunflower seeds and apples. I sneaked around the factory and knew where the biscuits were stored as well as the purple and red cordials we drank. I sneaked my bounty into the kitchen and shared it out amongst those that had no food. Had I been caught I would have been in for the high jump, but I felt I had to do something, Shlomo was obviously pocketing our allowance, refusing to give Ruth any more money and claiming she was just mishandling what she had, we knew he was on the make, but couldn't do anything about it. Eventually, a few years after we left, word got to me that Shlomo had been busted for keeping deposits and syphoning the volunteer's allowance, he was finally sent packing himself, oh how the mighty fall.

As time went by, I grew more impatient to leave Dafna but had no real plan of what to do next. I had no money, most of what I'd brought with me was gone on alcohol and cigarettes. Being barred from the Vol Bar meant that I could reduce my spending, but I still needed to survive and at Dafna, that meant drinking. One item we'd inherited from the previous volunteers was a large aluminium bowl, when I say large, it was large, it probably held about 30 gallons of liquid. It was 'borrowed' from the laundry in another time, handed down from generation to generation, and it's purpose was to be my saviour, it was our Punch bowl. Enterprising a chap as I am, I would collect a few shekels from each of the volunteers once a week. Every friday, I would pop into Qiryat Shmona and buy a whole load of fruit, fruit juice and other things I couldn't get from the kibbutz shop. I would buy dozens of bottles of vodka and tequila, the cheap stuff obviously, as well as plenty of red and white wine. The fruit would be sliced and skinned, mixed into the bowl with the tequila and vodka, left to soak before the wine was added to bulk it out. The bowl would be enough to get us all pissed for at least a weekend, with plenty to spare. Jim and I bottled up the spare and used that to get drunk on during the week, we weren't profiteering, just finishing off the leftovers. Everyone was happy, except Louie. He didn't like it when we all got together around the fire, drinking punch and having fun. He wanted us in the bar, buying his overpriced drinks, investing in his empire. Kiwi Karen had a guitar and would play and sing for us. Kenny would take over sometimes, bending our ears and shattering our teeth with his rendition of The Animal's 'House Of The Rising Sun.' The few occasions I wasn't drinking, I would find other things to do, play football, basketball, swimming, anything to keep myself occupied. I spent a lot of time up the water tower, writing letters, poetry and songs, anything that sprang to my mind.

Anne-Marie and I hitched up to Mount Hermon one weekend. We made it to the top, dressed in shorts and t-shirts we were poorly clothed for the drop in temperature up there. Snow lay on the ground, it was cold but the scenery was incredible. On one side, the beautiful lush green valleys of Israel. On the other side, the beautiful but barren desert lands of Syria, in the distance, Damascus lay like a dirty smudge on the horizon. I imagined a city of souhks and camels, of trucks passing through on their way to the Gulf. Drivers doing what I had, only going to the places I'd hoped one day to visit. As I looked down from the mountain top, a familiar voice came up from behind. It was Louie. He had driven up to the car park near the top, then come on foot the rest of the way. We were on neutral ground here, so there was no point being rude to the guy. Our disagreements had been over the running of the Vol Bar, nothing personal.

"How are you doing Louie?"

"I'm alright, thanks mate." He looked around at the scenery. "Wow, it's sure beautiful up here." We exchanged pleasantries for a while, enjoying the cold air on the mountain top.

"Say, do you guy's want a lift back? I've got my car here." We accepted his offer , it was already getting late and we were not dressed for the occasion. On the way back Louie and I buried the hatchet. I was allowed back in the Vol Bar if I wanted to go, it seemed that our Punch parties had taken a toll on his takings, most nights he sat alone in the Vol Bar, not happy that he had been busted for ripping off the volunteers, and Ruth was on the verge of a breakdown trying to get enough food for everyone with the limited resources she was being given. Their relationship was struggling and somehow I was his only hope. How or why, I had no idea. I had already spent the afternoon talking with Anne-Marie about Jack. There was no doubt that they both had strong feelings for each other, but it was also known that Jack had a roaming eye, he was a red blooded male who liked to look at women. He could spot an attractive woman a mile off and was a terrible flirt. Between Louie and Ruth, Jack and Anne-Marie, I was convinced that staying celibate was the best way to be right now, my head was full enough of regrets and woe, of guilt and anger. I just wanted a quiet life, to live long enough to make it home to see my girls, that was all I wanted, all I could plan for, but for the moment I was happy, I was no longer barred from the pub. Louie was still an ass though.

The water clicked. Drip after drip clicking into a stagnant pool. I circle around the basin, silent and slow. I can't hear my breath, my thoughts, just the constant slow clicking of the water from the tap. I am braver now, closer to the blue laminate doors than I had ever been, close enough to see one breathe, the swell going from the lock across to the hinges, bowing gently outwards before receding. My fingers are almost touching the door, almost there, ready to push it open and reveal what is behind it. ROARGH!

I jump up, disoriented and breathless in the daylight. My sleeping bag is damp and tacky, a reminder of the night on the beach at Jaffa, the salty Mediterranean air clinging to every fibre, never to feel dry again. I am outside by the fireplace, beside me lay a crumpled cigarette pack, breakfast.

"Something has to change" I thought to myself. I was a loose cannon, rolling and pitching around on an endless, empty sea. Nobody would touch me for fear I might explode, but all I really wanted was to be touched. To be held like I was still alive, I still mattered. I was desperate to feel that tenderness of trust between one person and another, to know that somebody cared enough to touch me, to hold me in their arms, to reach out to me. I was self-destructing, slowly going mad in full view of all those around me. My lack of sleep, the drinking, the endless lonely nights, staring at the stars. Ever since Adam's death, I had felt like I was in a permanent state of shock, I'd known death before and would again, far too often, but for some reason, Adam had got to me, it scared me. It was real and so brutally final. The break up of my marriage was real too, I had failed because I could not square the circle between want and need, between what Nikki wanted and the world needed. Life demanded more than we had, and eventually I had to pay the price. Dafna was my bolthole, my sanctuary. It was all I had, but I tried to deny it had any hold over me, that I could leave any time I wanted. I was denying the fragility of life, the uncertainty of existing beyond the next moment. I was pushing the limits because I was scared. Scared of my dreams, the faceless entity behind the door. I was scared that I was wrong, that Dafna held nothing for me, just cheap cigarettes and alcohol, I would find no comfort here, no peace, just a slow death, slower than Tracey's. I was scared to admit that I had once kissed her and touched her hair, as I wished so desperately now to be touched. I was scared to admit it because the doubt of that reality would question all I had ever said. That instead of being the victim, I would be the guilty party. It matters not, in my mind who did what, when and why, but that we were already so desperately removed from each other. The promises at the altar were long forgotten, the children had been put in peril and the only way forward was for me to take the hit. Me. I took it and it was crucifying me. I should have been at home with my family, but I had no family, no home. A shattered dream where once I lay, a dreamer with dreams to spare.

It was on the way to Domino's one night that Phil finally did it, he opened up and admitted he was gay.

"Phil, it doesn't bother me mate, you're my room mate and I take you as you are, you like what you like and I have my own preferences. I've known plenty of gay men in the past, so don't worry about it, I'm not going to treat you any differently."

"I was just worried that you'd think badly of me or something, you know, you'd treat me differently or whatever."

"Not at all mate, it's not like you've become an alien or a child beater or anything. I've got nothing against gay people, other than Marilyn, I nicked his dog once because he wasn't very nice to him."

"You knew Marilyn?" Phil was surprised, and a little impressed.

"No, not really, I didn't know who he was until I saw him on Top Of The Pops. But seriously, I'm not scared or shocked, nothing like that, you're still my mate Phil, so don't worry about it."

"Thanks Ribs, that means a lot to me."

Domino's was very busy that night, there was a special offer on drinks, but to get a drink, you first had to buy tokens, I guess it was a legal thing, not exchanging drinks for cash, I don't know, maybe they made more money with all the lost and unused tokens. Netta was running the bar, she was Yitzhak's daughter, someone I had been messing around with for a while. Netta and I got on really well, she was easy to get along with and a good laugh, almost flirty at times but always harmless. Each time I tried to pay for a drink, Netta would hand me back my tokens. I should have married that woman there and then, she was my kinda Gal. Somehow, I doubt Yitzhak would have been too pleased though.

There was a group of Dutch volunteers with us at this time, among them was one of the most beautiful women I had ever seen in my life. Her name was Pauline, and she was a police officer from s'Hertogenbosch. She had a fiancee back home and we got on really well as friends, mainly because I never tried hitting on her, trying to chat her up or anything. She knew I wasn't in the market for a girlfriend and so felt relaxed and at ease around me.

"Look at them all," she said as we stood at the side of the dance floor. "Throwing their lives away, why must they want sex all the time, can they not be friends and be happy, like us?" It was Pauline's last night at Dafna. She retired early to bed, along with Stephanie and Judy. They were all leaving in the morning and I was sad to see them go, but this was Dafna, people came and went, it's what happens here.

Kenny was busy swearing across the room at the DJ.

"Play something decent you motherfucker, Heavy Metal, not this rap shit, I hate this rap shit!" Kenny definitely missed his calling in the diplomatic corps. The Doobie Brother's song, Long Train Running came on and I was pulled onto the dance floor by Rachel Solomon, a volunteer from Canada. It was good to be up and dancing and when the next song came on, I continued to wiggle my funky stuff like an epileptic Orangutan on a hot tin roof. There was a new volunteer I hadn't seen before, she appeared on the dance floor as an Oasis song came on. I introduced myself and asked her name.

"Esmé" she said, smiling.

"I've never heard that name before, that's quite unique."

"It's Egyptian or African or something, it means 'Goat' in some language or other." Esmé had a really nice voice, aristocratic in a natural way, clean, well bred but without the arrogance or pomposity you find in some well spoken people's voices. I could listen to that voice for hours. Esmé was a keen walker, she told me she loved 'Power-walking'

"Have you ever tried it?" She asked me.

"No, I love walking but for my own pleasure. I try and get out and about from here as often as I can, this place is a cage. I often walk into Qiryat Shmona instead of getting the bus. Have you read Ffyona Campbell's book? She has actually walked around the world now, I'd love to do that, even here, just walk the whole length of the country."

"Hey, you guys-" it was Tree, Stuart's American girlfriend. "Do you want a night's work next week, you'll get paid for it?"

"Hell yeah, what, when and where?"

"It's a beach party, I need 10 Volunteers to help out, 100 NIS each, just serving food and drink, all you can eat once the job is done, I know the guy that's arranging it, it's for real."

"I'm up for that," I said turning to Esmé. "There's not many opportunities for earning extra cash here, so you have to take it when you can."

Working in the fields was great fun, everyday was a new adventure. We got to play with all the big boy's toys, tractors, sprayers, harvesting machines, we were spoiled. Jim and I would often be left for hours on our own, repairing drip pipes in the fields, spraying Round-up or playing water fights. Jim was a scream, a proper wide boy, loud, brash and physical. Play fighting was the norm between us. Whilst working outside, if we were caught short, we'd head off into the bushes, sometimes we'd even remember to bring some toilet paper to work with us, not that it ever survived the water fights. One morning I headed off into some bushes to do my thing. I assumed the position and began to fertilise the earth immediately behind me. Just then, I heard a noise, not the sort of noise you'd normally pretend to have a cough and cover up, but something different. I strained my neck and saw three little pigs running towards me, they wanted my breakfast, even though it was second hand. Right behind them came Mummy Boar, half a ton of angry bacon with sharp bits at the front end, I wasn't hanging around, I was out of there like a light, running as fast as I could with my shorts round my knees and a tissue streamer behind.

To stop the Boar from eating all our crops, some of the fields had electric fences around them. 10,000 Volts passed through a thin wire and gave a hell of a jolt if you touched it. It wouldn't normally kill you, the ampage was very low, something like a quarter of an amp, which means that it's gonna tickle a bit. Haim would often lock us into a field, then return later and laugh as we tried to jump over the wire without catching our family jewels on the sparky bits, that was not very pleasant. It was bad enough the first time I touched the wire, I got a jolt up my arm and what felt like a hammer blow in my armpit. Haim laughed and Jim was next. It was our inauguration, if we wanted to work the fields we had to pass the initiation test, apparently.

Sometimes we'd be interrupted by explosions, sometimes in the valley near us, sometimes on the Golan Heights. Sometimes it was artillery, sometimes Boar or cattle wandering on a forgotten mine, the livestock would be sent to graze with the aim of clearing any leftover surprises from the decades of war on the land. Most days though, we got on with our work, riding the antique tractors up and down rows of sweetcorn, sunflowers and cotton, laying new drip pipes, spraying and checking the crops. The crops were our babies, or at least, that's how it began to feel.

Jim and I became the dirtiest volunteers on site. Each day we worked outside there would be mud fights, or we'd be caked in mud from the work we were doing, repairing and laying drip lines was a dirty job and we loved it. At the canteen each day, we'd leave our muddy boots by the door, take our lunch and then go shower. Afterwards, because, we started work earlier than the factory workers, we were free to do as we pleased, which usually meant sleeping or swimming in the pool while it was empty. I spent a lot of afternoons in the pool, swimming from end to end, the chlorine in the water stung my eyes, the sun browned my skin and the water felt good around me, cool but not cold. I was finding it so very hard to sleep, and slowly but surely, my body began to let me know I was burning the candle at both ends, time was running out.

Esmé and I did a lot of walking together, just for the fun of it. We'd walk to Qiryat Shmona, or Kfar Szold some days. I told her about the caves at Mount Arbel one day and we decided to go there at the first opportunity. Esmé and I were friends, she had a thing for Juan Carlos, the Colombian, and I didn't blame her, he was a good looking lad, exotic too, and if I were a young woman, I'd probably be interested myself, if I hadn't already met me that is, I mean, why have cotton when you can have silk, huh? I enjoyed Esmé's company, being friends kept me on the straight and narrow, it took my mind off other things.

The night of the beach party we all met by the Hospital at Qiryat Shmona, Tree had told us we'd be picked up from there and taken to the coast. Sure enough, a minibus arrived and we jumped aboard. I sat on the floor with no idea of where we were or where we were going. All we knew was that it was somewhere between Tel Aviv and Haifa. We were driven to a car park by the beach, pretty much as close as we could get to the site. The car park was full of trucks and vans, caterers, event organisers and stage building teams were all over the place. It was pretty chaotic. The sun was setting and time was getting close for us to do our thing, about 3,000 people were due to descend on us at any minute and we had to get everything ready. There were large vats of food in the catering trucks. Huge pans of hot meats, vegetables and mixed dishes ready to be carried to the beach where a temporary canteen had been set up. It was open to the elements, a long table which we filled with the hot pans and trays. Further along the beach were tables, row after row of tables empty and waiting for the party to start. We had seven tables full of food, ready to go, behind each was a refill table with fresh trays ready to replenish what was used as it went. I volunteered to be a runner, collecting the food from the trucks each time a new tray or pan full was needed, returning with the empties, ready for washing. This was going to be a precision exercise, 3,000 meals in as short a time as possible. The organisation that had gone into this event was incredible, and it rested on our shoulders to make it work. We stocked the tables with piles of plates and bowls, glasses and cutlery. Two minutes to go and still no sign of anybody.

Exactly on time, almost to the second, we heard the throng of voices approach. They came from around a point on the beach, a huge group of people, all at once, like a swarm, calmly approaching from seemingly nowhere. The approach was calm enough, but once they hit the tables all hell broke out. The noise was deafening.

"More rice, get some meat, not that-the other stuff!"

"Houmous, houmous, I need more Houm-....."

"More plates!"

"Spoons!"

"Quicker, faster, more!"

For the next 30 minutes or so I ran to and fro, which is normally hard enough on a sandy beach, but carrying 10kgs of hot Kosher dead things in boiling juices, is almost insane. Our fingers burned, our knees throbbed, ankles twisted, we sweated, we swore, we smiled. The punters came first, they had to be catered for, quickly, fairly and without any additional sand in their dishes. For 30 minutes we worked our butts off to get the job done.

As the last meals were served, we began collecting the rubbish, clearing away the washing up and the emptying the tables. Everything had to go back in the trucks, everything, even the tables themselves. When this was done, we taken further down the beach where there was a bar, a stage, and a band playing live music. We had to help with the bar, collecting glasses, pouring drinks, whatever needed to be done. We brought cases of drinks from a storage tent to the bar, case after case of Rum, Tequila and Vodka. Strange not to see any Whiskey anywhere, or maybe after my last encounter with it as a teenager, I had stopped noticing it. The drinks flowed, like a river at first, and then slower and slower, to a trickle and then stop. Two English revellers stood at the bar talking between themselves before turning to us.

"Hey, you're all English?" One of them asked.

"Mostly," I said, "except Tree there, she's American, from Washington state. Oh, and Juan Carlos there, he's a Colombian drug trafficker on the run from a cartel in Bogota, he thinks we don't know, but we know."

The guys laughed.

"Neat, so how'd you get a job like this?"

"Tree arranged it, she know's someone who does this sort of thing a lot here. It's been a good night, better than hanging around on our kibbutz all night."

"Which kibbutz are you at?" Asked the other Brit.

"Dafna" I replied, thinking they'd never have heard of it.

"Dafna, by Qiryat Katyusha? Man that place is evil, it's surprising it's still there or that anyone wants to live in that hell-hole!" I'd never thought of calling it Qiryat Katyusha, it was funny in a twisted kind of way.

"It's not so bad," I countered, "how long have you guy's been here?"

"I've been here 8 years, and Charlie, 7. We met in Tel Aviv and have been working together ever since. No one checks your visa here and there's so much work on the black market, you could stay forever if you wanted to."

"Yeah, we've been all over the country" said Charlie, "Jerusalem rocks, it's fucking great there man, and Tel Aviv too, I love this country, and the birds are fucking awesome, I ain't never going home!"

"Who'd want to? It's fucking awesome here mate. I can't remember the last time I saw rain, man, it was a long time ago. You can't go back to London after living here, the fags are cheap, the birds are beautiful-you don't get birds like these in England, look at them, they're fucking beautiful."

He had a point, I tended to agree with both of them, I couldn't go back anyway, even if I wanted to.

"And this place is fucking weird too, I mean seriously. A couple of months ago, I was walking on the beach in Tel Aviv. My shoes were falling apart and I had no money so I just keep walking until they fell off my feet in bits. I gave up and said 'God, if you really do exist, I could do with some help here'. And do you know what happened?"

"You found a new pair of shoes in the sand beside you" I replied.

"How'd you know that?" His face shocked, jaw wide open.

"Because I heard the same story a couple of years ago from a guy in France who was hitching home for his brother's wedding."

"But I swear man, I fucking swear now to you, it's the truth. Look, see these?" He lifted his foot to show me an old pair of Adidas trainers. "Brand spanking new they were, I tell you, at 10 AM on a Sunday morning they just appeared next to me on the beach, still in the box. On my life, it's the truth." It seemed weird, hearing again this same story I had been told a couple of years earlier by someone I'd picked up in France. He was adamant that it was true, and I had no reason to doubt him either, both men were equally enthused and believable, both desperate to make me believe their story. If they were both telling the truth then Israel was indeed a very strange place indeed, anything is possible here, if you believe it enough.

The band finished playing and a DJ began to perform his set, the final event of the night. Soon, the crowd thinned out and we were told we could finish now. We bathed in the warm Mediterranean water, drinking bottles of Vodka and Rum. There was no beer left, the opened spirit bottles were ours to keep, and we made sure there were plenty, opening several dozen bottles before the bar shut, just to make sure.Once everything was cleared away, we all stripped off and bathed in the sea again, happy, refreshed and just a little bit drunk. Life couldn't get much better for us than it did that night. We lived like kings and queens of old. We were fed to bursting, drank enough liquor to fill a bathtub and when we eventually climbed back aboard the minibus, brought with us enough sand to bury the roundest of Grandmothers on the beach.

Shlomo was furious. He'd already sent instructions out that no volunteer was allowed to work the beach party. By the time we got back to Dafna, I was late for work and still drunk. Some of the team pulled sickies. Ruth scurried around in an attempt to find out who'd been and how she could avoid giving Shlomo any names.

"Tell him to stick it up his arse!" I told her. "It's none of his business what we do when we're not here."

We were standing on the grass outside 'Death Row' as a van pulled up and interrupted us.

"Hey, where are the volunteers?" A guy in the passenger seat asked.

"That's us" said Ruth, all perky. "I'm volunteer leader."

"We're from an organisation that promotes events in the region, and we are promoting a festival we wondered if any volunteers here would be interested in attending next Friday, here-" he reached over and pulled out some flyers, a banner and poster, "I brought some promotional stuff for you to put up in your volunteer's bar. It'll be a great party" We were already half way there but he kept selling it to us."It's from 12 'til 12, 24 hours, there's live music, a DJ, bar, and camping on site , it's called 'Welcome The World Festival' and is open to all Volunteers , free entry, all are welcome."

Ruth took the handful of papers and said she'd be pleased to help out. The van turned around a drove off, back out the gate, no doubt heading to Dan, the next kibbutz along the road.

Ruth had told the promoter there were about 40 volunteers in Dafna, and more still to come in the next couple of days. Nobody was due to leave so our number was to rise to over 50 but with no extra money from Shlomo, and no extra beds. Ruth had asked Shlomo for more money but he said there was none, that we could feed 50 volunteers just as easily as 40 by buying the right foods. The man was trying to starve us out.

"We'll have to talk to Benny, let him deal with Shlomo." I said to Ruth. Just then we were approached by a tall guy with a backpack. He had shoulder length dark hair and wore glasses.

"Hey guys!" He was American. "I've got to see a guy called Shlomo, I'm a volunteer."

"I'll take you to him, I'm Ruth-Volunteer leader" Ruth smiled.

"I'm Chuck" he replied, "nice to meet you."

Chuck had just arrived from London, he was travelling solo and had the misfortune to land at Dafna.

It was decided I would move rooms, I could take John's place in with Jim and Jason. Jason was rarely on site now, he had some bits and pieces of personal stuff in the room still, but spent most of his time in Qiryat Shmona with his American girlfriend Pam. Shlomo wanted him gone but could never find him to tell him he was sacked. Pam had started showing up at Dafna in her old VW Beetle. She would hang around for a while with the volunteers and then take Jason back home for a day or two. Chuck moved in to my room but soon moved to join Miami Steve and Jack. Steve was a Doctor, allegedly a surgeon in a practice in Miami, which was pretty disconcerting, Steve was one of the least confident people you could meet, hesitant, awkward and clumsy with long gangly legs and arms, ideal for basketball maybe but the fact that he worked in a 'Practice' made me wonder just how much more practice he needed and who he was practising on.

Chuck was a writer and I would frequently find him hiding behind a wall scribbling notes.

"Make me famous" I joked. I would often show him my own scribbling's, poems and songs that I was writing, he was a good critic to have on site.

The Welcome The World Festival was a long way from Dafna. Small groups of us hitch hiking and leap-frogging each other all the way to Netanya on the coast, just north of Tel Aviv. I went with Esmé, Kenny and his new girlfriend Stina. Louie and Ruth went by car, as did Jim, Jason, Pam and Rachel who arrived first and set up a base for us all to crash out in, basically just an area of ground, enough that we could comfortably lay our sleeping bags on it.

It's surprising how easy it was to hitch hike in Israel at the time. It could be quicker than taking the bus, most cars would stop for a traveller or volunteer. The important rule to remember was to point your first two fingers to the ground at about 45 degrees. If you put your thumb up, as we did in England, that would be interpreted as a 'Ride for a ride', not necessarily everyone's cup of tea.

When we arrived at the festival it was well underway. Some blankets had been put on the ground to mark our space in amongst the thousands of people that made up the crowd. Stupidly, I had chosen to wear a pair of thin rubber sandals, useless for walking in, equally useless for jumping around with a crowd. There was a band from Tel Aviv on stage, a great roar came up from the audience and they began to play cover versions of songs I loved, Billy Idol's 'Rebel Yell', The Jam's 'A Town Called Malice', 'Eton Rifles' and Elvis Costello's 'Oliver's Army'. I was bouncing around like a Jack in the box with a brand new spring, like Zebedee on speed, up and down, left and right and all over the bloody place. It was bloody on account of all the broken bottles and glasses on the floor, my feet were crushed by others in the crowd with their big heavy boots, landing on top of my little rubber covered tootsies, grinding them into the glass underfoot. My feet were an awful bloody mess, but still I carried on.

At some point in the night, I lay down and passed out on top of my sleeping bag. The music continued all around me, the festival kept going.

We left the following lunchtime and made it to Tiberias without too much trouble. Then we got a lift in a car with a Syrian driver who was pretty vague about where he was headed. We couldn't hear anything of what he said because all the windows were open and he took off like a rocket. I don't remember ever having travelled so fast in a car. The wind from outside contorted our faces, trying to breathe was difficult due to the pressure of the air blasting in through our mouths and nostrils. We were doing 90 MPH through the winding mountain road out of Tiberias, on the straight we hit 140-160 MPH I honestly thought we were going to die. We flew through Rosh Pina and in record time hit the outskirts of Qiryat Shmona just as the radiator blew. The driver pulled in to the garage on the main drag to check out the damage. We took the opportunity to thank him for our ride and head off to walk the rest of the way to Dafna. We hadn't got far when he caught up with us, a hose had come loose from his radiator, but he'd reattached it, refuelled and was ready to go again. We didn't hesitate to get back in his car and minutes later he dropped us off at Death Row.

Esmé accompanied me to Mount Arbel the following weekend. We hitched to the site on a Friday afternoon just before the start of Sabbath, when the roads emptied. Walking up from the road meant passing some old shanty like houses at the foot of the hills. They were the homes of local Arabs, Palestinians who'd lived and worked here all their lives. As we walked past one property, a dog came running out at us.

"Ignore it!" I said to Esmé, hoping to reassure her. "If we leave it alone it won't do anything."

The dog yapped continuously as we kept walking, not daring to look at it. Then, maybe out of frustration, it lunged at Esmé and sank it's teeth into her calves. It was still yapping as I kicked at it and pulled Esmé away, putting myself between it and her. We faced each other, froth and saliva dribbled over bared teeth, and the dog looked equally frightening. I made myself look big by lifting my arms and the dog stepped backwards. Just then, it's owners came running, a middle aged Arab woman and her children rushed up and one of them scooped the dog up in his arms, taking it back into the shanty home they all lived in. I was shocked that this had happened, as was Esmé, laying on the ground with blood oozing from her calves. The little mutt had really done a good job of chasing us off. We tried to play it down but the woman would have none of it, she insisted we go back to their house where we were invited to sit outside at a table. A first aid kit appeared and the woman tended to

Esmé's wound, first cleaning and washing it, before applying a cream and some bandages.

It was difficult to really understand each other, they spoke no English, we spoke no Arabic and very little Hebrew, but somehow we got by. We were invited to eat with the family and they brought out trays of delicious foods, pastry, breads and houmous, fruit and even drinks. We were spoiled and in return, all I could offer was to teach the young boys how to play with the chess board I had borrowed fro the volunteer's kitchen. I set up the pieces, drew pictures of how each piece moved and played a couple of games with them before handing it over and letting them keep it. I hoped one day to return and find them with the game still on the table, hopefully having mastered it properly.

We had planned on arriving early enough to collect some kindling and build a small fire in the caves, but the sky was already dark as we reached the top of the hill, having climbed up the route Kenny and I had raced down a few weeks earlier. We laid our sleeping bags down and then peered out across the Sea of Galilee, to the black silhouetted mountains in the distance. A million stars glistened in the sky and everything was quiet.

During the night we were visited by many different animals, it wasn't possible to see them in the intense darkness, but we could hear them, their little feet scurrying beneath them as they ran away once I'd made our presence known. A cough, a noisy turn in my sleeping bag was all it took.

In the morning we were awoken by the arrival of a group of tourists who'd come to see the caves, not expecting to find us laid out in our sleeping bags on the floor. They turned around and left as quickly as they'd arrived.

For me, the attraction of sleeping in the cave had been simple, I was hoping to find some peace. Esmé and I were friends, no more, just friends who enjoyed the other's company. I had been influenced by John, the short, football loving 'Baptist' of Dafna. I had begun to see things in ways I never had before, things like the beauty of water, the necessity for it was obvious, but the beauty was rarely appreciated. I began to see it for what it was, the giver and the taker of life. The one thing we could not live without, was the one thing that could destroy us. Finding the balance was the secret to life. I could taste the air too, more now than I ever had before. I was starting to wake from some slumber, from years and years of chasing falsehoods. I had been almost hellbent on a toxic demise for so long, that I had forgotten what it was like to really feel alive. Mount Arbel, Galilee, Nimrod and Hermon had opened my eyes, Israel opened my heart, and John, with our little chats from time to time, his voice so quiet as to be almost inaudible, had opened my mind. I felt free from the baggage of my past. The burden of my guilt, the hurt and betrayals, the violence, all seemed to be gone now. I was at peace with the universe, and myself.

Sitting with my legs draped over the wall of the cave, looking out over the scenery before me, I came to terms with my lot. I could never change what has been, I cannot undo what is done. I have only the ability and choice to choose what is next, who and what I will become.

I took Esmé to the kibbutz doctor next morning and explained what happened. We were sent to a specialist hospital in Safed, where her wounds were treated and she was put on a course of anti-Rabies injections.

"I should never have let that bloody dog near her" I thought to myself.

After a fair bit of waiting and going from room to room, we were finally sent back to Dafna with a bag full of medication. We were told someone would visit the dog and get it checked for any disease it may have, but in reality, they really meant it would be confiscated and destroyed. Now I felt double guilty.

While Esmé was suffering with sore calves and the threat of Rabies, I was starting to have problems of my own. What started as an irritation in my left eye, developed into something more sinister. I was despatched to the eye hospital in Qiryat Shmona where I was found to have Herpetic eye ulcers.

"Do you suffer from cold sores?" A doctor asked.

"Yes, from time to time I get them."

"Well, this is the same, only beneath the surface of your eye. It is the same virus, possibly transferred from your lips to your eye. You have to rest it as much as possible, no bright lights, no alcohol or cigarettes, they can all trigger another episode. Most importantly, plenty of rest and do not touch it, it is a contagious virus and you don't want to spread it."

It was because I couldn't sleep that I was so run down. I drank to put myself to sleep, and I smoked because, well, because I smoked I guess. Now I had to really let go of the past, I had to in order to rest, relax my mind and sleep, something I had been so deprived of for such a very long time. Each time I tried I would return to that same old dreams, either in the dirty the bathroom of my junior school, with something hiding behind the cubicle door. Or else, the squat in Earls Court, a dead body in the overflowing bath, or worse than both of these, the swimming pool dream, where I would be in a pool alone, but if I go underwater, I would see Kylie Mynogue wrapped around my waist, at bodies joined. (*Do not judge me, I got no pleasure from it, but I think she liked it!*)

I was stressed and could find no respite. Exercise, drinking, reading, nothing worked, nothing relaxed me. I only had one more month to go, one month until the Desert Trek I had booked, the only thing I had to look forward to at this point in time.

Whilst out walking one day by the river, I noticed something in the water. It was an old piece of metal, thin and almost wire like. It seemed to be a ring, a very, very old ring. I picked it up from the water and looked at it. It was definitely old, from when I hadn't a clue, recently, I have seen similar rings in collections of Roman antiquities found in the UK. Could it have been of similar age? I will never know. I gave the ring to Esmé, a parting gift. She was leaving Dafna, going home to finish her course of treatment. She hadn't contracted Rabies, but she'd had enough of a scare to want to leave.

I thought about the road ahead, things I should do, places to see and whatever else that I could find to occupy my mind. My walking buddy was gone and I had to get a grip on myself. I had to get my eye back to health, and save some money before I cut my own ties with Dafna. I wanted to see Petra, the 'Rose City' in Jordan. I also wanted to see the Sinai and Egypt, these were my goals, the things to aim for.

Tree and Stuart broke up. It wasn't a big surprise really, she was the hippy child from the west coast, he was a military man from East Anglia. One was a fighter, the other a lover, and no matter how hard he tried, Stuart never looked comfy in baggy leggings, the hippy look did not suit him. Tree was an environmentalist, feminist, vegetarian who came across as an air head, until you spoke to her. She was actually very intelligent, as if that were meant to be some surprise. It was Tree who introduced me to the wonder that is Houmous, and Tahini too. Tahini with honey on buttered bread was as good as peanut butter, without the nuts. Who knew? I certainly didn't, but I loved it all the same. Tree and I would eat it on the roof of the volunteers kitchen, away from the hubbub below.

Tree encouraged me to spend more time in the gym, playing basketball mainly. The pool was off limits due to my eye infection, so basketball became my new pastime, along with Chuck, Tree and an English lad called Kye, we would play for hours. At school, I had been in the basketball team. I used to be able to duck and dive, then run rings around my opponents, but that was a long time before, I had grown slow and less agile, but I still loved the game.

I was having regular check up's at the hospital, some days I would go even when I had no appointment, just to go to town and walk back again. One day, I had just left the hospital when the sirens sounded.

"An attack, now?" I hurried along to where the minibus usually picked us up, but it had already gone. Chuck had beaten me to it and neither him nor the minibus driver were hanging around. I had no choice but to walk back to Dafna and as I did so, a katyusha rocket slammed into a building in town. I heard the explosion and kept walking. It was not my war, there was no place in this for me, I was merely a visitor, an accidental witness.

A minibus pulled up one night as a group of us were sitting by our campfire. A rather large, thick set Israeli guy approached and introduced himself as the organiser of a new volunteer's disco night, starting the following week at Kfar Szold. He reckoned that hundreds of volunteers would be attending, from all over the Galilee region.

"How much is it to get in?" I asked.

"It's free, but you pay for drinks unless you bring your own."

"That's me sorted innit? I'm coming, how do we get there?"

"We will bring a bus, how many of you will be coming?" he asked around.

"About twenty." Rachel piped up immediately, "and I am going to drink you under the table" she declared.

Big Rachel, as she was known, was the undisputed Tequila Queen of Dafna, and she was throwing down the gauntlet, to me. Her reputation stemmed from having 11 shots on the trot, the night Andy left Dafna.

"Are you going to take her up on that, Ribs?"

"Of course, Chuck. It's what I do-innit?."

Chuck and Miami Steve were the only volunteers not to make it to Kfar Szold. They chose to go to Domino's instead and had a pretty quiet night compared to the shennanigans going down a few miles up the road.

The setting at Kfar Szold was wonderful, an outside event on a field, next to a lake. We were told on arrival that the lake was strictly 'Off Limits' and anyone entering the water would be removed from the site. There was a dance floor constructed under a huge canopy, collapsible tables made up the bar and DJ booth, with other tables and chairs spread around for the use of guests. Having not taken the challenge too seriously, I'd already seen off a bottle of Punch before leaving Dafna, I was on my second when I saw Jason, Rachel and Pam arrive. Jim and I were sitting on the grass when they came over to join us. Rachel had just got back from Jerusalem with Chuck, they'd been to see Neil Young in concert there. Rachel was a massive fan but other than the odd track, I can't bear his voice, so whiney and high pitched, he probably sounds just like me on a good day. Rachel was a slacker, a professional waster. She had not forgotten about the challenge, and as she sat down, she pulled out a bottle of tequila and I shuddered.

"Okay, Jason is gonna have to Judge, Jim can pour the shots. If you stop, you lose, but we both agree to a break we can stop and pick up where we left off. Are you ready for this?"

"I dunno, I mean, I...."

"Come on geezer, you can do it, she's a yank for fuck's sake" Jim cut in.

"Canadian" Rachel corrected him, "come on, dude, let's do this."

And that was how it started, Jim poured the shots, Pam and Jason bore witness, Rachel and I swallowed shot after shot of foul tasting liquid. Anyone that ever tells you they like the taste of Tequila is either a liar, or they have no taste buds. The only people allowed to like it are people who spend so much time in the sun that their senses are charred.

A small group of people had soon gathered around us, cheering us both on.

"Go!" called Jason and we poured the sour drink down our throats. Jim poured another. Five, Six, Seven. The cheers grew. Eight shots in and I wretched. My stomach wasn't enjoying this at all, but a challenge is a challenge and the cheers kept me in the competition. Rachel and I took a minute out to catch our breath, we were both feeling the pressure. I was regretting the drinks I'd had prior to the start of the contest, especially the beers we'd bought on our arrival, everything seemed to be sloshing around inside me and my head was getting light now, this was going to be a very colourful evening.

Number nine came, and then ten burned my throat. Rachel put her hands up to her own throat and paused, catching her breathe and trying to keep herself from wretching.

"This one equals your record" announced Pam, in a jubilant manner. She was enjoying this, more so than me or Rachel probably, both sitting face to face, our eye's rolling around like boules on the deck of a Hebridean ferry in the depths of winter. It was like being in a goldfish bowl, eyes everywhere we looked, staring in, willing us on, smiling. Jim, James, Kenny, Steve (the fireman from Walthamstow), Annabelle (the only volunteer whose voice could never be heard, she'd smile but rarely say anything aloud in public), Jack, Sheila and the others.

"Twelve!" I heard a blurry noise in the distance, nothing felt real anymore.

"Thirteen!" Called Jim triumphantly. Jim could do that because he didn't feel the burning sensation in my throat. The anticipatory muscle spasm in my stomach. I fought back and held everything in but my throat was constricting now, time to call a break. Rachel was wobbling, sitting crossed legged on the floor but in danger of falling off all the same. I put my hand over my mouth and my stomach went into spasm, I thought I was going to be sick but nothing came out, and then again, a second and third time. I pushed myself up off the floor.

"I need to dance, one song and then back..." I pulled Rachel up and turned toward the dance floor. 'Our House' by Madness had just started playing. I headed for the source of the sounds only to find my rudder chain had snapped and I was drifting at about 80 degrees to port. My legs were wobbling furiously as I gained momentum and continued sideways into the lake. About a dozen paces in I touched down with a splash, face first into the water. The shock brought me to my senses and I managed to get upright, standing thigh deep I raised my arms and started dancing. It was only a matter of seconds before security came after me. Half a dozen men in Israeli Defence Force uniforms stood at the water's edge yelling at me to get out, their guns slung over their shoulders, not sure what to do next, but knowing I had to be removed from the lake.

"Fuck you, this is my song, my lake and I wanna dance in my lake, so fu....."

I don't remember anything else. There were punches, apparently, a few kicks too and I did manage to get some of the soldiers wet, but it was Jim who took me down, Jim pounced on me to save me from a proper hiding. In doing so, he probably saved my life, knowing the state I was in.

I woke next morning in my bed. Chuck was saying goodbye through the open doorway, the light burned my eyes and made my head sore. He was leaving Dafna, moving on, something I very much wished I could do at this point.

"Write to me, won't you?" I said. "And have a good'un, yeah?" Then he was gone and I slipped back into my dreams. The same old familiar scene. The bulging door, the drip, drip, drip of the taps. When I eventually woke up, I discovered I had a black eye and a chipped tooth. I recalled nothing more of the night before, but I was annoyed at myself, not for not defeating Rachel, or getting drunk, or fighting with the soldiers, none of that. I was annoyed I'd made it home, back to my bed. I should have woken up in a field somewhere, anywhere but here.

Phil got invited to DJ at Domino's, so all the volunteers turned up to support him. Kenny stood near the bar shouting obscenities and demands for more heavy metal, not that he got any in the first place mind you, just that Kenny shouting obscenity's was just his default position, he didn't like any other music, he was a viking and ate virgins whole, for breakfast.

By the end of the evening I just wanted to get away and decided to sleep by the river. I collected my sleeping bag and crept out under the back gate, taking a short metal pole with me, just in case. Once beyond the fence I was in dangerous territory. If caught by an army patrol I could be shot as a suspected terrorist. If caught by a terrorist, I'd be killed silently, or maybe kidnapped and taken away to Beirut or somewhere maybe, a healthy ransom to be demanded. I knew this but still wanted out. I was feeling trapped in Dafna now, I was ready to leave. I had to wait for the desert trip, then I could go, only a few more days, 2 or 3 weeks, that is all.

The dusty track beyond the razor wired fence was silent. It was pitch black and when I raised my hand in front of my face I saw nothing, so dark was the night. I had walked the path many times and knew where I was going, using the metal bar like a blind person using a white stick, I tapped out my course between the trees and bushes on either side. Above me, the sky was full of stars, outlining the silhouettes of branches and leaves. I felt my way slowly along the path until something caught my attention, I was not alone. I froze, cold chills ran through me as I scanned the darkness around, waiting for a sound, a movement, maybe a shot and the searing heat that would burn right through me. This was for real, this was not high jinks, it wasn't tomfoolery, I was in real shit. My eyes darted from left to right and back, then again, delving deeper into the blackness until I sensed something to my right hand side, a few feet away. I slowly raised the metal bar and made ready to strike.

"Dear God make this painless" I thought to myself. Someone or something was there, right by me. I hadn't been shot yet, I hadn't been discovered but I felt sure we both knew of the other's presence. I knew because now I could smell it, a familiar smell I'd come across before, in the fields, in the bushes with my shorts around my ankles. It was a boar, not the cardboard ones I'd left out for Benny to shoot at, but the real thing.

"Aaargh!" I swung the bar at the bush beside me, slashing away at the foliage to create a noise immediate enough to scare the beast away. There was a snort, a squeal and the sound of departing wildlife. For a second I thought of killing it, taking it's life with my bar and bare hands just to drop it's carcass on Benny's desk and laugh at his ever present pistols holstered on his waist. Chances being, I was more likely to be lacerated by it's teeth and horns, that it would be my head mounted on a plaque in Benny's office, not the Boar's. I stood alone in the dark, the boar fled leaving me with my own deep breaths and the darkness once more. I slowly turned, and then tapped my way to the old bed frame on the river, to the pallets where I laid my sleeping bag, smoked a Noblesse and slept soundly to the tune of the waters rushing beneath me. There was no basin, no doors, no hidden demons, just deep beautiful sleep.

"Don't you ever do that again!" It was Haim's turn to be furious with me. "They will kill you, you understand that? You will die out there."

"It's alright Haim, I'm still here, they didn't kill me"

"But you can die out there!" He wasn't letting go this time.

"But I am here, I am alive, see. Nobody killed me."

Jim sat quietly eating a biscuit, for Jim to be quiet was a rare thing at a time like this, maybe he was was with Haim on this, maybe he didn't think I would really have done something so crazy, I mean, really? Everybody knew the IDF would shoot first and ask questions later, or that Benny would have taken me out as easily as a Boar if he'd stumbled across my path. The truth was, Haim actually liked me (I think....) and he didn't want me getting all dead and stuff because I had a penchant for reckless behaviour. I let him have the last word and promised not to ever do anything so foolish again, then he stepped outside our work room and began loading the van. I hid a packet of biscuits in my sleeping bag, food for the volunteers tonight.

Another new wave of volunteers arrived, young Brit's mostly. They seemed to be following Paul, a tallish, skinny guy with brown hair and ears that stuck out just a little bit too far. He was a bit of wide-boy, a small town cheeky lad, with a smile to cover his villainy. I liked him already. He was the sort of lad that could either get you anything you wanted, or knew somebody that could. They had only just arrived when trouble struck. Shlomo had left the office open for a few moments to get something, when he returned the keys to the safe were missing. He threatened to have everyone thrown off the kibbutz. As usual, I was the prime suspect, but much to his annoyance, I had an alibi and a witness. I had been in Benny's office receiving my final, final warning. Someone had turned me in for pissing on the fan that drew cold air into Domino's, on the night Phil was DJ. I admitted doing it, but that it was an accident and I didn't mean to give everyone on the dance floor a golden shower. "Oops!"

Word came about that Jeremy, a bit of a scoundrel if left unsupervised, have lifted Shlomo's keys. I urged him to return them via a third party if he preferred, however he did it, he had to do it soon. Little Rachel and Kiwi Karen couldn't leave until they got their passports back, which were in the safe. They had flights booked the next day and were panicking about getting away in the morning. Before long, the keys were returned, the girls got their passports and Jeremy was invited quietly to leave, the next day.

The next day, Sarah, a small black woman from North London, got into a fight in the canteen and threatened to stab another volunteer. Paul and Sarah seemed to be quite close and he managed to calm things down, but word got around quickly at Dafna, and Sarah was being shortlisted for early departure. Jason and Big Rachel, the Tequila Queen, were both expelled for absenteeism, but Jason still managed to get in at night time and bring his washing for Jim and I to send through the laundry.

My time at Dafna was finally coming to an end too. I was leaving for the much anticipated desert trek, on my return, we had a few more days, before going to Eilat on a Kibbutz trip, a 5 day trek for free, after which, I was planning on leaving.

The night before Stuart and I left Dafna, I was given a a copy of a poem written by one of the Turkish volunteers I had become friends with. His name was Semih. Semih and I would often talk about our writing, about life and the world in general. He wanted to be a writer and Journalist when he left university in Ankara.

Stuart was unusually quiet at breakfast, unlike me, I was excited and rearing to go. We were going to Tel Aviv and then would meet up with the rest of our group on the desert trek. As everyone left for work, we collected our passports and Shlomo wished us a pleasant journey, and it seemed to me, he really meant it too. We were just pulling out the gates when Stuart sighed.

"Thank god for that. I am so glad to be out of there."

"What? What's been bugging you mate?"

"Tree. I'm not very good at breaking up with people, she really got to me. I like her, I like her a lot but I can't stand to be around her anymore, now we're not together."

Stuart had separation issues and didn't like to see Tree enjoying herself now that they'd split up. Tree was busy spending a lot of time with a Kibbutznik friend called Nilli, they both loved working out, exercise, sports- especially swimming. Nilli was from Denmark, and was as fit as a fiddle, she put all us volunteers to shame. Tall, slim, muscular, Nilli was a lean, clean fighting machine, and very good looking to boot. Tree was active, and fit, but Stuart was never going to make the grade. They were two totally different people and it was never going to work, no matter how much Stuart pretended to be a new-born hippy, he was still a military man in his heart and she was a feminist vegetarian, it was never going to end well. By the time we reached Tel Aviv, Tree was all but a memory and Stuart was smiling again.

We booked into the Dizengoff Hostel, a cheap little place to crash for the night, in the centre of the city, by Dizengoff Plaza. The receptionist asked if we were looking for work.

"Not today" I said, "we're off on a desert trek, but maybe in a couple of weeks."

"Come and see me then, I can keep you working, very busy."

Stuart and I walked around town for a bit, treated ourselves to Nutella covered pancakes from a street vendor, then ambled around aimlessly, taking in the sights, every doorway was another temptation, something else to lighten our pockets, coffee, alcohol, falafel's and waffles, coke and chips.

We all met the next morning, outside the offices of the tour company, Tracks. It was a couple of blocks away from our hostel on Dubnov Street. Stuart and I arrived nice and early. The two Stuarts were reunited and went immediately into soldier mode, exchanging tales of their conquests since our last meeting. It seemed the younger Stuart had a better time than the elder. He now had an Israeli girlfriend and was thinking of joining the IDF.

I mingled with some others in our group, there were about 20 of us in all. I was soon talking to a young lady from London, Tiziana. She was petite, very jovial, constantly smiling with bright white teeth highlighting her dark skin and black hair, she was half Italian, half Iranian and totally swamped by her backpack. Surely I thought, smaller people have smaller clothes and therefore smaller backpacks, no?

Our guide finally arrived, strolling up like one of us but even more laid back, he had the best job in the world, getting paid to take us through the desert. His name was Armed, he was about 6 ft tall, with long corkscrew hair. He looked like a cross between Marc Bolan and Slash, with a gold tooth that glinted in the sunlight from time to time, dark sun drenched skin and a long Roman nose. He wore mirrored sunglasses and flip flops. Armed was a hippy, a quiet, peace loving man with a great love, respect and knowledge of the natural environment into which we were about to enter. He walked this trail every week, we would be lucky to see it more than once in our lives. A coach arrived and we boarded it, Armed making sure we were all present and accounted for. As the door shut, the bus pulled away and Armed spoke through a microphone.

"Hello everyone, welcome aboard our bus today. We will be travelling to Ein Gedi today, passing around Jerusalem and through the Judaean desert. Some of our journey will be with Camels and walking, some by bus for security and time purposes. We will be visiting also Masada, Timna Park, the Dead Sea and finish up with a yacht cruise in Eilat. If anyone has any questions, please come to see me and I will do my best to answer them."

9 ARABIAN KNIGHTS

Razor wire on the inside of a hell you can't escape, 15 metre cables, 15 minutes late.
Looking out from my machine, clocks ticking all the while, smiles wiped clean my empty
face, mile after mile.
Switching on the radio the newspapers' on strike, something about the razor wire and
gunshots in the night.
She said she never loved me though I loved her too much, I slip into my fantasy and
memories of a touch.
Misinterpretation of things I never said, the things I said I think I said, I never really said.
Gone in the morning like milk floats in the night, plastic bags and clothing tags, the things
that make life right.
Television, radio, dog fights, deep red wine, the problem's not for solving, just finding out the
time.
Bread rolls and stereos, urine stains and coke, round and around the porcelain, nothing left
to smoke.
Misinterpretation of things I never said, the things I said I think I said, I never really said.

I'd come to Israel to escape the drunken, rat-race debauchery I'd been very
much involved in for so long. I had come to find some semblance of society,
community, togetherness. I'd also wanted to to escape from own failings, my
inability to deal with a wife who'd gone off the rails, and the guilt I felt for
having been so inept at dealing with everything at home. Instead of finding
peace and solitude, I'd stumbled into a club 18-30 style experiment in
socialism. An experiment that had long since failed, was less than scientific
and totally without observation or conclusion, other than my own. Life as a
volunteer on a kibbutz like Dafna, was nothing like the place I'd imagined. I
had hoped to find reflection and the opportunity to learn and develop as a
person, a chance to become able and strong enough mentally to deal with the
situation I found myself in. Homeless, separated from my family and

confused, all I had found was cheap escapism and sunshine, within the backdrop of a war nobody was talking about. I had found people who's lives had seen more trauma than I could possibly imagine, who still went to work each morning, who continued to live inside the razor wired fence that kept their minds captive, kept them in their place. I'd found people who believed in the system, others who were exploiting it, and the volunteers who ambled in and out, that came and went with no sense of propriety, no sense of right and wrong in a land that was not their own. Dafna had done nothing to alleviate the damage in my heart and mind. It had given me experiences I could never have had elsewhere, but it fed me a constant supply of my own worse medicine. Easy access to cheap alcohol was my downfall, the thing that brought out the very worst in me, and those about me. Could I have survived without it? I don't know, I was so highly strung that I would probably have done exactly the same crazy stunts all the same, only sober.

Leaving Tel Aviv, I finally felt as though something was changing. We were heading away from the crazy cities, away from the bars, clubs and crazy people. We were riding out into the desert, the vast wasteland I had admired so much in the back of my mind. I loved the feel of the sun on my skin, the thought of being in the desert, the dry air, the heat, the vast emptiness all around, it was so enticingly close, just a few hours away now.

The landscape around us was changing now, there were fewer green fields filled with lush green crops. Everything around us looked dry and the ground itself grew more barren the further we went.

The 2 Stuarts and I sat by each other across the aisle. Stuart the younger telling us again of his desire to stay in Israel and join the IDF. Stuart the elder took it all in before urging him to go back to the UK and join the British Army. Stuart the younger, had not been to Metulla. He hadn't seen the look on the faces of the young conscripts as they crossed into Lebanon for the first time. The lines of trucks and tanks that crawled steadily through the border to an uncertain future. The odd thing being, all traffic was going north, I don't recall ever seeing anything coming back. I'd been to Metulla several times, and it was the same each time, scared, insecure faces heading north on the back of trucks. Dust, engine fumes and the roar of tanks and heavy transporters.

It wasn't long before we reached our first stop, a lay-by on the outskirts of Jerusalem. We were on a hill and had a great view of the city from where we stood. The golden dome of Temple Mount, also known as Qubbat al-Sakhrah, reflected brightly against a clear blue sky as it had done for the last 1300 years. The city sprawled out over the hillsides around, every street, every house had it's own history to tell. Every inch of this city built on the blood of a previous generation. For thousands of years this tiny corner of the earth has been fought over, it's riches and people taken again and again. It's children enslaved by one religion, or another, one flag or other, one nation or another. Violence was the foundation upon which it's walls stand, foundations built on the ghosts of the dead, the martyrs, the victims, the human waste upon which belief and trust is still fought over on a daily basis. How could it be that such a beautiful place as this could make monsters of men? How could two religions, with so much commonality be so diametrically opposed, so violently at odds when they preach the same bloody message? I looked at this holiest of cities and wondered, just how many people had perished in order that one school of thought could lay claim to it over the other? How many lives, how many tears? The wailing wall so perfectly placed to absorb the torrents of sadness, day after day, atrocity following atrocity, year after year.

I had no desire to enter the city, none whatsoever. For me, it was enough to see it from afar. My footsteps were not needed to disturb the dead, not anymore than the many tourists that already woke them. My place was far from here, there was nothing holy in my being, nothing to bring peace to the troubled souls in this city of love and death.

Our coach moved on, our journey continued beyond the city limits, out into the wilderness of the Judaean desert. We were taken to Ein Gedi, a nature reserve at the northern end of the Dead Sea. We left the coach and walked through a Wadi, a dried river bed. Our feet creating tiny clouds of dust where water should run. There were lines in the sand, dips and grooves where in other times, fresh water ran through, carving a path down to the sea. Rocks lay strewn, left where they'd stopped rolling when the flood had once been a torrent. I loved this landscape. I loved how it could be the source of life one moment, and the taker of life another. I loved the feel of the sun, the warm air tasted so dry and clean.

I was grateful at having worn my work boots, they were ideal for hiking through the desert. Our bags were kept on board the coach and taken to where we would sleep, at a Bedouin camp somewhere in the wilderness. We were to be reunited with them later in the day, for now, we carried only bottles of water, and a towel each.

After clambering over, through and around a whole host of rock formations, sand dunes and river beds, we came across an oasis, a real genuine oasis in the desert. We came around a rock face, deep in a ravine to discover a handful of green trees, so vibrant and rich as to look like they'd been manufactured in a plastic's factory somewhere in China.

"You see there?" Asked Armed. "That is an oasis. Why do you think the tree's are so green when there is no water?"

"Is there a pond ahead?" Someone replied.

"Could be" he smiled, and headed towards the trees. As we grew closer we could hear water, rushing water. We could hear it and only saw it once we close enough, a waterfall. The trees were as green and lush as they were because of the moisture in the air from the spray of the falls, minute droplets blew about in the breeze bringing life to an otherwise desolate place.

The water was clean and fresh, we drank it, bathed in it and stood beneath the falls, the water pummelled our backs, heads and shoulders. The weight of the falling water hit like a Masseuse who'd just discovered his boyfriend had left town with his ex, it was brutal, cold but invigorating, and so welcome after our short walk from the bus. We stayed a short while, messing about in the water before drying ourselves and eventually continuing towards our camp under the stars, somewhere out in the desert.

Our camp was a genuine Bedouin tent about the size of a tennis court. Inside were rugs and cushions decorated with beautifully intricate Persian designs. Armed led us to the entrance, the sides of the tent were open to allow air to flow through, it would be too hot to be under enclosed canvas and the chance of rain was virtually nil, for a couple of months yet.

"An Arab will invite a stranger into his home, he will feed them, give them water and shelter without asking them who they are, where they have come from. If the guest wishes to speak, he may tell his host all that he wishes. If after 3 days he has said nothing, the guest must leave and continue on his travels. He may stay longer, but only if the host invites him. It is tradition that all travellers are welcome in the desert".

We slept under the stars that night, between a sand dune and rocky cliffs. There were huge birds of prey nesting in the cliffs, when a couple of the girls decided to climb the massive sand dune, Armed became weary.

"What's wrong?" I asked, looking out at the group slowly vanishing up the side of the dune, growing ever smaller as they went.

"Up there, you see?" He pointed at the circling birds. "Vultures, Griffon Vultures, they think the women are food, we must get them down from there, if the sand doesn't get them the birds might." I looked up at the sky and saw the birds circling high above the sand dune, it was like a scene from a western, if you want to find someone in the desert, look for the birdies circling hungrily overhead. I ran to the dune and called up at the girls, then scrambled up to help them down. The sand fell away with each step and I had to zig-zag lightly across the surface to make any ground upwards. It was much harder than I could have imagined. The girls were struggling too, the sand tumbling away beneath them, swallowing their legs up to the knee with each step. Once they realised the situation they were in, they headed back down keeping a close eye on the Vultures overhead.

Out here in the desert, there was nothing to drink, only water. Alcohol could prove deadly in the heat, dehydration was a real danger.

"You must drink 5 -10 litres of water each per day here. When you are walking and climbing, you may not feel thirsty, but you must sip water, if you feel thirsty then you are already dehydrated. There are 5 stages to dehydration, feeling thirsty is stage 3, stage 5 is death, so you must drink, and keep drinking".

There seemed to be lot's of things that could kill us out here, snakes were favourite with at least 4 species that are deadly to man. The Israeli Viper, Rattle Snakes, Israeli Mole Viper and the most deadly, the Black Adder, known across the globe for tight leggings, Ratatouille and a sidekick called Baldrick. Poisonous Scorpions also live in the desert, along with Black Widow Spiders and the Mediterranean Recluse Spider, for which there is no anti-venom. Armed was doing a good job of scaring us all half to death, we didn't need to get bitten, we just needed another half hour of his welcome to the desert lesson and we would all have been showing symptoms of one illness or other.

As the sun set behind the cliffs around us, the temperature dropped and the sky opened up into the clearest most magical sight. There was absolutely no light pollution in the desert, nothing to deflect the billions of tiny lights in the night sky above us. We stared upwards, our mouths wide in awe of the heavens above us. I had never seen so many stars, even at Dafna when I would lay on the rooftops looking upwards all night. I could see the Milky Way, hundreds of thousands of lights twinkling above me. It was incredible to see, something so awesome, and so easily ignored so often. I loved the night sky and being in the desert gave me a much greater appreciation of what I was seeing. A billion or more suns, planets, solar systems, all hanging in space, each in its own place, like the individual pieces of an atom, all separate, but still together. Was this the universe I was looking at, or as I'd thought in my youth, just a cell inside something so much bigger, something so huge we could have no concept of it.

Next morning, we had breakfast and were taken to an ancient Synagogue nearby. There was a huge mosaic on the floor and the remains of the walls lay only a couple of feet high. We wandered around the site for a while and then were taken to rejoin the bus. Our next stop was The Dead Sea itself, we could see it from Ein Gedi but had yet to experience it first hand. Dave and Craig had told me you could lay in the water and read a news paper, the water was so thick that your body would just float naturally, this I was looking forward to trying out.

Before getting into the water, Armed took us to a section of the beach where there were mud pools, the mud was meant to be full of nutrients and really good for the skin. We caked ourselves in thick black mud and then lay still as it dried on our faces, arms, legs and stomachs. As it dried it was meant to make us younger and better looking.

"You do this every week, Armed?"

"Yes, every week".

"You want to get a refund mate" I said, "Either the mud isn't working or you're actually about 132 years old and still going strong".

It has to be one of the strangest sensations in this world. Stepping into the Dead Sea. A huge evaporating lake with water so thick it feels like you're stepping into olive oil. There are virtually no waves, the few there are slop slowly and quietly onto the shore. It's warm, like a perfectly regulated bath and it highlights every tiny cut and scratch on your body. Every wound, regardless how small becomes a saline sponge, soaking up the stinging minerals from the thick gloopey liquid, each one feeling like a brand new scratch opening out. The thickness of the water is a really strange sensation, it's very tempting to want to submerge yourself totally, but if the water gets in your eyes it would hurt like hell. My eyes were delicate enough as it was, I was certain I'd go blind if I got any of this stuff in them. I stepped out into deeper water, gently laid back and lifted my feet, half expecting to sink backwards, I prepared to get a face full of thick salty water, but instead I was actually floating on the water.

Above me, the cloudless sky was deep blue, the sun burned brightly and reflected off the flat surface of the water. To one side of the Sea stood the mountains of the Ghawr Almazra'a District of Jordan. On the other, the mountains of the Negev desert. I lay between them on the surface of the Dead Sea, afloat and in awe. This was what I had come for. This peace and beauty, this heaven on earth far from the madding crowd of Dafna, a whole world away from the life I'd lived in Coventry and London. This was what I had been searching for all my life.

We showered and returned to our coach, next stop was Masada, the fortified mountain palace overlooking the Dead Sea. Built by Herod The Great, it sits atop a mountain and is virtually impenetrable from below. The site was taken over by the Sicarii, an offshoot of the Zealots, a tribe of Jewish people. The Sicarii and the Zealots were causing the Romans a few headaches, you know, sacking villages, slaughtering the inhabitants, stealing their produce and driving away in uninsured or taxed motor cars, that sort of thing. Anyway, the geezer in charge of the Romans got a little peeved and sent in around 15,000 soldiers to besiege the little hilltop palace. The Romans spent 3 years building a ramp up to the city gates, some 1,300 feet above the ground. Thousands of tons of rock and earth were dumped to create access for a battering ram to break into the site.

According to historic legend, the inhabitants didn't fancy the idea of becoming Roman Slaves, they'd seen the prospectus and compared the whole thing to Iain Duncan Smith's Workfare scheme, only better. On April 16th, in the year 73 AD, 15,000 Romans stormed the city, with swords drawn and blood in their hearts they liberated almost nothing. The storehouses were all alight, food, fodder and stores had been set ablaze, there was nothing to save. The water cistern had been poisoned, and all 960 inhabitants, men, women and children were dead. There were only 2 women and 5 children left alive. It was through them that the story of the mass suicide of the Sicarii was known.

On the eve of the invasion, the Sicarii elders had a meeting. It was decided that they could not withstand the mighty force of the Romans encamped below. Rather than allow the Romans the honour of victory, they chose to burn everything of use to them, food, buildings, furniture, everything. They contaminated the water to make it unusable, and picked 10 of their best men to slaughter each and every person in the city. One of those then had to kill the other 9 and finally himself, thus leaving nothing for the Romans but an empty victory. The 2 women and their 5 children had other ideas and hid themselves away while this slaughter was going on, their names were lost to history, but I bet there must have been one hell of a party in Masada on the 15th April, 73 AD.

Access to Masada is via the 'Snake Pass', a long winding path that leads up to the site from the eastern edge of the mountain. It takes about an hour to an hour and a half to climb and is bloody knackering. It is well worth the hike though. Once we made it inside the city wall, we saw the remnants of the buildings, the wall that encircled the site and some of the towers that protected it. We climbed the walls to take our first look out over the desert and the sea below. The view was breathtaking. I sat on the wall looking out as Armed told the story of Masada. I took it all in and felt chills running through my body. How such a beautiful place could have such a violent and catastrophic history was beyond contemplation. The anguish and suffering, knowing that all must die to spite one's victors, the wives, children, livestock, everything.

The sky was bright blue, the Dead Sea reflected magnificently below with it's white mineral encrusted edging, outlined against the pale yellow and brown sand. The red rocks of the mountains beyond the sea, in Jordan, on the eastern side of the water, struck a harsh but shimmering line against the sky. Everything was quiet, silent as a deep sleep, as calm as the grave. Masada still holds many secrets, for 2,000 years it lay uninhabited, it's ghosts left to roam unseen. Their rusty cars still in the parking lot, uninsured, untaxed, their tyres well and truly flat.

There is a magic in the air at Masada, the warm breeze that kisses your skin is filled with it the intoxicating imagery of history, strife and siege. Of life carrying on, despite the building of the Roman camp below. Despite the threat of siege and guerrilla warfare, the tunnels that led to the foot of the mountain were never discovered by the Romans, they couldn't understand how the Sicarii were able to raid their supplies and livestock at night. The Summer Palace Herod had built, overlooking the sea and the desert, was an incredible feat of engineering and foresight. To have lived within these walls would have been to have lived without many of the fears endured by other peoples of the day, those who lived on the floor of the valleys, those most at risk of invasion and plunder, those with little protection from marauding gangs. Masada was security, safety in a time of uncertainty. Masada stands as a symbol of defiance, the few against the many, holding out to the bitter end and in the last moment, in the face of overwhelming odds, having the nerve to say "Fuck you! You will never own me."

My heart and soul lie in the dusty earth, 1,300 feet above the dry desert sand. In a place where one can no longer tell the size of an object in the valley below, where there is nothing with which to compare scale or distance. Where the sun rises each day, with such magnificence from beyond the eastern horizon, behind the mountains, beyond the thick, still waters of a dead sea, on a mountain's top, I discovered the real meaning of defiance, the very essence of Punk Rock, "You'll never take me alive....."

We travelled further south, deep into the desert to where we would stop for the night. We arrived at Sede Boker later in the evening, it was already dark and

once we'd eaten supper, Armed took us on a tour of the 'Museum of the desert'. There were stuffed snakes, rats, and Ibex, those strange mountain goats that manage to find tufts of grass on a ledge that even Chris Bonnington wouldn't ever want to climb up to.

"They're not real though are they?" I asked Armed.

"What do you mean?"

"Those one's on the mountain sides, 500 feet off the ground, 200 feet from the top on a vertical face standing on a ledge 3 inches wide and they've got 4 legs, come off it, they're not real are they? they're robots put there to bring in tourists, I mean, how come they don't fall- and why aren't there loads of dead ones at the bottom of the cliffs?"

Armed smiled a little ironically, but it was a smile all the same, he knew where I was coming from and appreciated my sense of humour.

"The desert is full of wonder and mystery, innit?"

We woke next morning and headed off to the dining room for breakfast. "SUGAR PUFFS!" I blurted, "They've got Sugar Puffs!" I shoved a bowl into the open box, pulled out an overflowing bowl of cereal and grabbed a pitcher of milk. I hadn't seen a sugar puff for months, possibly years. The food at Dafna had been superb, wonderful fresh fruit, vegetables, yogurts etc, but no bloody sugar puffs, not a single one. I gulped my bowlful down and went back for seconds, then thirds. No matter how many i ate, I could not quell the hunger inside me for these little puffs of sweet honey goodness, I was in breakfast heaven, even the milk was perfectly chilled and refreshing. Bowls 10, 11, and 12 hardly touched the sides, but by the time I made it to 17 I noticed some of the funny looks I was getting from other diners in the room. Maybe I overdid it a little, but wow, sugar puffs, in the desert, happy days indeed.

"Now that we've all eaten" announced Armed, "we can start our day, with a short walk to the site of the grave of David Ben Gurion, the first president of the state of Israel".

Armed led us outside, beyond the museum we'd visited the previous night, along a pathway, behind a row of trees. The track was well worn, a sign of it being a popular attraction, the first president had obviously been a well respected man, not only did he have an airport named after him in Tel Aviv, but they let him pick anywhere he wanted, for his grave site. He had the whole country to choose from and he chose here. We walked past the row of trees, tall conifer like things about 50 feet high with a hedge beneath, obscuring our view. Once we turned the corner the scenery unfolded before us. Side by side lay two graves next to a monument and a flag pole, the Star Of David hung limply from the mast, there was no breeze to lift its bulk into the air. Beyond the gravestones lay the true beauty of the picture, I understood immediately why this spot had been chosen for his final resting place, the Zin Valley opened out before us, a beautiful wilderness of white, yellow, red and green sand, stones and mountains. I caught my breath and stood silently gazing out into the wilderness.

"This is the tomb of David Ben Gurion, the other, his wife, Paula". Armed spoke with much reverence. "This was chosen by themselves to be their final resting place, looking out onto the Wilderness of Zin".

If ever I could have chosen a place for myself, I could never improve on this. There are many beautiful places on Earth, many it seemed, were in Israel, but in all my travels I had never seen such a place. I was gobsmacked and maybe even a little overawed, the valley, the mountains, the sky, a belly full of sugar puffs and it was barely 9 AM.

We admired the view for a while, photo's were taken and I drew a mental picture of a third grave on this site, my own. If only I could find somewhere like this, a place of my own to be laid to rest, so far away from the world.

Armed gathered us up and we walked out a few miles into the desert. There was a track that seemed to head out into the desert, to and over a large hill in the distance.

"Here we wait, our camels will join us soon".

We sat on the ground as Armed took the opportunity to chat about how to behave around camels, what to expect from them and that we shouldn't be upset if the handlers hit the camels to control them.

"Camels are beasts of burden, they are powerful animals and can kill you if things go wrong. When we hit them with a stick, they feel it, but they have very thick skins and it's not as painful as it may look. The main thing is to keep them well behaved, and to keep all of you safe".

His words may have been meant to reassure, but I felt as though it was going to be a lot worse than it turned out to be in practice.

It wasn't long before a train of camels approached from beyond a nearby hill. They were herded by a gang of young Arab boys, maybe mid teens, there were 6 camels and an equal number of handlers. Armed welcomed them and they chatted for a while in Arabic, they all seemed very friendly.

The idea was that each camel would have 3 people assigned to it, one would walk at the side of the camel and the others would ride, swapping places every half an hour or so, in order to change places and give the camels a rest. But to start with, we had to show the animals that we were in charge. To do this we had to stand by the head of the beast,facing forward so as not to make eye contact, pull it's rein so the head came level with our own at which point we had to make a noise like trying to honk up a particularly nasty gremlin. A rasping KKKKKHHHHHHRRRR! sound from the back from the back of our throats, translated into camel, it meant something along the lines of "Fuck with me and I will be toasting your testicles for supper!"

Having asserted our mastery, we then had to pull the rein down further, forcing the animal down on it's front legs, once down the back followed and it was safe then for the riders to climb into their saddles. Getting back up was a lumbering jolt. The camels moved in such a way as to almost give you whiplash if you didn't cling on tight. From my place on the ground, it didn't look like the most comfortable of rides. I walked at the side for the first leg of the trip, happy enough to be out in the desert, the sand and dust beneath my feet rising in tiny dust clouds to coat my boots and shins. This was it, the Wilderness of Zin, about as far removed from the world I'd grown up in as I could imagine.

We walked in convoy, nose to tail at a steady pace further into the desert, it was hot and dry, dusty underfoot. I kept my eyes open, scanning for snakes and scorpions, it would be just my luck to step on a Rattlesnake or stick my boot in a scorpions' nest. I need not have worried, the path was clear as we approached the base of the hill we'd been heading toward, Armed called a halt, everyone switched places and I rode a camel for the first time in my life.

We followed the path as it rose up the long back of the narrow, diamond shaped hill . The path narrowed as we climbed and before too long there was a long drop on both sides. Looking down made me feel nauseous, I hate heights and being on top of a lumbering camel, walking a razor track on the top of bloody great hill in the middle of nowhere, left me feeling just a tad green in the gills. The view was beautiful. We could see for miles in all directions. Nothing but empty desert lay in all directions, rocky hills breaking out from the sandy floor, red, yellow, white and green mineral rich rock coloured the wilderness as far as the eye could see. Between sky and desert, nothing stirred, no life other than our own could be seen, it was as desolate a place as one could imagine. It was beautiful.

We walked and rode hour after hour, through wadi's, canyons and desert wilderness. I was riding on the back of one camel when the Sugar Puffs began to filter through. If ever there's a time when you really don't need to take a dump, it's when you're travelling in a group, in the desert, with no visible cover anywhere in sight. I looked around for somewhere to go, my cheeks clenched but also spread open by my position in the saddle, the urge to go becoming greater with every step and sway of the camels' movement. There was a hill off to our left, and way up near to the top of it, I spotted a small bush, it was the only cover I could see for miles, somehow I knew I would have to get up there, it was my only chance for a moment of privacy.

"Okay everybody, we'll stop now" Armed's timing could not have been better, I felt as though he must have known what I was thinking.

"I'll just be a minute mate, gotta go" I said, climbing down from my camel and hot footing it up the hill. I didn't bother looking back, nobody would leave without me and I couldn't do my business anywhere else but behind the bush, way up on the hillside. I made it just in time, there was a pretty big turtle popping it's head out to say hello. Behind the bush I found a deep hole in the ground and thought for a second about spreading my axles across the divide, but something seemed odd, like why it was here, on the hillside, with a bush in front of it? I decided not to unload into the chasm and instead squatted off to one side evacuating as I went down. My relief was instant, a massive jobby that back home would have equated to a six flush pan monster, was born of my bowel. As quick as I went down, I bolted upright, my shorts around my knees and not a doc leaf or square of paper in sight. Only the familiar faces of my fellow travellers as they too reached the hole behind the bush. I pulled up my shorts, and hastily joined the group, infiltrating a position away from the warm beast on the floor.

"What we have here, is a desert water hole. The Bedouin use this to collect water from deep down in the ground. A bucket would be tied to a rope and lowered down to collect fresh water, it is clean and drinkable. Without these holes, life in the desert would be impossible. Knowing the position of these water holes is an important aspect to Bedouin life. They are closely guarded secrets, critical for the survival of the camel and the travelling man." Armed was a font of knowledge, I wish I knew a fraction of what he did. "Any questions, anybody?"

"Yes, I have one," A voice piped up from beyond the hole. Stuart the Elder was pushing something on the floor with a twig. "What sort of animal does a shit like this?"

We spent the night out under the stars once more, the sky full of the most amazing clusters of stars and heavenly bodies. It was silent, save for the occasional grunt of a camel, and the breathing of sleeping travellers. Armed had disappeared with some of the young boys at one point. When they returned, he was more relaxed, smiling and giggling a little more than he should have. He was a stoner, out here in the desert alcohol could dehydrate and kill a man, but cannabis, well, that just you through the night. In the morning Armed took us for a short stroll from the camp and stopped in a wadi where he urged us all to sit down.

"One thing I like to do on these tours, is to bring you out and away from the background noise. The desert is a quiet place, there is no traffic, no conversation, no noise pollution. Instead, there is silence, pure beautiful silence that you will never find anywhere else. But what you may not know, is just how loud that silence can be. I want you all to relax, close your eyes and listen to the desert".

Everybody relaxed, someone sniffed, another coughed. It seemed that some people hadn't quite understood what Armed was trying to get across to them. I pulled myself up and walked away quietly, I went about 100 yards down the dry river bed, just around a corner to escape the coughs and sniffing. I lay down on the ground, closed my eyes and listened. The blood in my body coursed noisily through my head, filling my ears with a strange sound I'd never noticed before. I concentrated a little more and suddenly there was a loud buzz in my head, a background noise that seemed to boom all around me, it came from all directions at once. It was the sound Armed had wanted us to hear, the deafening sound of silence. It was a little overwhelming and somewhat disconcerting, I jumped up and returned to the group, I had heard it, on my own, away from the others. I told Armed later on that day, he smiled knowingly, there was a bond there, a commonality we both recognised in each other.

"You have the best job in the world, Armed. You're a very lucky man".

"You like the desert, but you should come in the spring, when the flowers bloom and cover the land with colours, that is when it is most beautiful".

We walked and rode the whole day until we came upon our bus in a lay-by. We said goodbye to the camels, and the young Arab handlers and took a short ride to the edge of the world.

We stood amazed, our mouths wide open. Before us was the Ramon Crater, a massive natural crater known locally as the Makhtesh Ramon. We stood like visitors at the Grand Canyon, looking down into the abyss. Incredible rock formations,with bright coloured layers lay before us. For the umpteenth time in the last few months, I was speechless. I had never heard of this place, and yet it was a spectacularly beautiful scene. A massive crater as deep as a mountain is high, running for miles from one horizon to the next. As we look out two fighter jets fly through the canyon, I feel as though I could reach out and swat them from the air but I know it's an optical illusion. It's not normal to look down upon a speeding aircraft, not when you're standing on Terra Firma. The planes are followed by the familiar sound of roaring engines, echoing off the sides of the canyon, the roar is amplified as the sound waves reverberate and spill outward into the open sky as the craft themselves rose in the far distance returning high up into the atmosphere, their manoeuvres continuing as they disappeared from view.

We returned to the coach and headed south, once more on the road to Eilat. Our next stopover was at a Hotel by the side of the road. It was dark and we could see nothing beyond the perimeter of the complex. There was a shop, a filling station and restaurant. We ate hungrily and eventually went off to our dormitory like accommodation.

After breakfast we drove to Timna Park and were taken by foot to see more incredible rock formations, and the famous copper mines for which the park is famous. The mines date back to around 500 BC and there are carvings and writings on many of the rock faces in the park, writings in Egyptian Heiroglyphics, Roman and ancient Hebrew too. It's also the home of the King Solomon's Pillars, a place where erosion has carved out some magnificent columns of rock, which were alleged to have something to do with the King himself, although there is no proof. We wandered around the park for a couple of hours, had lunch and then took the bus to our last port of call, Eilat. Eilat is Israels Costa Del Sunshine, the most southerly town, the only town in Israel on the Red Sea coast. It is the go-to place for young Israeli's and worldwide traveller's looking for water sports action. Eilat has 2 airports, one in the town itself, and another out in the desert some 40 Km's from the town. It is a port city too, and boasts a spectacular harbour, Sea Life Centre and Marina. Our last night of the tour was spent in the Yacht Pub, drinking beer and listening to some live music, a local band had set up in a far corner of the bar and were entertaining the punters. It wasn't punk rock, it wasn't even rock, but it was live and there was beer, so life was good. It was even better since when we arrived at the hotel, Armed invited me to his room.

"Don't say anything" he whispered to me as I went into my room to dump my bag. I had no idea what he wanted and the potential scenario's played out in my mind.

Scenario one; He likes that I spent the week helping when I could, and he wanted to thank me for being a good fellow traveller. Downside being he might like me a little too much and I may get raped.

Scenario two; he didn't appreciate my help or the huge turd I nearly dropped into his mates' water source, in which case I may get beaten unconscious and raped. Scenario three; he likes me, we smoke a couple of joints together and exit his room like the giggling schoolkids we were, stoned, sworn to secrecy and not a rapist in sight.

Thankfully, Armed liked me in a scenario three kinda way, we were it seemed, very naughty schoolkids.

Next morning, we ate some breakfast at the hotel and headed down to the Marina. We were going on a yacht cruise, on the Red Sea.

The marina was a hubbub of activity, it seemed that all the charter yachts left the marina at about the same time each day, hundreds of passengers milled about on the jetty climbing aboard one boat or another. There were several large schooners, tall ships with huge masts and enough deck space to carry a hundred or more passengers. Motor boats with glass bottoms for seeing the coral and sea life below the water's surface, even a yellow submarine. Vessels of all shapes and sizes took on their passengers. Once counted, checked and given the go ahead, the boats pulled out of the marina and headed south to where 4 nations' borders met. We were in Israeli water, to our east

Jordan.Here In the Gulf of Aqaba lay another frontier, to the south west Egypt, to the south east, Saudi Arabia.

Aqaba is the Jordanian port made famous by a mister T E Lawrence, better known as Lawrence of Arabia. The attack on Aqaba in 1917 nearly cost Lawrence his life, he accidentally shot his own camel in the head and was thrown from the dead animal as it fell to the ground. Lawrence the Camel killer, went on to capture the town from the Turks and bought himself a motorbike.

We were taken aboard one of the schooners, the crew were a mix of former kibbutz volunteers from all over the world, I got talking to one, Oleg, he was from Russia and lived and worked on the boat. An idea began to seed, maybe, just maybe, I could do this too.

Our cruise lasted a couple of hours. We were taken out toward the Jordanian border and then turned southwest to head back towards Dolphin Beach, just past the Naval Dockyard. The captain of the boat made an announcement over the tannoy, in a very heavily accented voice, he told us that the dolphins were free to come and go as they pleased, they were not captive, but they enjoyed the company of the bathers and the treats they were given, so they would hang around by the beach and let children pet them. If you are really lucky, you could swim with them too, but no guesses as to who would be the fastest. Beyond Dolphin Beach, we followed the coast down past green, yellow red and white hills and cliffs. The bright blue sky highlighted their colours magnificently against the dark blue sea. Dark blue, not Red. The Red Sea is not Red it's blue, the same colour as every other Sea I'd seen, and from what I could tell, it didn't taste like wine either. We motored on until we reached the border at Taba, the gateway to the Sinai peninsular. Here we stopped and were allowed to dive into the water. For the next 30 minutes, we dived into the water and climbed back on board, dived back in and swam around the boat as much as we could. We savoured every moment of our swim, having spent the last few days in the desert, being immersed in the sea was heavenly, the warm water soothed my sun baked skin and I could have stayed in there all day if I could, floating, swimming and looking down at the multitude of different coloured fish swimming around beneath me.

When eventually, it was time to go, I climbed back on board and was immediately handed a plate of food. Kebab meat, salad, rice, houmous, salsa and a big glass of the same purple shit we drank at Dafna. Life was good.

Many of us swapped names and addresses once we arrived back on shore. I thanked Armed for having done such a good job of looking after us. His really was the best job in the world and when I grow up, I wanted to be just like him.

Stuart and I returned to Dafna, our minds blown by the fantastic journey we'd just been on. It felt strange being back, when we left it felt as though it would be for good, as if we weren't returning, but we did. Now we were here, the dynamic's of the place had changed. New volunteers had arrived, others had left. I worked a couple of days in the fields and then began to teach another volunteer what to do. My time at Dafna was coming to an end, and I wasn't really prepared. Shlomo had my passport again, he took it both for safekeeping and to renew my visa. I could stay in Israel for another 6 months once it was granted, but I had no plans whatsoever to stay at Dafna. I wanted to get out, to go to Tel Aviv and work, or maybe even Eilat, I wasn't sure which would be best, slaving on a construction site in Tel Aviv or hoping for a job on a boat in Eilat, there was construction work in Eilat too, plenty of people queued each morning outside the Peace Café in the hope of getting a job, but I wanted something more regular, and I was hoping to find it soon.

We were only back a week when it was time to go again. This time, it was the Kibbutz's quarterly trip to Eilat. A carbon copy of the trip Stuart and I had just been on, but without the camels and the surprise 6 flusher behind a bush. Our journey was to be by coach all the way. Kenny and I were back together, along with Jim too.

Our first stop was the Youth Hostel at Masada. Stuart and I revelled in telling everyone about this place, and also in building up the challenge for the ascent up the Snake Pass. If Craig and Dave could do it in 32 minutes, Kenny and I would beat them. That was the mantra, but in reality, I knew what lay ahead and as much as I would give it a shot, I had no plans to kill myself trying to beat anybody's record.

Sure enough as soon as we gathered at the foot of the mountain, half a dozen couples and some single volunteers jockeyed for position to get away up the path. It was still dark, cool enough to run, but dark enough to stumble and hurt one's self.

"And Go!" called Kenny, before I was ready, he was off like a light, at least 10 paces ahead of me before I really got going. The little viking was away and running like he meant it. I gave chase in a halfhearted way, I knew just how steep it was ahead and paced myself. There were steps cut into the path, some short, some narrow, some very steep, it was hard to know where to put your feet in the dark, but we kept going, hoping not to twist an ankle or fall and break something. Up and up we went, higher and further away from the bulk of the group who'd sensibly chosen to walk up the path. Time was on their side, competition was our driving force. The higher we went, the slower I ran, Kenny was way ahead of me and I really didn't care, I was struggling for air and by the half way point, had all but given up.

I reached the top and Kenny was waiting, triumphantly. He was still out of breath, but he was happy, happy he'd beaten me, happy he'd won and happy he'd beaten the record, so he claimed. There was no way of knowing, but I let him gloat, 28 minutes, was the new record.

"Kenny, Jim, over here". I called the others over to the city wall. It was still dark when we entered the site and I rushed over to get the best position I could to see the sun rise from beyond the Jordanian horizon.

There were photographers setting up their cameras on huge tripod. Massive telephoto lenses taking aim at one spot in the distance, all waiting for that first sign of the sun breaking above the horizon. When it came, none were disappointed. A huge gasp of air followed the first rays of light, it was audible all along the wall. As many as a hundred people stopped breathing for a second as the dark sky began to lighten, the ridges of the mountains beyond the Dead Sea came into view properly and the stars were turned off for another day. The darkness moved above us, like a silk sheet sliding silently from a bed, behind it came the light in great beams across the sky until the first piece of the corona surfaced and rose majestically above the black line of the land. To us it was a beautiful sunrise. For the Sicarii who'd lived and died here, 2,000 years earlier, and the Romans before them, this must have been a truly awesome spectacle. The moment when Luna gives way to Sol and another new day begins, relief for those who survived the night, only to struggle on once more through the next day.

As the light spread over the sky, the great sea below shimmered and reflected in return, silvery blue amid the black silhouette of the land. The air came to life with birdsong and a gentle breeze blew warm about us. Masada was alive once more.

From Masada, we were taken to Ein Gedi, to bathe in the waterfall before lunch, after which we took a mud bath and once again floated on the waters of the Dead Sea at Ein Bokek. I loved these places and felt no less in awe being here again so soon after the desert trek.

At Sede Boker we settled in for the night. I didn't want to spoil anything for any of the other volunteers, so I said nothing about the view by the tombs of David and Paula Ben Gurion. They would have to see for themselves the beautiful view of the Zin Valley.

I avoided the sugar puffs at breakfast, 17 bowls in one morning had been enough to see me through for a few months longer, instead, I had toast, omelettes and fresh fruit and peppers, and maybe some pickled Herring.

As we came out of the Desert Museum, Yitzhak led us towards the tombs. "Do you trust me?" I asked one of the new volunteers, she was from Sweden and looked at me in a confused way.

"Yes, why?" she asked.

"Then do as I say and you won't regret this". I stood behind her and placed my hands over her eyes. "Now keep walking, just keep going straight unless I say otherwise".

I guided her along the footpath, around the corner and out to the tombs, to a spot where she could take in the entire view without having had it open up in tantalising bits and pieces. I had thought about this and wondered if it would work.

"Oh my GOD!" Her reaction when I told her to open her eyes, told me I was right, that she wasn't prepared to see such a fantastic view in front of her. "Oh my god, oh my god, thank you so much, this is.... Wow!"

A simple act of trust, repaid.

Our next stop was the Ramon Crater near Mitzpe Ramon. Again we stood near the edge the edge, tiny little dots peering into the chasm before us. To see so many beautiful sights in one's lifetime is fortunate and an honour, to do so twice, within a couple of weeks is very humbling. The pain and misfortune, bad choices and whatever else that had led me to be where I was, were all worthwhile. I was living a life I could never have previously imagined, and in many ways, I was doing so less for myself than for those I'd lost, for my kids, in order that one day I would still be around to see them, not that they would necessarily understand, but because it would keep me going. They had their own problems now, problems I had brought about by not being there, not just now, but right from the start. It was, also, for those that could and those that would never see these things. I felt deeply about living for those who'd lost their lives, those who'd never see what I could, would and should. For those too, the many that would never be able to see, but wished they could. Maybe it is for them now, that I am writing this, so they can see through my words, the pictures in my mind. Or was it all just selfishness. Just me doing what I wanted again, not caring about other people. Did I? Do I? I know what I feel and how I felt at those times, the best times and the darkest. When life tasted so bitter as to make me wish it would end there and then, without warning, without mercy. When only the words of Helen or her sister Nicky, could be enough to stop me from harming myself. Those were truly dark times for me, times I hid from the outside world, times I was saved from, with a cup of tea and a shoulder to cry on.

Looking out at an almost lunar landscape, with the sun on my skin and the wind in my ears, all I could think of was to say, "Thank You!" The words drifted in the wind, joined with those from the Swedish girl whose eyes I'd covered at Sede Boker and fluttered off into the great beyond. Two solitary 'Thank You's in a world of noise and chatter.

In Eilat, we were booked in to stay at the Red Mountain Hostel. Jim and I got talking to a South African woman on the desk. She told us there was plenty of work going in Eilat, and if we stayed at the hostel, they'd look after our bags for us while we were out in the day. She showed us a cupboard with a couple of bags already hidden, everything was falling into place. Once we got back to Dafna, we'd get our passports from Shlomo, head back down to Eilat and look for work, once we were settled, we could take things from there.

Once more I was taken on a boat ride to Taba. This time however, we were on a much smaller yacht, not that it really mattered, it was a freebie, a treat from Dafna for all the hard work we'd put in.

Yitzhak had overheard us talking of finding work in Eilat, he said there were always jobs going on the yachts and he would put in a good word for us. Nothing came of it though, and later that evening we were back on the bus.

10 REDEMPTION SONG

Somewhere on the road from Eilat, about 100 km's north lies a truck stop. A little place, with a shop, a zoo and hotel. We stopped for the night and after breakfast Yatzhik introduced Jim and myself to the manager of the place.
"You are from England?"
"Yes, I've been here 3 months now, love it." I replied, hardly noticing Yitzhak as he slipped off out of the way.
"You want to work here?"
"Doing what?..."
"I need two peoples to help here, you can live in the staff accommodation, sometimes you help in the hotel, sometimes work around the site, I need guys who can build walls and clean beds, maybe help in shop. Lots of different things, but I need you now, 100 shekels a day plus accommodation, you get one day a week off. Are you interesting?"
As job interviews go, this was pretty quick and to the point, there was nothing stopping us staying here right now and getting started, nothing except Shlomo, and our passports sitting in his safe.
"If you can wait until the day after tommorrow, we will be here, definitely. We have to go back to Dafna for our passports but will come straight back, as soon as we get them, we'll get the first bus back, what d'you say Jim?"
"Sweet, geezer, yeah, I'll have some of that, 'appy days innit?"
Jim was on board and -at last, it felt like the shackles of Dafna were finally coming off. It had only been 3 months since I arrived. So much had happened that it felt like a lifetime, a life sentence-lifted.
"We have also the Lion to feed, and the Snakes and other animals here, you are not afraid of to be feeding them, no?"
"Hell no, that would be a pleasure".
The ride back to Dafna went by in a flash of excitement and joking around. Jim said I was welcome to feed the Lion, as it was kept on a chain and without

a cage, he didn't fancy getting too close to the business end of it, even with an armful of dinner to keep it's attention from gnawing on his lanky legs.

We arrived back at the kibbutz late in the afternoon. Shlomo was nowhere to be found and so we would have to see him in the morning when he came to his office. Until then, there was a bunch of new arrivals to meet, fresh blood from England had arrived the day we left for Eilat. They'd been met by those volunteers who hadn't come on the Eilat trip, the ones that were planning to leave, were themselves new arrivals, or had not been interested in the trip.

Everyone was gathered on the grass outside the entrance to the Vol Bar, all sitting neatly in a big circle, drinking from bottles, smoking the last of their duty-free Marlboro's. It wouldn't be long before they were chugging along with the rest of us, smoking cheap Noblesse and drinking Wodka.

I had spent the week between the Eilat trips, teaching Paul the secrets of the punch bowl. How to source the ingredients, the mix and the profit it offered. Being a bit of a 'wide-boy', Paul loved the chance of making a few Shekels on the side. My time here was coming to an end, I had trained my successor, done my work and had a bloody good time having a bloody awful time. My poorly eyes were improving, I was starting to sleep better at night and I had survived everything the Hezbollah had thrown at us. I was ready to go now, it was time to move on to the next chapter, living in the desert, on an oasis hotel/truck stop/zoo miles from anywhere.

"Chocolate..... You have chocolate?"

"Yes, I've got a big bar of Dairy Milk and some Fruit and Nut". It was a wonder if not an an absolute miracle this girl sitting opposite me in the circle of volunteers, had not been robbed already. I hadn't tasted chocolate since before I left England (the Nutella pancakes I'd had with Stuart in Tel Aviv didn't count as chocolate, not in my reckoning anyway).

I had noticed the girl with with the short dark hair and big eyes as soon as I sat down. She sat opposite me and I caught her looking at me a couple of times, her eyes seemed to be fixed on me from time to time, and then she'd look away when I looked back at her. There was a glint, *that glint,* and as a bonus, she not only had Marlboro, but chocolate too.

Her name was Tara, and once we got over the avoiding eye contact thing, it became obvious that we would be sharing her Dairy Milk before too long.

"Have you been up the water tower yet?"

"What water tower?"

"What-you've been here 4 days and nobody's shown you the tower yet? Paul, you're sacked mate, you've been caught slacking, c'mon you lot, let's show you what you've been missing".

We headed over to the tower and taking one look at it, Tara said she couldn't climb up the ladder.

"You'll be fine, I'll help you up there".

Slowly but surely I guided her up the rusty steel steps, one step at a time. As nervous as I had been my first time climbing up there, Tara was twice as bad. "....And over there is Mount Hermon" I said, in my best Jack like voice. "The highest point in Israel, and that my friends, is the end of this tour...." I had done my bit now, passed on the knowledge to the new arrivals, all that remained now was the river, seeing as Paul hadn't even shown them that either. I was beginning to wonder if my choice of successor had been a good one or not, but decided to let it go, maybe all this legacy and inheritance stuff was only important to me, maybe nobody else really cared, after all, they were here for cheap beer and giggles.

I descended the ladder last, keen to make sure everyone else got down okay. About 15 feet off the ground, one of the rungs gave way, it broke away and I fell still holding the sides of the ladder, I slipped straight down and landed with a thump on the ground. Nothing broken other than another rung in the ladder, I took it in my stride and acted like it was part of the plan, I didn't want anyone thinking it was too dangerous to go up the tower, it was an important part of being here, so I thought. Next morning however, the ladder was taped off, a large red 'DANGER' warning sign was placed at the foot of it, and it was temporarily off limits.

Jim and I went to Shlomo's office only to find a sign on the door.

"YOM KIPPUR, CLOSED"

It was a national holiday. Nothing moved in Israel, nobody worked, there were no buses and no Shlomo.

We splashed about at the river for most of the day, Tara and I got very close. She came from High Wycombe and had just left an abusive relationship with her long term partner. Dafna was a new start for her too, somewhere she wanted to regroup and get back to her old self, just like many of us, looking for new beginnings in a far off place. I told her about myself, my past, my hopes for the future, about the job I was going to, even though today was a holiday, tomorrow Jim and I would get our passports and leave as we'd planned, a little late, but it was all we could do seeing as we hadn't known the country was going to sleep for a day.

Jim and I left the next morning, Tara waved us off at the bus stop, she was having pains in her legs and after we'd gone went to see the nurse. It turned out she had DVT (Deep Vein Thrombosis), basically a blood clot in the leg which if passed to the heart would be fatal. She was given a course of blood thinning medication and told to do only light work around the kibbutz, basically, this meant bed rest for a couple of weeks.

Jim and I got the bus to Qiryat Shmona, then another to Tel Aviv. We had about an hour to wait until our next bus to take us south to the Oasis Truck Stop and the start of our new lives. I was hoping to get myself settled and when the time was right, to send for Tara once a vacancy existed for her too. We stood looking over the balcony of the bus station. From the upper floor we were able to watch the people hurrying along below. Tel Aviv bus station was an incredibly busy place. Tourists, business people, families, soldiers, sailors, volunteers and everyone you could imagine passed through this place. Some dithering, others running or walking determinedly towards their allotted space at one corner or another of this chaotic building. I looked below and saw a sea of people milling, rushing, ambling and darting in and out, an endless flow of bodies. Then one stood out, a woman in an IDF uniform, with long blonde hair. In another time and place she was outstanding, beautiful and so very much in control of her destiny. Here, in her olive green uniform, she was stunning, powerful and determined, but vulnerable too. Her long hair a target for those who'd wish to hurt her because of her uniform. She was a target because she was a prize, a beautiful woman, captive and very vulnerable. Could I harm her in battle, could I fight her? Ha, she'd kick ten barrels of shit out of me before breaking into a sweat. But she was beautiful, and of all the people in that building, I noticed only her.

We stopped at Be'er Sheva, just long enough for a stretch of the legs, cigarette and a cold can of Coke from a machine. Next stop would be our new home.

We pulled up at the bus stop, got our bags and waited for the bus to leave. Our new home lay before us, new adventures, experiences and friendships in the middle of the desert. Other than the desert, there was nothing around us for miles and miles. The next town was Eilat, we could go there on our day's off, maybe have a few beers in the Underground Pub, or treat ourselves to a full English breakfast whenever we could. It was just a bus ride away, just an hour down the road.

"Can I help you?" The young woman on the reception desk looked at us strangely, I don't think she liked us.

"Yes, we've come to start working here".

"Working?"

"Yes, we were talking with the manager the other day, he offered us a job here, we were meant to be here yesterday but couldn't get our passports from the kibbutz because it was Yom Kippur. Anyway, we're here now".

"Jobs? I'm sorry I don't know anything about any jobs. Who did you speak to?"

"A big fellow, don't remember his name-he was sitting over here in this chair, big bloke, y'know, fat guy with a bit of a beard".

"I think I know who you mean, let me go and check for you." She went into a back room and returned a few minutes later.

"I'm sorry, but you were supposed to be here yesterday, you didn't come and it seems we have taken on some other people now. The jobs are gone".

Oh well that's alright then, the jobs are gone and we are stuck here in the middle of the fucking desert with no money, no water and enough food for a fucking anorexic hamster to live on for about a day, said no one, ever.

"Are you sure? I mean, he did promise us..." The futility of these words were even more audible once they'd left my mouth. I couldn't stop myself from saying them, but I knew they meant nothing. There would be no change in the status quo. Jim and I were up the creek, without a paddle, in fact, even shit creek was a dried up wadi.

We walked outside to the bus stop.

"What're we doin' then geezer?" Jim had nominated me as boss, thanks.

"Well, we have virtually no money, food or water. We're in the middle of nowhere and nowhere else to go........ Let's make the most of it mate, we'll go for a walk out there, build a shelter somewhere and chill for a couple of days. If we want water we can come back here and get some, but we've got biscuits, sardines and a tin of potatoes, we'll be okay for a couple of days, chill out in the desert, then go to Eilat and get some work, yeah?"

"Sounds like a plan to me, fella".

We picked up our bags and crossed the road, heading out into the wilderness. A couple of miles away from the road, we started to work on our plan some more.

"If we wait until we're really hungry, then eat, we can stay longer, you know, make it last".

"What about fags? I've only got a couple of smokes left, I was going to get some once we settled in, like"

"I've got about half a packet left, that should do us until tomorrow," I replied. "But we have to watch our money too, not buy any fags if we can help it, food is more important now mate". Jim didn't seem too keen on having to go without a smoke for a while, his face seemed to take on a more serious look. The broad grin that usually spanned his face from one side to the other was gone. Jim, the pill popping, Trance loving cool geezer from the shires was out of his comfort zone. This was not his idea of a good idea.

"No mate. No" He'd stopped dead in his tracks. "No, this is wrong mate"

"What's up?"

"Look, I know you love it 'ere an' all, but like, the desert ain't going nowhere is it?" He had a point.

"No, I guess not". I replied, "So what are you thinking?"

"Well, I reckon we should go to Eilat, get some work and money and then come out to the desert". Fuck me, who slipped Jim a sensible pill when I wasn't looking, this was just plain weird. Jim, being sensible and there wasn't an adult in sight, in fact, there wasn't anything in sight. Nothing. Nowhere to hide, nowhere to shelter, nothing to shelter under. Bollocks, bollocks, bollocks.

"You want to go back. Hitch a lift to Eilat and take it from there?"

"I reckon we can go doss on the beach, get some work, ditch our bags at the Red Mountain and once we have somewhere to live, we can come back here anytime we like".

My dream of living in the desert, catching and eating whatever we could kill with my little penknife, seemed to be fading, Jim had been poisoned with a lethal dose of sensibility, and nothing I said now could bring him back. We turned around and there was no sign of where we'd come from. We were too far away to see the road, the hotel, nothing.

"Fuckin' 'ell mush, where's the road gone?"

"Don't move. We have to find our footprints and retrace our steps or we'll end up walking in circles forever. Look, there. That's the direction we came in, keep looking for more footprints and we'll find our way back alright". Now it was me that was being sensible. I blame that tin of Coke at Be'er Sheva.

We followed our footprints where there were some to follow. The ground was quite firm but occasionally there were areas of soft sand and ours were the only footprints out here. About a mile back toward the road, I saw something on the floor, between some footprints where we'd walked half an hour earlier.

"Hey, what's this-are these yours, did you drop these on the way out here?"

Right there on the ground in front of us, between both our footprints, was an unopened, brand spanking new, packet of Time cigarettes.

"They ain't mine, I've never bought a packet of Time". Jim looked serious.

"Well, if they ain't yours...." I picked the packet up and inspected it. "They weren't mine, but who...." I looked all around. Nothing. Nobody. If anyone else had dropped them, they would have left tracks in the sand. They weren't mine, and I was pretty sure they weren't Jim's either. Then I remembered the guy at the beach party, his trainers. The other guy I picked up in France. How they both needed new shoes and they were desperate, then they both looked up to the sky and pleaded, only to find a few minutes later, exactly what they needed, without any reason for them to be there. Jim and I needed cigarettes. I knew I hadn't prayed, but what about Jim, was he praying silently in his head, Could this be.... ?

Could it?

We waited by the bus stop trying to hitch a lift, nothing came through. Eventually a bus stopped.

"Get on!" Called the driver, and we did. A free ride to Eilat, on top of a free packet of fags, somebody somewhere was looking out for us.

It was evening time in Eilat, Jim and I walked down to the beach and tried to find a secluded area, settling for a spot away from the noisy bars and clubs. We laid out our sleeping bags and crashed.

For the next 3 days we roamed the town, hung around by the Peace Café for work offers, nothing. When we tried to leave our bags at the Red Mountain, a new receptionist told us we couldn't and so now we were burdened with having to carry our rucksacks with us everywhere we went. This had the knock on effect of making us as good as unemployable. Things were not going well. We hung around on the marina, asking all the crew's of all the boats if there were any vacancies. It turned out, for the most part, that the crew were hired by the 1st mate or the skipper of each boat. The skipper was the boss but he got the 1st mate to do all the work, but if a skipper didn't like someone, they were out, off the boat and gone immediately. There was no redress, the skipper's acted with total impunity, and were a pretty feared bunch.

I asked around all the crew's, the 1st mates, the skippers whenever I could. There was nothing going, but I kept trying. Morning, noon, evening, I was there, again and again. Something had to come up soon, we were starving and desperate, we would do anything, almost.

There was a daily meeting at a Christian Meeting House in Eilat. At the end of the service, a free meal was given out to all present. We decided we were just about hungry enough to sing Hallelujah and praise anyone handing out free grub. We joined a group of about 20 Happy-clappers in the garden of a building about 10 minutes walk away from the town centre. We took a seat on the back bench quietly watching, doing our very best not to look as though we were only there for the food. A congregation of about 30 Senegalese and Kenyan Christians sang enthusiastically, their arms waving, their bottoms wriggling, all I could think of was Kenny Everett with big hands pointing his fingers to the 'Lord above' and urging everyone to donate into the bucket- for the good lord's work. We put our hands into the bucket and pretended to donate, flicking a coin around the inside for effect. We were skint, we were only there for the food, and once we had been served, we made our excuses and left Kenny and his big hands to continue their ministry, without us.

We tried again and again to find work, we were hopeful but starting to think of who we could call back home to send us some money. I decided to try my luck at the Fairground, just behind the Marina. I heard they sometimes hired extra workers and went in search of something, anything. I couldn't believe my luck when I was offered a job on a little kid's ride. A miniature Big Wheel about 20 ft high, spun gently round to the sound of pop music.

"You press this button, it goes round 3 times, then you press this and stop. Then you let the parents get the children out. You got that?"

"Yes, how much is the ride?" I asked.

"It's a token, no cash, they buy a token from the kiosk, they give you 1 token each child. 1 token okay?"

I was more than Okay, I was hired, I could buy food tomorrow and we would live another day at least. I was over the bloody moon. I stayed on the ride all night, collecting tokens, opening the gate, letting the little darlings and their mothers in pressing the start button once they were ready. Sometimes I would give an extra spin, or accidentally forget to take a token so the kids could have another go. It was fun, I actually enjoyed it, even arguing with some the parents about the 1 token + 1 child = 1 ride rule. Some would push it and try to get 2 kids for 1 token, which again, I sometimes allowed, my stance being that it was just a bit of harmless fun. The machine was running so why not?

At the end of the night, my boss came back and we shut the machine down.

"So, what do you think, you like it?"

"Yes that was alright, I don't mind it at all" I said.

"Come back tomorrow and you can do it again. Here- take this."

He put out his hand and gave me 20 Shekels. It felt like a fortune, 20 NIS, about £4 in real money. I headed back to the beach and found Jim, he had a bottle of beer and was smoking a cigarette he'd managed to scrounge from someone on one of the boats. He'd saved me half of a pitta bread and some rice he'd been given too. Suddenly, we were kings, we had food, beer and cash. We may have been living on the beach, but we were proper Royalty.

Next morning I was back on the jetty at the marina, touting for work.

"See Jez, on the Zorba, he's looking for someone, I think he is anyway".

The Zorba was one of the bigger boats on the marina, a big wooden schooner and a job on here would be a dream come true. Wood, ropes and sails, what's not to love about it? I was excited at the possibly of working on board and went in search of Jez. He turned out to be a couple of years younger than myself. He was from Brighton, with sun bleached, blond and brown dreadlocks. A former punk rocker who'd sold his soul to E's (Ecstacy) and dance music, he looked like a 'Crusty' or hippy throwback with a brightly coloured but filthy bandanna, a whole raft of different stringed necklaces and ties around his wrists and neck, the biggest being a string full of keys. His feet were bare and dirty, his shorts, an old pair of denims cut off at the knee.

"I hear you might be looking for crew" I said. I recognised Jez as someone I'd been hassling ever since I arrived at the marina. Everyday I had asked him, the answer had been the same, No!

"Look, come back and see me when we get back from our cruise later, there might be a job coming up, I will have a word with our skipper first, but come back later and I'll let you know then".

This was the closest I'd been to a job, other than the fair, which was good, but didn't pay enough to get us off the beach. Working on a boat meant having a job, food, drink and a place to live. There was no money in it, but everything else was catered for.

Jim and I had made friends with quite a few people on the marina, mostly crew of the boats, but also the photographers who would snap people's pictures as they boarded the various boats. While the passengers headed off on their cruises, the 'Togs' would hurry to their studio, print off the negatives and sell the finished pic's when the passengers returned to the marina. There was good money to be made doing this, but the opportunity to do so was pretty much non-existent. The guy's doing this had the market and were not leaving any time soon. Other opportunities existed on the sport's boats, usually these were reserved for the better looking females. The macho owners only wanted someone beside them who'd boost their own ego's as they raced around the bay. Some had winches on board for Para-sailing, others, water skiing, or pulling doughnuts and banana boats. There were the casino boats too. If you looked and played the part, you could earn a lot working as a croupier or waiter/waitress. I had no chance at these sort of jobs, the tattoo on my head did nothing for my job prospects there, even if I had any smart clothes with me, I would still look like a thug to some people.

Jim and I bought some biscuits, cigarettes and bread. We were able to get water from a tap on the marina and so our bottles were always full. Some of the friendlier crew members on the boats would sneak us some food if they could get away with it. We sat around on the beach for the rest of the day watching the boats come and go, eventually, the Zorba came into view and I went to meet her. As soon as the passengers had disembarked, I let Jez know I was waiting for him. He scuttled around doing shipmate type things, such as telling people to do stuff, tidying up messy ropes, and then he climbed up the rigging, a good 20 ft off the deck before diving into the water. As he surfaced, someone else appeared on the rigging and swallow dived in after him. There was a huge splash, and then more, from the other side of the boat. It seemed as though all the crew were joining in. If this is what you got to do working on the boats, then I was definitely wanting to join in. " Gi's a job, I can do that!"

"One of our crew is leaving tonight, I have to sack him, Skipper said so, so yes, come back in the morning and I'll run you through everything. Ever worked on a boat before?"

"I used to be in the Sea Cadets, I've been on plenty of boats, and ships for that matter too. I can splice a rope, send and receive Morse Code, not brilliant at Semaphore but I know how to do it".

"You should be alright on here then," Jez cut me short, "we don't do much of that technical stuff, but if you can handle ropes you'll do okay, come back at 8 AM and we'll sort you out".

To say I was happy was a real understatement, I had a job at the fair in the evening, and a job on the Zorba, starting tomorrow. This meant I could ditch my rucksack on the boat when I was at the fair, sleep on board, eat, drink and get 2 wages, I was loaded. Jim was pleased too, this meant he could leave his bag with me and go looking for work at the Peace Café each morning. We were "Sorted, geezer, well sorted, innit?"

I worked the fair that night, taking tokens, stopping and starting the ride, arguing with customers in a mix of Arabic, Hebrew and English. Some of the mothers would put 2 or 3 kids on the ride but only give me 1 token. Sometimes I'd smile and let them off, sometimes I would try to say 'No'.

"Lo, lo, lo. Ichad token, ichad ride, Ken?" I would say.

(no,no,no. One token, one ride, yes?)

"Huh....?" Normally accompanied with a confused look.

"Wahid token ken? Wahid *(one)* token, ichad,ichad"- points at child. "Ichad, wahid, one, yes, Ken?"

"Huh.....?" Still confused.

"Ichad.....Wahid?" Signals with one finger, "Ken?"

"Ken...." Smiles, offers one token.

"Ichad child..." Points at child in seat, "Ichad.....?"

"Ken...." Points at child.

"Shteim child...." Points at 2 kids, "Shteim tokens, ken?"

"Ken..." Still offering only 1 token. At this point I give up and start the ride anyway. Ken and wahid would have to fight it out later, I knew what I was on about, even if they didn't.

Next morning, I arrived at the Zorba ready for work. Jez took me below deck and showed me around.

"This is our area, at night you sleep here if you want, or take one of the foam mats up onto the deck to sleep if you want, but make sure the skipper's don't catch you, they don't like it. Anyway, the cabins at the front there are for the crew as well, Tony and mike share the one on the left, the right is for the girls. You can store your bag in one of these cupboards here," He lifted a seat behind one of the four tables that lined the room and I looked into the empty space below. "That should be safe in there, we've never had any problems. Anyway, over here is the kitchen, just behind the bar, that's out of bounds once the chef starts to cook lunch, nobody goes in unless requested to do so. You got that?"

"Yes, seems about right, erm, what are those other doors down there by the cabins?"

"Oh those, I forgot them, that's the heads, Gents on the left, ladies on the right, and whatever you do, don't press the switch next to the Gent's light switch here, you can switch that on when we're at sea, it's for the shit tank, pumps it out into the sea, it's illegal to use near the marina, don't ever get caught with it on or you can get a big fine for that."

Jez took me on a tour of the boat, showed me everything as quickly as he could, then we ate breakfast. Cornflakes, coffee, bread and jam. Suddenly I felt like I was back in the Human Race. Living rough, directionless and skint for the last week was much harder than I had realised, but I had made it through, I was back, with food in my belly and a job to do.

"So what exactly is my job?" I asked

"Oh that, yes, you just come down here before dinner and when it's ready, take the plates of food up to the passengers, quick as you can, everyone has to be fed at the same time. Afterwards, you help bring everything back down, clean up the decks and unless there's anything to do, just stay out of sight. The cruise is for the passengers, we're here to run the boat and feed them, clean up after then stay out of the way."

As I had no specific job to do, I was just meant to hide, serve dinner and tidy up. I could do that. I stowed my bag after breakfast and tried to look eager. Jez took me to the company's office, I had to surrender my passport and fill out a job form. It was all legal and above board, I had a job, on a schooner and they were going to pay me too.

"How much?" I said.

"50 Shekels a month, it's shit, I know, but you get a share of the tips and whatever food and drink is left over each day".

This was about all we got at Dafna too, it was the going rate for volunteers wishing to stay in Israel at the time, everyone knew it, and everyone paid the same, unless they had a real job to offer. Black market workers like us, were paid the same money as the kibbutzim, a little less than the Moshav's paid, but the work was not as strenuous and demanding. A kibbutz is like a socialist farm, everyone chips in, everyone gets the same benefits. A Moshav is like a normal farm, where labourers have to earn their pay a little harder than we did on the kibbutz. Black market construction paid around 50-100 NIS a day, but you had to have somewhere to live and feed yourself, normally.

My papers done, I was welcomed to the firm and swiftly taken back on board, my first cruise about to begin. As per my instructions, I stayed below deck, playing chess, backgammon- which I still don't understand to this day, and cards. At lunchtime I helped to take plates of food upstairs onto the deck, and offer them around to the passengers, once they'd all eaten, we took the rubbish and leftovers back down to the kitchen, it was orderly chaos, nothing seemed to be fully functional, but somehow it just about worked. We were not allowed into the water on the cruises, we had to wait until we were finished for the day. At the end of the cruise, when all the passengers had disembarked, we had to tidy up, and only then could we go swimming. I couldn't hang around too long, I had to get off to the fair for my evening job. Jim was waiting for me on the jetty and I gave half of the food I'd been given for lunch. A blackened steak, lamb kebab, with rice and houmous in a pitta bread. It was a feast to what we had been surviving on. Jim was over the moon an ate hungrily.

"Right fella, have fun, I'm off to the fair, I'll sneak you on board later when I get back from the fair."

I went to work, leaving Jim on the jetty. I was just in time to set up up the ride and apologised to my boss for cutting it fine. The night went well and it seemed as everything was going very well.

"Night cruise, what do you mean a night cruise?" Jez had just informed me that we were to go on a night cruise the following evening. I couldn't do it as I had to be at the fair, but then, I had to if I wanted to stay on the boat. I had got into a regular routine, getting back in the nick of time to make it to the fair and then back to the boat to sleep. Jim had become friends with some of the crew and would stay on deck overnight, he was usually drunk when I got back from the fair, and I was giving him half of my money to keep himself going until he got a job. Instead of looking for work, Jim stayed on the beach all day, ate what I shared with him and spent the evenings drinking with my crew mates while I worked at the fair. He definitely had the better luck. Luck now, it seemed, was running out. I had to make a choice, the fair or the Zorba.

I told my boss I'd be leaving that night, that I had to stick with the boat and at the end of the night, I was paid off as normal and walked away from the fair for the last time. *Ken?*

Our first few days on board had been pretty easy, hiding below decks, serving, clearing up and not a lot else. I'd begun getting used to the routine but it all about to change. The Zorba had not had a full time skipper for a while. The skipper's that had been aboard had been pretty lenient and left us alone, but the company wanted to improve things. They wanted a more professional look, a permanent skipper and tidy ship and crew. Enter Mula.

Mula had a fierce reputation. He was a tough guy, Special Services in the Israeli Army, if his pager went off you knew something serious was happening somewhere, and Mula would leave immediately, even in the middle of a cruise, he would take the tender (Dinghy) and go. Where he went, we never knew. It was said that his team had been involved in the rescue of hostages from a hijacked plane, a lot of things were said about Mula, some of it was true, some beyond belief. All that I knew of him was not to get on his bad side. I had seen him on the jetty a couple of times, even asked him for a job. He'd looked at me with disapproval, paused and declined. I should have disliked him there and then, but there was something about him though, something I sort of liked and recognised. I wasn't at all sure if he felt the same, so when he came on board the Zorba, I stayed out of his way.

Doing as we had always done, the crew stayed below deck, except for Tony and Jez, they would disappear and do things, then come back wet and full of adrenaline. We were half way through a game of cards and some Turkish coffee when Mula came below, furious.

"What is this, where is my crew? Up, up, everybody out."

We jumped up from the bench and went up on deck, as I passed Mula our eyes met and he recognised me. I saw he wasn't pleased and so took my eye off him, climbed up to the deck and looked to see what I was supposed to do. I had no idea what happened during the cruises, where we went or what we were doing, save for my memories from when I was a passenger a few weeks earlier. I went toward the bow and saw Mike sitting on top of the entrance to the chain locker. This was a room below deck, in front of the kitchen (Galley to give it it's proper nautical term) where the anchor chains were secured to the ship. The chains fed up through a hole in the deck around a winch and out through the bow, where the anchors hung ready to be dropped if needed. We never used them as we always moored up to buoys which were secured on the sea bed.

"Hey Mike, what are you doing up there?" I asked.

"I'm on lookout duty, keeping an eye open for little boats, divers or whatever, there's never anything to see, so I just sit here and get a tan." Mike was from South Africa, as was Tony, Jez's number 2. That was where the similarities ended. Mike was short, quiet and well spoken. Tony was huge, muscular, with long blond hair and a big barrel chest, he was loud, funny and so in your face that he was unavoidable. Tony was never obnoxious though, he was a laugh a minute guy, an adrenaline junkie and great fun to be around. He was also a pretty good guy to have onside, you may not wish to have to tangle with him.

"So if you're a lookout, how does that work?"

Just then Mula was back on deck behind me, he'd heard me ask my question and for a moment, just a short moment, I thought I saw his lips move, a bit like a smile, on one side, ever so faintly.

Jez came round and told all the crew that we were to be having a meeting at the end of the cruise, Mula wasn't happy.

The crew gathered around the tables in the 'mess' and waited for Mula, when he arrived nobody spoke until invited to. His message was clear, he was taking over the boat, he was the boss and things would change. No more hiding b elow deck, all crew to be on deck at all times, except the chef. There would be regular daily maintenance to clean and maintain the vessel. No guests to be allowed on board, anyone inviting people on board would be sacked. All crew were to buck their ideas up and anyone falling short would be fired immediately. Mula was the boss, and he was laying down the law.

Once he'd left, Jez told me I had to stop Jim from coming aboard, we would both be thrown off if caught. Jim took it in his stride and ended up sleeping on another boat instead, it was the beginning of the end for our friendship, Jim stayed on for a while, but eventually I stopped seeing him and he returned the UK.

I was on lookout duty, we had just left Eilat and were heading towards the Navy buoy which marked the border into Jordanian water. All the boats did this, crossed over the border, I was told it was to annoy the Jordanians, but nobody was ever arrested or chased away, the Jordanians were a little too relaxed for that nonsense, apparently. As we approached the buoy I saw a small wooden dinghy over in the distance, in line with where we would be going once we turned. I waved at Mula and pointed to the little boat with 4 little fishermen aboard, calmly minding their own business. Mula was giving his normal speech to today's passengers about the port of Aqaba, the fish farm behind us and the Navy buoy marking the territorial border. I waved and he continued his speech.

"Do you want a drink?" It was Mike, checking I was okay.

"Yes please mate, when you're done can you get Mula for me, there's a boat over there".

"Yeah, no worries". He returned a few minutes later and before I could remind him, we were distracted by a passenger asking a question, something stupid like 'Do you work on here, then?'

Suddenly there was a shout, and a scream and another shout just as the fishermen's heads disappeared beneath the bowsprit. I jumped down from the hatch and saw them beneath the forward port quarter, pushing themselves along the side of our hull so as not to be pulled under. As they passed to our stern, I caught sight of Mula's face glaring, he exchanged some choice words with the fishermen then looked at me with THAT look, the one that says 'I am a dead man walking'.

Colliding with another vessel at sea is a serious charge, one that could get the skipper imprisoned, it could also get me Mula'd....

Jez came to get me a few minutes later, I stood on the rear deck, my knees almost knocking as I told Mula that I had tried to get his attention before being distracted. Never again would I let him down. For the rest of the cruise I did everything I could to do everything right.

"You!" Mula called me to him at the end of the cruise. This was it, I was history. "Normally I say bye bye, I give you chance. No good, bye bye, one chance only, today you lucky, huh?"

"Yes sir, thank you...."

I'd been in touch with Tara a few times since arriving in Eilat, once her legs were better, she planned to come to Eilat, she didn't want to stay at Dafna, she wasn't happy there. I was hoping to get her a job on one of the boats.

I was dozing on the floor of the saloon when I heard footsteps on the deck above. Tony, Jez and some other crew members were returning from the Yacht Pub. I could hear some messing around and then Tony's voice.

"Woohoo, Shiiiii..." It sounded like he was falling from the sky, there was a crash and a splash followed by a scream. He'd climbed the mast and slipped from the platform by the yard arm, hitting the side rail on his way down and then bouncing off into the water. Thankfully he was not killed, no bones broken, but he was in a lot of pain. He'd put his shoulder out and was soon covered in bruises from his neck to his toes.

The morning after, Jez called me to one side.

"I've decided it's time to go, I've been here long enough, had my time, now it's time to go. So I thought I'd give you first refusal on my job".

"What, me? I don't know enough about the boat or anything, I'm going to need some help, but yes, I'm interested, mate".

"Good, I'm not going for another week, so I can show you all I know, you're a natural though, you'll be good as 1st mate. You'll get more money, double what you're on now, and you get to do everything I do. Hiring and firing, training, managing the boat and the crew. Whatever Mula wants, you have to do it. I don't get on with him myself, but you'll be okay, he seems to like you".

From that minute on, I had to shadow Jez. I had to do every job on the boat, learn every job on the boat and become the best at everything on the boat. I had a week to become the boss, a week learn everything I could. I learned how to prepare the boat in the morning, pre-cruise stores ordering and delivery, in other words, the shopping list. Where and how the electricity was supplied, the water, the toilets. How the Galley should work, the cooking, storage and supplies. How to start the engine, the generator, the bilge pumps. How to maintain the engine room, the decks, the rigging, the dinghy. How to moor up to a buoy, how to moor up to the marina. Every little job, I was there, watching, doing, learning. It was hands on and full on. I loved it. I loved learning about it all, and I loved the boat itself.

The Zorba was a 114 ft long schooner, she had a displacement weight of 200 tons. Built in Denmark around 1918 with a wooden hull, twin masts and bowsprit. Originally the main deck and saloon would have been a cargo storage area, timber or coal mainly, the only cabin being the skipper's cabin beneath the rear deck, which now became my quarters. I had my own bedroom, shower and toilet next to the engine room. The Zorba was powered by a Caterpillar marine diesel engine, about the size of a decent dinner table, noisy, powerful but never pushed to the limit.

Following Tony's fall from the mast, I took over his role on the bow lines as well as everything else I was having to do and learn. It was repetitive but simple requiring a certain amount of speed, agility and physical strength. Each time we moored we would perform the same routine. A small rope called a heaving line, was secured to the bow line, a much bigger, heavier rope which had to bear the weight of the vessel. The 'heaving line' would then be thrown to a crewman in the dinghy below, he would then take the bow line and secure it to a buoy with a very large shackle. It was easy to learn, physical and enjoyable.

When the time came for Jez to leave, Tony left too. I inherited the big bunch of keys Jez wore around his neck. Keys to the stores cupboards, the engine room, lockers etc etc. Suddenly I was an important part of the crew, I was the only person with access to the most valuable parts of the boat.

So just to make things perfectly clear, you are sitting comfortably I hope, here goes. The Zorba was/is a Yacht, not a Motorised Yacht (M/Y) but a sailing Yacht (S/Y). It is also a Schooner, which is a boat with fore and aft sails on two or more masts, the foremast typically being shorter than the main mast. A boat is not a ship because a boat is not big enough to carry a ship, and a ship is not a boat because it can carry a boat, which makes it a ship, although a yacht can be a boat or a ship, unless it is under 30 ft long, then it's a pleasure boat. So to clarify, if it's under 30 ft, it's not a yacht, but over 40 ft it's a boat, a yacht or a ship (so long as it has 3 square rigged masts and weighs over 40 tons). The Zorba was 140 ft long, weighed 200 tons and had 2 masts and a bowsprit, which means she's a Yacht and a boat, even though she's big enough to carry a boat, which would make her a ship, except she's not. Got it? Good.

Tara eventually arrived in Eilat, along with Paul and a couple of other Dafna volunteers. Over the course of a few days I managed to get Paul and Tara onto the firm, Tara was on the Zorba only a day or two before she was taken onto another of our boats, The Sea Princess, a few days later, she too was made 1st mate. Suddenly we were both important figures on the marina, we both did the hiring and firing and everything else that was expected of us.

We had been separated as Mula had declared that no crew members could have girlfriends on board, an extension of the no visitors rule. Someone had complained and we were separated but because I had the skipper's cabin, we were allowed to share as Tara would need her privacy too, something she could not have got on The Sea Princess because it was a different type of vessel, it was a Motorised Yacht with two decks for disco cruises, it was a party boat, not a sailing vessel.

I eventually had to sack Paul. Mula was strict about the no visitors rule, and one morning arrived a little early to find Jim on board. I had already had to sack one guy a few day's before for having his girlfriend on board when Mula arrived, this time I had to sack my friend, and I hated it. I had no choice. I either sacked Paul, or I lost authority over the crew and my only option would be to resign.

People came and went on an almost daily basis. I had some really hard working, trustworthy crew members. I also had some trouble makers, a few people who Mula took a dislike to immediately, and I would have to send them on their way after only one or two cruises. Others would be sent packing after a couple of weeks. The most dramatic being the 'Frenchman'. I needed a new cook and miraculously had a chef turn up asking for a job. He was from Yorkshire and had a bit of an accent, but most important of all, he had a set of chef's coverall's, black and white checked trousers and a white linen jacket. He was the real deal but no matter how much I told him how Mula wanted his dinner cooked, or how the rice had to be done, he wanted to do it his way. This resulted in Mula dragging him onto the deck and verbally tearing him a new arsehole before chasing him around the boat throwing chairs at his head. I managed to get between the two and took the 'Frenchman' (Mula called him the Frenchman because he couldn't understand his accent) below deck, away from Mula and away from the passengers. Once we docked he left the boat and was never seen again.

There were two cruises available. The cruise I'd done myself prior to moving to Eilat, and the Coral Island cruise. Both cruises left Eilat, passed the Jordanian border and headed back toward Dolphin Beach and then down past the Navy yard to Taba. If we were going to Coral Island, we would pause at Taba, despatch our dinghy to meet Dadi, one of the company's owners whose job it was to produce the passports of all passengers and crew on board to the

Egyptian authorities at the border, in the town of Taba. Once checked they would allow the boat to enter Egyptian water, the dinghy would race back, the passports handed to the skipper for safekeeping, and we would head south for about another half hour until we reached Coral Island.

The Island sits off the Sinai coast and hosts a castle built by Saladin, the first Sultan of Egypt and Syria. All around the island are coral reefs and it is the perfect place for snorkelling or scuba diving. Sometimes the Egyptians would come out to us in their dinghy, and demand our passports, they may ask to see someone, but we never had any problems. The Coral Island cruise was the favourite for both crew and passengers. For us, the tips were better, we usually ate well and we got to have a good splash about in the sea. The dinghy would ferry passengers over to the island to visit the castle and others would snorkel around near the coral. It was heaven on Earth. Beautiful blue waters, amazing clear sky and a 900 year old castle on an island, what more could we ask for?

Only once did it nearly go wrong, well twice actually. Three times if you include the two Israeli girls I hired who didn't have passports. We got to Taba and they hid out of sight. When we got back to Eilat, I had to send them on their way, which was hard, they'd begged me for work and cried when they left, they were runaways, just like the rest of, but with no passports, we couldn't keep them on.

One time, we had a passenger on board, a middle aged lady who said she thought I was the guy from that film, Waterworld. I had a bit of a beard due to not having shaved for about a month and I did move around the boat like it I owned it, but I'd never seen the film so didn't know who I was meant to look like. When we got to Coral Island, she wanted to snorkel and swim but was afraid of the fish, there were fish in the sea, how unexpected was that? Seeing her struggling, I dived in and tried to help her, calming her down and keeping her afloat. In return, she held onto me and managed to keep pushing my head under the water. I'm not keen on the taste of sea water at the best of times, but when you're trying to help someone and they respond by attempting to drown you, it can be a bit much having to take in a belly full of salt water. Needless to say, I was as quick to jump in to someone's assistance again after that. Every so often I still catch a glimpse of a fish tail in the corner of my eye, circling around inside my head, looking for the exit.

A problem I inherited when taking the position of 1st Mate, was looking after the engine room. As a truck driver in my previous life, I knew one end of an engine from the other, but other than a few repairs here and there, I'd never had to do too much in the way of diagnostics or marine engine maintenance. The Zorba had a big Caterpillar engine, which ran like a dream, once started. On some cold mornings, she would need some coercion in the form of a shot of easy start up the air intake, a bit like the kiss of life when your girlfriend passes out at a party. Once fired up, there's no stopping her.

Next to the engine was a diesel engine generator, which provided 24 volts of electricity to a bank of batteries stored behind the on-deck bar. These then powered the lights, pumps, radio, stereo, fridges, freezer and all other electric users on board. Should the generator pack up, which I will get to in a minute, we had back-up power in 12 volt form purely to power the boats bilge pumps.

We were at Coral Island one day when the generator packed up. This had been a regular problem and both Mula and I were stumped as to what was causing the salt water pump to fail. The pump was powered by a fan belt connected to the fly wheel of the generator. This turned a pulley on the pump which turned the pump and salt water into the generator, cooling the engine before passing back out through the exhaust. The shaft on the pulleys kept bending, the seals kept melting and the generator kept breaking down. (Mula eventually realised it was because the fly wheel on the generator was about 10 times larger than that on the pulley, but with a RPM of 1500 the pulley was therefore spinning at about 15000 RPM but only had a max RPM of 2500, no wonder we were having problems).

The generator was off, but that was okay, we had enough 24 volts stored to get us back to Eilat. Our bilge was constantly needing to be pumped as our stern tube was leaking, the tube was misshapen by being put into reverse to quickly and causing the prop shaft to bounce, thankfully it had never sheared the bolts at one end or the other, that would have paralysed the vessel. We were taking on a lot of water, but this was not a problem, because our bilge pumps kept up with the flow coming in, so long as we had plenty of electricity.

Using the 24 Volt pumps meant draining the battery's very quickly, so I switched over to the 12 Volt pump, it worked, but not as well as the 24's. This was not a problem though, because the engine was fitted with a bilge pump too and I could put this on as back up for the 12 volt system.

Unfortunately, there was a clunk and a whirr and little bits of fan belt flew around the engine room. This was not a problem though, as I had spares. I fitted a spare as the water level rose and the boat seemed to slow a little with the excess weight on board. This was not a problem though, until I put the engine pump back into gear and that shredded too. This too was not a problem, I had an emergency fan belt which I cut to size, connected the ends and clunk. This was not a problem, I could do without the engine pump, I would use the 12 volt pump and back it up with the emergency hand pump fitted to the hull near the stern tube. I pumped as hard as I could and the water continued to rise, I pumped some more and realised the pump hadn't even been primed yet. This was not a problem. I grabbed a socket set and opened the pump, poured some water in, closed it and began to pump, it was working, I was pumping the water by hand. The 12 Volt kept going but being fixed to the hull lower down was in danger of being inundated, I waited as long as I could before switching off the power so as not to blow the electrics, which we needed to radio the coastguard and harbour master on our return to the marina. This was not a problem, the boat was taking on more water and getting more sluggish to handle. Mula knew something was wrong and came down into the engine room to find me. I would always let him know when I was going below, it was protocol. Normally I would only be 5 minutes at most. It was 44 degrees outside in the sun, in the engine room, it was hotter than hell itself. With the engine running and little ventilation, I would normally resurface after 5 minutes looking like I'd just crawled out of the sauna in a particularly dodgy 1970's porn film. I was dripping with sweat.

I told Mula what was happening and he sent for two other crewmen to help. As they began pumping the hand pump, the handle snapped. This was not a problem. I gave them both a bucket each and told them not to get near to the propeller shaft, just to get what they could from near the engine's gearbox and pour the water out of the port hole in my shower room. The water was rising and we were slowly sinking. This was not a problem though, I clambered up on deck, the cold air of the afternoon hit me, I felt like I'd been staring into a blast furnace for the last hour, compared to down below, 44 degrees was pretty cool in comparison. Dripping with sweat I sidled between and around passengers, whispering instructions to my crew to make sure nobody else knew what was going on. Matt collected the fire pump from the starboard fore deck, James collected the hoses and pretended all was well, smiling as he passed along the deck. I felt a tap on my saturated shoulder. It was the Rep from the company who'd chartered the boat.

"Is everything Okay?" She asked, staring straight into my eyes. I looked past her as the pump was passed down into the engine room. The rest of the crew had come to the rear of the deck and were obstructing the view of the passengers, making sure nobody could see the flurry of activity going on behind the Skipper.

"It's not a problem. Everything is fine" I said.

"Are you sure? Only, Mula always plays his Beatles cassette on the return leg, and for some reason he isn't today, I thought there might be a problem he wasn't telling me about." She smiled and I returned the compliment.

"There is no problem, honestly, just relax and enjoy the view, it's beautiful here isn't it?" I slid further and further away from her, crawling out of her grasp and then running for the hatch, throwing myself down the steps into the lower deck and then down the second flight into the engine room. A hose was fitted to the pump and out of the porthole as I had ordered. Another set into the ever rising water. Some of the wooden sheets that made up the floor of the engine room were already floating, we were running out of time, half an hour from the marina and barely 20 minutes before the engine would flood and we would be left floating and then sinking in a sea full of sharks, Rays, Eels, dolphins and the occasional Ford Fiesta car tyre.

We took turns to pump and pump as furiously as we could, an irregular stream of water coughing out of the porthole as we did so. The closer we got to Eilat the slower and lower in the water the boat became. Mula used the last of the electricity to radio the harbour master, then we dispatched James and Matt in the Dinghy, much earlier than normal, with them they took another crewman to jump ashore so that we had no delays in getting our lines over, he knew what was happening and understood our urgency. Mula spun the wheel furiously and in a manoeuvre I'd never seen before spun the Zorba on a sixpence whilst ordering the stern lines and shore power cable be thrown across immediately. Within seconds the shore power was connected our stern lines attached even before the bow lines attached to our buoy at the front end of the vessel. Suddenly the pumps kicked in and the Caterpillar engine had come to within about an inch of being inundated. Nothing had been a problem, a challenge maybe, but not a problem.

Tara took on her new role as 1st mate quite well, it wasn't a position she particularly wanted but served it well. The one thing she didn't like was being treated differently by the rest of the crew, she liked to be one of the gang, not an outsider. She didn't want to have to sack anyone either, so left that to her skipper and to Dadi, who supplied both boats with our stores each and everyday. Being first mate meant some crew were weary of us, we were not on the same level as them and we were paid more. There was always some drama or other going on, hardly surprising really as most of the people working on the marina were runaways, misfits and miscreants of some degree or other.

One day, one of the girls working the bar on another boat was being abused by her boss. He suspected her of stealing money and supplies from him and there was a scuffle. I heard a scream and looked over to see he had her by the hair and had just slapped her. I dropped what I was doing and before he knew what was happening I run across and pulled the two of them apart. I stood between them and told him in no uncertain terms that I'd knock him into the water if he touched her again. He began to shout and I pulled my arm back, fist clenched. His hands went up and he stepped backwards.

"Don't you ever hit a woman, you understand me? I don't care what you think she's done, you don't lay a finger on her or anyone else!!"

They calmed down and eventually the girl was assumed innocent, to a point, but the experience had been too much and she left the job. She found work on one of the Parasailing boats. Her previous boss left the marina, word got around he'd had a nervous breakdown and was hospitalised. I had no idea if the girl had been stealing, but I knew that she didn't deserve the beating and I was no fan of this form of summary justice, not here like this. We were travellers, homeless nomads maybe, migrant workers, we were not slaves nor were we to be treated as such. Only on one other occasion did I have to stand up to anyone on the marina. That person, was Dadi, the calmest, quietest of the 3 brothers that owned the company we worked for.

Dadi was a lovely guy, a good looking, bald headed, well built man with a cute smile and gentle voice. We got along really well together and had a few laughs too. I had never thought of him to be someone to lose it with anybody, but one night he did just that.

It was one of Tara's crew, a Canadian lad who failed to pull his weight, was a slacker and a bit of a mouthy git. He'd push my buttons too if I'd had to work with him, but I didn't. One night, out of nowhere, a row broke out next door aboard the Sea Princess. This led to Dadi losing his rag big time and beating the crap out of this lad. The shock of seeing Dadi lose it, the sudden violent outburst, without warning, scared some of the crew, some of the girls on both the Sea Princess and the Zorba became scared and demanded I protect them or stop Dadi from coming aboard any more. These were his boats, I could hardly stop him coming aboard, but I could try to calm the situation.

We were gathered in the saloon when someone ran down the deck above.

"Dadi's coming, with Roni and someone else!"

"Everybody stay here," I demanded, "I'll deal with this".

Dadi, Roni and another guy were halfway down the deck. The third guy was a stranger to me, maybe came along for a fight, maybe. He stepped in front of Dadi and looked down at me, maybe it was going to kick off now.

"Hold it there" I warned, my arm out to show authority. "You can't come aboard, not tonight".

"I have come to talk to the crew" said Dadi, and he meant it.

"You can't, not after earlier, you want to say something, say it to me."

"I just want to apologise for earlier."

"I know mate, but at the minute they're feeling a little vulnerable and I don't want to be losing anyone right now. Everyone's heard what happened earlier, and they're feeling concerned it might happen again. As their superior, I have to make them do things they don't want because you tell me to, so now that something bad has happened, I have to look after them, otherwise I have no authority. If I can't protect them when things go wrong how can I get them to do things right or ever even tell them what to do?"

"Then tell them they are safe, it will not happen again and that I did not mean to upset anyone".

"I will do, but do me a favour, don't be coming aboard any boats just yet, it's gonna take some time to get things back to normal".

They accepted this, or rather Dadi accepted it, Roni and his mate said nothing, maybe I'd been wrong, maybe they hadn't been looking for trouble after all. I knew I couldn't trust them right now because to do so would have been like a let down to the crew. Nobody really knew why Dadi had erupted the way he had, but suddenly everyone was scared of him. Me, I just thought he'd blown a fuse and the Canadian guy had pushed his luck too far. But by keeping Dadi away, just for now, I could at least gain the respect of the crew and keep the peace.

Since Mula and I had joined the Zorba, there had been some changes, starting immediately with the no visitor's rule, the no drinking rule and a shit load of on board maintenance. Everything was being given a new lick of paint, new coats of oil or replacing. Our old tattered flags that were so weather beaten were replaced. Those that were on halyards up amongst the rigging were pulled down and replaced with new flags, those that were fixed had to be cut down by hand. I took on this job while the rest of the crew were sanding and oiling the decks one day. I heaved myself up a steel cable about 30 feet above the deck. Barefoot, I was able to trap my legs around the thick cable and hold myself aloft using the strength in my legs and stomach. I held the flag in my left hand and cut the cable ties holding it in position with my right. I dropped the flag down to the deck and pulled out a new replacement from my pocket, secured it nice and tightly to the rigging before sliding back down the cable and onto the side of the Yacht. I crossed to the opposite side and pulled myself up to replace the flag on the port side. Unfortunately, I could feel my legs struggling to hold my weight, we had no harness or safety gear at all, if I let go or slip, it's either crunch time on the deck if I'm lucky and the wind blows me hard enough, I could splash over the side. Neither scenario really appealed to me so I clenched my legs tighter and cut at the cables with extra vigour, going through the plastic and through the bed of my fingernail right behind it. I felt the blood immediately as it soaked the Star Of David in my hand. I had cut through to the bone and needed to get down pretty sharpish.

"Someone get the first aid kit!" I shouted down to the crew below. The urgency in my voice worked as Matt headed off to get fetch it from the galley. Everybody else looked up as I slid down the cable faster than I really should, I had nothing to hold on with and so basically fell 30 ft with the cable between my chest and elbows, the flag filling with blood faster than I would have liked. Sarah, who was from Nottingham and was probably my most faithful crew member as well as being our latest cook, tended to my injury and Mula took me to the Hospital. A doctor checked the wound and decided it didn't need stitches, just to be kept clean and left to heal. I was scarred, but not defeated.

Our revamping of the Zorba went on for a couple of months, at night we would work late, cleaning painting, sanding, oiling the decks. It meant for hard work and long hours. Some of the crew left, others moaned, some just on with it. Mula would give me a list of jobs to have done by the morning, and I would ensure they were. On top of that, I was also working in the engine room, cleaning, changing bulbs, rigging extra lights, painting, oiling and greasing. I set about putting all the tools in useful easy to get places, painted the walls white so as to lighten the room, painted the floor panels. Everything was bright and clean, accessible and in some sort of order. Between us all, we really had transformed the boat. Even the anchor chains had been taken out and relaid in their hold. It was a good job we'd never had to use them though, when we took them out we discovered they'd never been secured to anything. If we'd dropped anchor at any time, we would never have seen it again.

One thing thing had always bugged me about the Red Sea was the fact that it wasn't, or at least not normally. The sea is the same colour as any other large body of water, the difference here being that sometimes, when the sun sets below the mountains in the Sinai, the sky turns orange, then red, the deepest bloody red you can imagine, with bright yellow fingers reaching out from any clouds drifting in the sky. From the black silhouetted mountains comes a fire show so brilliant as to take your breath away. The whole sky appears to be in flames, this reflects on the surface and hence the name, the Red Sea.

We were often asked this by passengers, and I would always teach the crew to explain it as best they could. They would often ask us about the colours on the mountains too. The red was Iron, green was copper, the white was salt or other minerals while the yellow was sandstone. If anyone ever asked, and they did, frequently, I would point to dip in the hills near the Saudi border and say that was where Moses parted the water.

Eilat sits at the top of the Gulf Of Aqaba, or Gulf of Eilat, it's the same Gulf but it has two names, and is the top end of the Red Sea. Head south and you spill out into the Indian Ocean just above The Seychelles. Twice a year, the wind direction would change, normally the wind would pass from North to South or even sideways, East to West or vice versa, only when it turned and came from the South would there be any problems. Air from the South brought storms and high water, as the wind blew it would push the water up the gulf and water levels at the marina would rise, the beach would be inundated and some vessels could be damaged.

The Zorba was the only vessel on the marina unable to shelter inside the marina at these times. The boats draught was too deep, roughly translated, this meant our arse was too big and we didn't fit in the bath. Whenever the wind turned and storms were predicted, we would have to be ready to leave immediately and ride the storm out moored up to the Navy buoy at the Jordanian border.

After a week or so of false alarms and no shows, some of the crew-who were barred from taking shore leave at this time, became a little peeved at having not been out to play for a while. Mula had left strict instructions that 'NOBODY' was to go ashore tonight. Despite this, when the wind picked up and the flags turned North, some people were missing, and to make things worse, others were present who were not meant to be.

It was 2230 when I rang Mula, that's 10.30 PM to most folks. I told him the wind had turned, the barometer had dropped below 900 and the water was rising.

"I am on my way, start the engine, get the dinghy ready and lines prepared to go immediately".

I had already sent Brett off to the Yacht pub to bring the rest of the crew back, I trusted Brett, he was from Perth, Australia, and struck me as a good reliable guy for his age, he was only 18. Back on the boat I hurried round and warned everyone to get off the boat if they had no place being aboard, Mula was on his way and we were going to sea in a storm.

Brett came running back and arrived just before Mula. Matt and James were in the dinghy ready to go, I'd got the engine ticking over and we were all set, all but for 2 guys still at the pub. As soon as he stepped aboard I hoisted the gangway, the wind was pretty strong and there was a lot more resistance in the pulleys. Everything on deck had already been secured, nothing was left to chance. We had already seen the mattresses we used on deck flying off into the sea or bounce over the marina on other days, we didn't want anything like that happening now.

We slipped our moorings just in time to see our absent crewmen appear on the jetty, Mula saw them too, and cursed in Arabic. We left them behind and Mula tore a strip off me for letting them go ashore. I hadn't, but I could not stop them sneaking off when I was in my cabin. Mula knew this and told me they had to be gone at the end of the week.

We arrived at the buoy and the dinghy was dispatched with the bow line. The little dinghy bounced up and down in the waves, rising about 6 ft with each wave and then falling away again as soon as it passed. The lads were taking a battering but eventually managed to connect the shackle despite the movements of the dinghy. Neither were harnessed or strapped into the boat in any way, there were no lifelines, it was a rubber dinghy, battling against the force of the sea. I stood on the deck of the Zorba as they finally backed away and gave Mula the signal to say we were secured. At this point he would reduce the throttle on the engine and allow the buoy to slowly take the weight of the Zorba. I looked down into the dark water watching as the buoy bobbed and moved in a strange way, something was wrong, I didn't know what, but something wasn't right. The buoy wasn't in line with the bow line. The boat was secured to the buoy, but the weight was being held by the chain beneath it.

I called Mula to let him see for himself.

"Look, something's not right, the bow line is straight but it's loose on the buoy".

"It's on the chain, it will break..... Fix it....."

Mula's words were few but they had the desired effect. I ran to where the dinghy was bouncing against the hull of our boat and jumped over the side, landing with a thud next to Matt. James was already clambering back aboard the mothership.

"Take us back to the buoy,Matt, we've got a problem".

Matt turned us into the wind and we rose about 6 ft as a wave passed along beneath us. I had no life jacket, no shoes, harness or anything to hold onto the little dinghy with, but none of that was important, I had a 200 ton boat and 10 crew to take care of, once they were safe, I would worry about myself.

We slid down the back of the wave and I got a face full of the next one before being lifted up again, he hit 3 more waves before reaching the buoy, I could see now the difficulty James had faced first time around. I crawled as far forward as I could, my feet slipping around in the rubber boat, as always, my feet were bare and I found little grip beneath them. In front of me, the buoy rose up, bigger than I realised from my vantage point on the deck, this thing was pretty huge, probably 8 ft in diameter, trying to grab a hold of the shackle on top was not an easy feat, especially in these waves. Eventually I got a hold and as Matt kept the dinghy butted up to the buoy I removed the shackle, taking care not to drop the pin before setting it back into the shackle and whipping the thick rope around to untangle it from the chain below. I was blasted with another wave and gripped the buoy tight with my left hand as the dinghy fell away behind me. Matt pulled the throttle and the boat was back beneath my feet, I felt the rubber under my toes and momentarily realised that this was not going well. I paused to let the next wave pass through before swinging the rope once more, it was heavy but I had to do this, I had to free the rope from the chain.

Mula had pulled the Zorba forward a few feet, enough to slacken the bowline, this took the weight off the rope and when I swung my third loop the whole lot was freed from the mooring chain. I clung to the buoy as the dinghy fell away and turned off to one side, Matt had let go to try to grab my legs and stop me falling out of the boat, but it was too late. I held the buoy with my left hand as my feet dangled in the water, the Zorba reared up and fell back pulling the bow line with her. Suddenly I was a human shackle. My left arm firmly attached to the buoy with my all my strength, clinging on for dear life. In my right arm was 200 tons of timber, a few good people and several bottles of Hebron wine, all at the end of a very taut rope. I was lifted out of the water, clinging on like some Stretch Armstrong toy in the hands of a 7 year old, pulled to my very limits in both directions, my dirty yellow shorts with the cigarette burn hole in the bum, suspended in the air, highlighted against the dark sea. I thought I was going to start spinning, my head and feet furiously chasing each other, first one way, then the other. Little old me, dangling on a tight rope spinning furiously in a blur of yellow shorts and skin tone. Mula hit the throttle and I was unceremoniously dumped in the briny. Just another day at the office, just another mouthful of water. I pulled myself up with expert timing and in a furious blur of motion somehow managed to undo the shackle pin, position it and twist it back into place before the next wave hit. Matt had brought the dinghy back and once I finished securing the bow line, I slipped back into the dinghy. We rose up on the crest of the next wave as we turned and headed back to the safety of the Zorba.

Once on board, I knew something major had just occurred by the faces of the crew about me, for the first time that I could be sure, there was respect in their eyes, and a few slack jaws.

Mula inspected the bowline, his weathered face peering into the dark. Then he turned to me and smiled, a very tiny half smile at the side of his mouth that looked almost alien. He was softening up, no, surely not.

"You did good".

We spent the night riding the waves, the wind blowing through the rigging keeping us from sleep. With each pitch of the waves the unsettling creak and bending of the masts. I'd never realised before now why it was essential for the masts to be flexible, not rigid in their fixing with the decks. In high sea's the boat needed to flex and move, it was this movement that held it together, stopped it from snapping with deadly consequences. Where such movement allowed the rain to enter was not a problem, the water was minimal and would find it's way into the bilge, only then to be pumped out into the sea, when the pumps worked, that is.

In the early hours, the wind eased off, and we made our way back to the Jetty. Coming in to dock as the rest of the marina was just coming to life felt strange, the calm after the storm. We were adventurers returning from a story out there in the dark night, those who'd seen us, anxiously waiting to hear what had happened. We were the only vessel out on the water, that made us different, it made us veterans of the storm, and just a little bit sea sick.

We managed to cruise to Coral Island and got back again just as the wind was picking up again. There was a flurry of excitement as our passengers were disembarked hurriedly, the gangway barely touching the jetty. Mula kept the engine running and once everyone was off, we slipped our lines and headed back to the buoy. For 3 days we sat at sea, riding the waves, listening to the wind. For 3 days we waited for calm, eventually it came, by which time we had heard most of Mula's stories, those he was able to tell.

We were returning from a cruise one evening when Mula's pager went off. This was not a good sign. We pulled the dinghy up alongside and he jumped in, fired the outboard engine and raced off ahead of us. Dadi came out to meet us when we arrived back in Eilat. Our 2nd Skipper, we also had a 2nd Skipper aboard for just such an emergency, was Hugo. A quiet, unassuming guy who had none of Mula's air of command. Mula was in charge and you felt it the moment he stepped aboard, Hugo was like the crewman who just happened to have a commercial skipper's licence. Hugo took us in to dock, he lacked the confidence of Mula, his approach was slow and nervous, overly cautious, and he used the throttle too much too late, it was a surprise to all of us on board that we never hit ant of the other boats as we swung around from one side to another, trying to get onto our mooring. As soon as we landed, we could see something was wrong. There were police everywhere, sirens rang around the town and the people milling around on the jetty looked worried. Concern contorted their faces, lines and cracks were visible.

Prime Minister Yitshak Rabin had been assassinated in Tel Aviv, at Dizengof plaza. The country was on lock down.

There was quiet, and a sense of concern all throughout Israel, even in Eilat, so far detached from the capital, there was a palpable feeling of loss and worry. How would the state respond, who had done this? It all came out quickly, he'd been shot by an Israeli, thankfully. This meant Israel had to look at and question itself, not the Palestinians, not Hezbollah, itself. There were no retaliatory strikes, no mass imprisonments, just a time of reflection and peace.

Mula returned 3 days later, nothing was said, his absence ignored. Life continued as per normal.

I'd gone to the office one morning as I often had to, there was always an errand, paperwork or some other thing I needed to do before we set off for the day. On my return, there was a group of people on the jetty, an argument had erupted and was turning into a fistfight between an Australian and South African, both crewmen from other boats. As I got closer, the cat calls rose, a circle formed and the two went head to head. I tried to get in to break it up, nobody wanted to see this especially when passengers were arriving for their cruises. As I tried pushing my way in Mula appeared and the circled opened up to him. He said nothing, but calmly put his arm out and grabbed one of the guys by his neck and lifted him up. He had him in a pinch between his thumb and forefinger but was able to physically lift him off of his competitor. The guy's face contorted in pain as his body froze and Mula dumped him unceremoniously to one side. The fight was over, nobody won, or did they? Mula had a reputation, and for good reason too.

Christmas was coming, and with it the inevitable change of crew. Some folk heading home, others for Dahab or Petra. Some stayed on and others got the call they didn't want. Brett was a good lad, a reliable crewman who I liked and got on well with. Christmas day consisted of 3 cruises for the Zorba, Coral Island, followed by Taba and a late cruise for 100 American Friends Of Israel, all wealthy donors to the state and it's institutions. We ate well this day, and the tips were good, everyone was happy, looking forward to having the next day off. Brett was called to the office, his brother had been seriously injured in a car crash in Perth, he was booked on the first available flight and headed home. He was devastated, he loved his little brother and was desperate to get home to him.

Mula invited Tara and myself to dinner at his apartment. I'll say that again only with added gravitas. Mula, invited Tara and myself to dinner at his apartment. Dadi nearly fell overboard when I told him.

"Mula invited you to his home?" This was unheard of. Nobody, but nobody was ever invited to his home. People who'd known him for years had never seen his apartment or met his wife, some even believed she was made up, a story to make Mula seem more human, Mula never spoke about his wife, never invited anyone round and never for dinner.

Tara and I were very privileged, we put on our best clothes and I even had a shower and made myself smell nice. I hadn't shaved for about 3 months and had a beard which I trimmed and combed before or dinner date. I was a hipster before the concept had even been thought of or made fashionable on the streets of Shoreditch. You guys, you are so last year.....

Mula's apartment was in a block in the centre of town and had a great view of the marina and especially the jetty. Mula could see what was going on aboard, all he had to do was pick up his binoculars and he could see who was doing what at any time. No wonder he knew things we'd never told him. He had a front row view and nobody knew about it. Access to the apartment was by way of an intercom, nobody got into the building without permission from those that lived there. His home was spacious, clean and well decorated. Furnishings comfortable and in good taste. Mula had a bookshelf, with only a handful of books, one was a hardback he was particularly proud of, it was the story of a couple's cruise through the Nile and around the Red Sea, a diving adventure, and there in the credits, was a big 'Thank You' to the boat's skipper, a certain Mula Weinstein. No wonder he prized it so much.

Mula's wife was lovely, a little younger and easier to get along with than her husband, but here, in their home, the guards were down. Mula was the most amiable I'd ever known him, a different person to the character he portrayed on the outside. He laughed, smiled and poured plenty of wine. Dinner was served, Fish with rice and vegetables. I hadn't had fish for months and relished in this feast, unfortunately for Tara, she was not a fan but did her best to eat it without chucking up. Her last words before we left the Zorba had been;

"I hope he's not cooking Fish, I can't eat fish, especially if has bones in" and it did.

"I am thinking of leaving" declared Mula as we sat on his sofa. This couldn't be true, why would he leave?

"Why, what are you going to do?" I asked.

"I have some options, one is to take a diving boat, it's in the Seychelles. I have been offered the position and am thinking about it. I have other options too".

Mula had plenty of options, he was a very competent master/sailor. He had captained merchant vessels all over the world, ships that made the Zorba look like a Dinky toy.

"We are thinking of going to Jordan for New Year, to visit Aqaba and Petra"

I wasn't trying to change the subject, just let it sink in.

"That is good, Petra is good. You have been before?"

"No, but it's so close and this is the only chance we are likely to get for a while".

Other than having doubled the wages for the crew and myself, Mula had also redoubled my pay and secured a new contract for all our staff, which included paid Holiday's. Unheard of on the marina at the time. We had earned it, there was no doubt about that, but all the same, it was previously unthinkable. Tara and I had booked a few days off to go to Jordan, something I was really looking forward to. Tara was keen, but not as much as I was, it would be different for her, being a woman.

"The Zorba is going in to dry dock soon, when it does, I have arranged for you to have an apartment, the rest of the crew will share another. There is a lot of work to do but after that we will have a much better ship. I have decided to wait until after to leave, Don't tell anyone, only you and I know this".

Mula was inviting me to go with him. I had not prepared for this, and I needed time to think, it was very tempting, very.

Tara and I made it to the Jordanian border. It felt strange to leave the Zorba behind, to hand my keys over and walk away. I felt vulnerable and suddenly homeless again, it was very unnerving. At the Jordanian border we were invited into a room to drink Chai with the head of the border post. This well groomed officer had the ability to allow us in or deny entry to us on the basis of a one to one interview over a cup of tea. I knew nothing of football, something officials throughout the middle east seemed to be obsessed with, especially Manchester United. A phenomenon I have never come to grips with, 22 overpaid, idolised idiots kicking a ball around, it does nothing for me, not when juxtaposed against images of starving women and children. I hope that one day those people actually do some real good with all their wealth, somehow though, I have yet to see any evidence of it.

We were finally given the go ahead, our passports stamped and returned, we jumped into a taxi and taken to the Red Mountain Hotel in Aqaba, it was run by a good friend of our taxi driver, a very good friend. We were given a room and after a short walk that evening to a nearby coffee house, we stayed in and made full use of room service. Tara had not enjoyed the prying eyes of the locals as we passed them on the streets, the looks on their faces seemed almost hostile, very unfriendly. I could ignore it, she couldn't. Petra was cancelled and we headed back to Eilat a day early, choosing to stay our last night in a hotel before going back to work.

Tara called her mother from the hotel room, she talked, and talked, and talked. I tried to tell her it was going to be an expensive call, but she continued to talk anyway. At breakfast the following morning we were interrupted by the receptionist.

"I am so very sorry, but there is a bit of a problem with your bill, you made a call to England from your room last night and the bill is rather a lot of money". I assured him there was no problem and asked how much. "$127 for the phone call".

"That's not a problem, I'll go and get it now". I ran to the marina just in time to catch Mula before he left for Coral Island. He handed me $100 without flinching. I thanked him and ran back in time to finish breakfast. Tara was looking nervous.

"Did you get it?"

"Yes, Mula saved our skin, I told you that was going to be expensive, anyway, we'll have to pay him back as soon as we can".

Dadi came aboard one morning with our stores.

"There is no cruise for you today, but I have a special job for you to do". The company, or should I say the brothers, Roni, Dadi and Adi who each owned an equal share in the business, had bought a new yacht. A little boat about 30 ft long, with a mast and enough space for no more than maybe 10 passengers at a push. We had been offered to live aboard and maintain the boat but had turned it down, it seemed like a step backwards, and anyway, I preferred the bigger boats. Another couple, from Sweden, eventually took over the little yacht and ran it happily for a few months before going home to Sweden to buy a boat of their own. They called me and offered me a position aboard to bring their new yacht from Stockholm to Eilat. A 6 month schedule, stopping off anywhere we liked on route.

Dadi pointed at the mast and told me that there was a problem with the rigging, my job today,was to fix it. I shimmied up the mast, once again with only the strength in my legs to hold me up there. No harness, no safety net, 30 ft up above the deck as the boat swayed gently below. One moment I may fall into the marina, the next, flat on the deck. Honestly kids, don't try this at home, not only is it not safe, but your parents are going to hate you for putting holes in their living room ceiling.

At the top of the mast I found some of the rigging to be twisted and intertwined. Somehow, one of the halyards had been fed around a shroud a could not possible function. I slipped back down to the deck and collected a marlin spike and some pliers from my toolkit. Before long I was back up the mast, my legs fixed against the aluminium pole as I worked to correct the faulty rigging. Beneath me a small crowd gathered and I caught odd phrases like "he's got no harness..." "Look, he's going to fall..." "Oh my god, what's he doing up there?" I smiled to myself, but was fully aware that they were not too wrong. My legs were starting to turn to jelly, the strength draining the longer I stayed aloft. By the time I'd succeeded in fixing all the problems aloft, my legs could barely hold me upright, but that was okay, I'd done what needed to be done and returned to my own boat to discover the gangway had just fallen into the water. Several crew members had gathered at the stern to see what was happening.

"Get me one of those ropes from the locker, Nick give me a hand here mate!"

Nick was Australian, he had a bent nose and full mane of sun bleached blond hair for which he took on the nickname of the Lion King. I liked Nick a lot, I really did, but there was an air of jealousy about him. I'd left him in charge when I had gone to Aqaba with Tara. I thought he was the most competent of all the crew, but Mula thought differently and eventually I had to sack him. He'd undermined me a couple of times and even put the boat at risk. Today was an example of that. He'd been told to paint the bollards on the stern of the Zorba, in order to get at them he released the stern lines and the boat was floating away from the jetty. I threw the stern lines back over and the boat was secured once more. Then, Nick and I dived with ropes to attach to the gangway. The crew then pulled on the lines and the gangway heaved back onto the boat. This was not the last time we had to dive. There were some fishing nets and rope caught around the propeller. Nick had allowed the boat to go straight over these and the engine had to be cut before the clutch burned out. Mula was glad to have me back, and once we'd hacked away at the tangled web of ropes and netting around the prop, Nick was eventually dispatched ashore for the last time. We bumped into each other a few days later and he squared up to me on the jetty, it was such a shame it had come to this, I liked Nick, for all his faults, I thought we could have been much closer. He eventually left for Dahab, and I felt the whole thing was misunderstood. Nick was popular with the crew, I wasn't, but they didn't know what I had done for them behind the scenes. Such is life, innit?

Do you ever have a moment when you see something and it looks familiar but you don't know why because it's too out of place?

We were coming back from Coral Island one day when I saw somebody standing on the jetty wearing a Motorhead t-shirt. I hadn't seen one for so long I was fixed on it. 'Fair play' I thought, the fellow had good taste. As we got closer I saw he had a mohawk. 'Fuck me, fair play to him' I thought, the fellow's got some balls out here, looking like that, looking like, well a bit like... "Fuck my old boot's!" As my old boss Malc used to say, it's Dave, *not that one,* Big Nosed Dave was here, in Eilat, standing on the jetty.

Dave and Julie had come out to see me. They'd arrived in Cairo and thought it would be a good idea to pop across the Sinai and come say hello. I was gobsmacked. It was the singularly most wonderful thing anyone could have done. It was so nice to see them, here, in my world, a million miles from home. We hugged, chatted and spent the evening catching up before they finally left to get back to the border. I later found out they'd had to bribe their way back into Egypt as Dave had not realised his Egyptian Visa was single entry only. By coming to Eilat, the visa was expired and they had no right to re-entry, even if their luggage was in a hotel, in Cairo.

Dave wasn't the only friend from Coventry in Eilat. Unbeknown to me 'Ratty Ray' Kelleher was there too. We discovered this on our way to a Sex Pistols gig in Crystal Palace some years later, both of us working on the marina, at the same time. It's a small world.

The Zorba was finally taken into dry dock. We sailed her over to the Navy Dockyard, positioned her in a dock, the gates closed and water drained out. The boat settled onto a huge cradle, the deck warped and creased unnaturally as the weight settled. She was manoeuvred into a position where she would rest and dry out for the next few days, water seeping from the timber hull like a sponge hung up to dry. For the next month we worked our nuts off, grinding off rotten timbers, replacing with new, plating the hull with sheets of copper, repainting everything beneath the water line with non-stick paint. New electric's were fitted, the whole boat sealed and fumigated against cockroaches, one the worst aspects of living on board, the thousands of uninvited visitors who scuttled around in the dark recesses. One night, a crewman felt something in his ear. Next morning he was screaming in pain. We took him to hospital where a huge cockroach was pulled from his ear. It had bored into his inner ear and laid its eggs. His ear was full of puss, eggs and baby roaches, all trying to feed on the inside of his skull. He made a full recovery but was later busted on a drugs raid in the marina, he was caught with cannabis in his possession, arrested and taken away for a short holiday at a secluded institute somewhere out in the desert.

Once the boat was finished, complete with a new stern tube, propeller shaft and bilge pumps, she was returned to the water. The gaps in the hull flooded with water and our new pumps worked overtime until the swollen timbers closed on one another and the bilge was eventually dry. We returned to Eilat with our new look Zorba and spent another week tidying up the inside and the decks, resealing where the boards had warped in dry dock.

I'd taken on a French girl, a young woman who'd seemed friendly enough. I got on very well with her and after Sarah left she took over the galley. I taught her what was expected of her and she fitted in well until we were on our way back from a cruise to Taba. There was a cold wind on the deck and she had no jacket, so I gave her mine to wear. Apparently this wasn't a good move, Tara was not best pleased and I had to let the French girl go.

"I'm pregnant" Tara told me.

"She's pregnant" I told Dadi.

"She's pregnant?" Mula gasped.

"She's what?" said the crew.....

This was most definitely not in the script. It wasn't planned for but it wasn't unwelcome either. It was what it was. A baby in the making. Tara and I were offered an apartment in town, courtesy of the company. Dadi offered to sort out our visa's and if we stayed would get our residency sorted out. Our child would be born Israeli and we could stay, but I would be required to do Military Service, as would the baby, in time. Tara wasn't keen on this option and headed home to England, I stayed behind to work my notice and train my successor. Dadi continued to bribe me with offers.

"Please don't go, we can make you a good life here, it is your choice, but we would really like you to stay".

Mula too would keep reminding me of his offer, a diving boat, in the Seychelles. I could only imagine how beautiful it would be there. I was offered more and more money, everyone wanted a bit of me, everyone had a deal on the table. I had to choose. I had to make a decision.

I had loved many people in my past, loved them and left them. I had a history any 'Wanderer' would have been proud of, but it hadn't made me happy. Don't get me wrong, I loved each and every woman I'd loved, I still did, still do. The heart never stops loving unless it is hurt, then it stops, it breaks and that love can never be retrieved. I had been broken but still felt love, especially for my daughters, more than any words or attempts at explanation could ever express. They were and are my blood, my creation. My yet to be born son, Jordan, whom I so desperately wanted, he was mine too and still to this day I love with the whole of my heart.

I had to choose, I could walk away again, sail off into the beautiful red sunset or I could try once more, redeem myself to those who'd criticised me, to those who didn't know how broken I had been. I could live a free man, with Mula, on a boat in the Seychelles, or in Eilat with the company, both had their appeal, or I could return to England. Tie up the loose ends, be a father and face the music. This was my chance at a second chance, a second chance to get it right, to build a home and family. I had always been willing to take a chance, come what may, that's life, innit?.........

ABOUT THE AUTHOR

Born in Romford 1965, everything was going well until the midwife slapped his arse. From that moment on, life was always going to be a fight one way or another. Trained for the Sea, Wayne Reid gave it up for sex,drugs and rock and roll, or more precisely, Bakery.

Well travelled, if mostly in steerage or handcuffed on the back seat, his life is one of happy endings and happy new beginnings.

Thrice married, and now living with his american wife Laurel in Sudbury, Suffolk, UK. He spawned 2 daughters, Sian and Christina, and a son, Jordan.

He has written many stories for *Trucking International* (now *Trucking*) as well as songs and poems nobody wants to know about.

Wayne appeared in Chuck Kershenblatt's book *Mile End,* 1997 on ITV's *May The Best House Win,* 2011 and had a part in Eileen Daly's film's Daly *Does The Dead, Exorcism,*2013, and *Mr Crispin,* 2018.

His first book, *My Book-Innit?* sold both copies and yet can still be purchased from the usual dodgy geezers you meet on street corners.

He currently writes freelance for online music websites, and collaborates with Costa Rican band *Last Dusk.*

Printed in Poland
by Amazon Fulfillment
Poland Sp. z o.o., Wrocław